Global Creative Industries

Global Media and Communication

Global Creative Industries

TERRY FLEW

polity

First published in 2013 by Polity Press

Polity Press
65 Bridge Street
Cambridge CB2 1UR, UK

Polity Press
350 Main Street
Malden, MA 02148, USA

ISBN-13: 978-0-7456-4839-2
ISBN-13: 978-0-7456-4840-8(pb)

A catalogue record for this book is available from the British Library.

Typeset in 11 on 13pt Adobe Garamond Pro
by Servis Filmsetting Ltd, Stockport, Cheshire
Printed and bound by Clays Ltd, St Ives plc

The publisher has used its best endeavours to ensure that the URLs for external websites referred to in this book are correct and active at the time of going to press. However, the publisher has no responsibility for the websites and can make no guarantee that a site will remain live or that the content is or will remain appropriate.

Every effort has been made to trace all copyright holders, but if any have been inadvertently overlooked the publisher will be pleased to include any necessary credits in any subsequent reprint or edition.

For further information on Polity, visit our website: www.politybooks.com

Contents

Figures and Tables

Acknowledgements

While there has been much work published in recent years on the creative industries, and associated concepts such as the cultural economy, the creative class, creative cities and so on, these analyses have typically been national in their orientation. Perhaps reflecting the origins of creative industries in policy discourse, there has been a focus on what the idea has meant for cities or nations; fewer attempts have been made to situate this discussion in a global context. Moreover, it has hitherto been a metropolitan discourse, focused either on the opportunities presented for advanced industrial nations to acquire new wealth through combining creativity and intellectual property, or condemning this discourse as inappropriately imposing economic imperatives upon the autonomous realms of art and culture.

An important guiding principle of *Global Creative Industries* is that many of the most important developments in the creative industries are now happening outside of Europe and North America, whether it be the flourishing of creative cities strategies in East Asia, the low-budget film scene in Nigeria, the creative economy policy prescriptions being proposed by agencies such as UNCTAD, or the identification of popular music as a new developmental as well as a creative outlet in Africa and the Caribbean.

In providing maps for creative industries development outside of the metropolitan centres, this book works with six core concepts: Industries; Production; Consumption; Markets; Places; and Policies. The book does not uncritically present the creative industries as providing a universal developmental panacea, nor does it simply condemn them as harbingers of an oppressive and homogenizing global culture. Instead, the book uses case studies as a way of illustrating some of the complexities and nuances of creative industries in practice. Among the case studies developed in the book are: design thinking; fashion as a creative industry; global advertising; gathering data on work in creative occupations; the meaning of 'global culture'; monopoly and competition in media markets; Shanghai and Seoul as creative cities; popular music and urban cultural policy; and the 'Nollywood' film industry in Nigeria.

Two of the key ideas informing the book are that culture and economy are becoming increasingly intertwined, and that institutional formations matter, including those involved with public policy settings at all levels of government. It is hoped that the presentation of such ideas is done in a way that is insightful to the non-specialist, and works across disciplinary divides and boundaries such as those between the creative practitioner, the policy maker, the academic and the student.

This book was written while I was in the Creative Industries Faculty at the Queensland University of Technology in Brisbane, Australia, and I have benefited from discussions with colleagues there, including Stuart Cunningham, John Hartley, Christy Collis, Lucy Montgomery, Jean Burgess, Axel Bruns, Christina Spurgeon, Stephen Harrington, Brian McNair, Alan McKee, Nicolas Suzor and Michael Keane. I was assisted in the research undertaken for the book by Adam Swift, Mimi Tsai, Bonnie Liu, Angela Lin Huang and Anna Daniel, and I thank them for their support. I also thank the anonymous readers of the draft manuscript that were approached by Polity. The work has benefited considerably from their observations and insights.

Sections of the book have been presented at the Chinese University of Hong Kong, the Institute for Culture and Society at the University of Western Sydney, Monash University, Hong Kong Baptist University, the Beijing University of Science and Technology, and Ming Chuan University, and I thank those who invited me to their academic institutions. I would also like to thank Andrea Drugan and Lauren Mulholland from Polity for their support as publishers. Finally, thanks to my daughter, Charlotte, who is always a source of new knowledge and inspiration.

I am grateful to the following authors and publishers for permission to use their work in this book: Table 1.2, Bloomsbury Academic, for Dwayne Winseck, *Political Economies of the Media: The Transformation of the Global Media Industries*, 2011, pp. 8–9; Tables 2.2 and 2.3, Taylor & Francis Social Science and Humanities Library, for Stuart Cunningham, *Cultural Trends* 20(1), pp. 28 and 30. Figure 1.1, United Nations Commission for Trade and Development, *Creative Economy Report 2010*, p. 8; Figures 1.2 and 2.1, United Nations Educational, Scientific and Cultural Organization, *The 2009 UNESCO Framework for Cultural Statistics (FCS)*, pp. 24 and 20; Table 2.1 and Figure 2.3, Centre for International Economics, *Creative Industries Economic Analysis Final Report*, p. 29; Table 4.1, American Economic Association, for Oliver E. Williamson, *Journal of Economic Literature* 38(3), p. 597; Table 4.3 and Figure 4.1, United Nations Commission for Trade and Development, *World Investment Report 2011*, p. 3; Figure 5.1, Sage, for Helmut K. Anheier and Yudhishthir Raj Isar, *Cities, Cultural Policy and Governance*, p. 2.

1   Industries

The Growing Significance of Creative Industries

The concept of creative industries has a somewhat unusual genealogy, in that it was first articulated in policy discourse, rather than in academia. The United Kingdom (UK) Labour government led by Tony Blair, first elected in 1997, established a Department for Culture, Media and Sport (DCMS) with specific responsibility for defining, mapping and developing a set of industries related to the arts, media, culture and digital technologies, that it termed the creative industries. From this work, the DCMS estimated that these creative industries accounted for 5 per cent of the UK economy in 1997, and were one of the fastest-growing economic segments of contemporary Britain (DCMS, 1998). Such impressive statistics justified an adventurous rebranding of what had previously been the Department of National Heritage, and a rethinking of the arts sector out of a historic association with public subsidy. It promoted a more holistic approach to thinking about the arts, media and design, associating their future with digital technologies, creativity and intellectual capital, and warranting a place at the table in wider debates about the economic future of Great Britain (Leadbeater, 1999; Howkins, 2001).

The UK DCMS study acted as a catalyst to a number of studies internationally that identified the growing size, scope and significance of the creative industries. In the United States, it was estimated that the 'core' *copyright industries* accounted for 6.56 per cent of US gross domestic product (GDP) in 2005, and all copyright-related industries made up 11.12 per cent of US GDP in 2005 (Siwek, 2006). The concept of creative industries has been taken up in many parts of the world, with pioneering studies in Europe, Asia, Australia, New Zealand and Latin America (for an overview, see Flew, 2012a).

Internationally, it has been estimated that the creative industries account for as much as 7 per cent of world GDP, as well as constituting a growing share of international trade. The United Nations Conference on Trade and Development (UNCTAD) found that exports of creative goods and services were worth US$592 billion in 2008, showing 14 per cent annual growth over the 2000s; this meant that the size of creative goods and

1

services exports in 2008 was double that in 2002 (UNCTAD, 2010: xxiii). Importantly, such exports continued to grow in the wake of the global financial crisis of 2008–9, which saw exports more generally contract by 12 per cent.

Such figures have suggested that the creative industries are not only a growing part of the world economy, but that their growth has developed its own dynamics, and is not contingent upon developments in other sectors of the economy, such as manufacturing, services or finance. The creative industries can therefore be seen as harbingers of what has been referred to as a *creative economy* (Howkins, 2001; UNCTAD, 2010). The concept of a creative economy places creativity and knowledge at the core of economic growth and development, identifying the products and services associated with the arts, media and culture as intangible goods embodying unique creative inputs that take the form of tradable intellectual property, and becoming more central to the future of cities, regions, nations, communities and the world.

Jing Wang (2008) observed that the term 'creative industries' was itself an effective piece of British marketing, while Andrew Ross noted that 'few could have predicted that the creative industries model would itself become a successful export' (Ross, 2007: 18). The economist Richard Caves (2000) identified the creative industries as being central to the dynamics of contemporary organizations, due to the centrality of networks, contracts and project-based work to these sectors. Jeremy Rifkin (2000) identified such developments, associated with what he termed the 'Hollywood model' of cultural production, as becoming a feature of twenty-first-century service-based economies more generally. The urban geographer and policy entrepreneur Richard Florida popularized the concept of the *'creative class'*, at whose core were those working in the creative industries, who he proposed were now at the centre of the dynamism of leading global cities (Florida, 2002, 2007, 2008). The evolutionary economist Jason Potts has argued that the creative industries are not only at the forefront of 'the experimental use of new technologies . . . developing new content and applications, and in creating new business models', but that by promoting 'new lifestyles, new meanings and new ways of being', they are 'resetting the definition of normal' (Potts, 2011: 5).

Defining the Creative Industries

Behind these impressive statistics and larger claims of significance lie some tricky definitional issues about the creative industries. Indeed, the term 'creative industries' coexists with a variety of other broadly cognate terms, including cultural industries, copyright industries, content industries, cultural-products industries, cultural creative industries, cultural economy, creative economy, and even the experience economy. In the course of providing an overview of the field for economic geographers, Jeff Boggs observed that 'while individual authors are often consistent in the terms that they use . . . when viewed collectively, these terms appear as an imprecise muddle' (Boggs, 2009: 1484).

One of the difficulties is that there is no single business or production model that encompasses all of the creative industries sectors; nor are they sectors that typically speak with a common voice. Hesmondhalgh (2007a) has distinguished between 'publishing' and 'broadcasting' models of the creative industries in terms of the relationship between production and distribution, while Caves (2000) differentiated between what he termed simple cultural goods, which are typically produced by individuals or small groups (e.g., a painter or a rock band), and complex cultural goods, that arise out of complex divisions of labour, such as films, television programmes or video games. The National Endowment for Science, Technology and the Arts (NESTA) developed a four-fold differentiation between: (1) *creative originals producers* (visual arts and crafts, antiques, writing, photography); (2) *creative content producers* (film, TV and radio, publishing, recorded music, interactive media; (3) *creative experience providers* (performing arts, museums, galleries and libraries, live concerts, heritage and tourism); and (4) *creative service providers* (advertising, architecture, graphic design) (NESTA, 2006).

I have discussed these distinctions elsewhere (Flew, 2012a), but it is important to note that it may be possible for one creative industries sector to be defined across several of these taxonomies. Music has elements of simple cultural production, elements of large-scale industrial distribution, and important elements of creative experience through live performances: it also relies heavily upon the providers of creative services, such as agents, venue owners and concert promoters. Very similar points can be made about the multi-dimensional nature of fields such as writing, games design and development, and the performing arts. The creative industries seem by their nature to generate variations and innovations in organization and practice that defy simple definitions and classificatory schemes.

There has been considerable progress over the last decade – at least in official policy discourse – in establishing agreed definitions, shared understandings and transferable measurement techniques for the creative industries, and in assessing their size, scope and significance. The first widely used definition was that of the UK DCMS, which defined the creative industries as engaged in 'those activities which have their origin in individual creativity, skill and talent and which have the potential for wealth and job creation

3

through the generation and exploitation of intellectual property' (DCMS, 1998). While this definition has been useful, it has also been contentious for three reasons.

First, there is the issue of why creativity is believed to be essential to some industries and not others. Pratt (2005: 33) observed that 'it would be difficult to identify a non-creative industry or activity', while Bilton and Leary (2002: 50) pointed out that 'every industry would surely lay claim to some measure of individual creativity, skill and talent'. Moreover, if 'creativity inputs' such as design are becoming more central to value-adding throughout all sectors of the economy, which is one of the propositions behind claims that we are moving towards a creative economy, then the demarcation lines between creative and other industries can appear somewhat arbitrary.

Second, it is not clear why the focus should be on individual creativity, except in terms of a conception of creativity as something that springs from the artist as an individual genius. By contrast, Bilton (2007) argued that the production of commercially successful complex cultural goods – films, television programmes, recorded music, live performances, etc. – was based upon a team-based model of production that mixed together so-called 'creative' and 'non-creative' activities as the necessary condition of its success.

Third, the focus on intellectual property in the DCMS definition has proven increasingly contentious in an environment where influential arguments have been made that the collaborative use of knowledge through open source models works better in a digital economy increasingly driven through open global networks than in proprietary models of knowledge 'ownership' subject to stringent forms of copyright protection (Lessig, 2004; Benkler, 2006). As Ruth Towse has observed in relation to these debates, 'it is very easy to slip between the use of copyright as a way of defining the creative industries and the idea that their contribution to the economy is *caused* by the presence of copyright' (Towse, 2010: 382; emphasis added).

In its work on the creative economy, UNCTAD (2010: 8) offered an extended definition of the creative industries, proposing that they:

- are the cycles of creation, production and distribution of goods and services that use creativity and intellectual capital as primary inputs;
- constitute a set of knowledge-based activities, focused on but not limited to the arts, potentially generating revenues from trade and intellectual property rights;
- comprise tangible products and intangible intellectual or artistic services with creative content, economic value and market objectives;
- are at the crossroads among the artistic, services and industrial sectors.

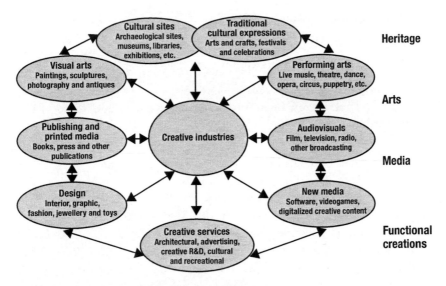

Figure 1.1. UNCTAD model of creative industries

Source: UNCTAD, 2010: 8.

The UNCTAD model pointed to nine sectors across the domains of arts, media and design, as well as heritage and what they term functional creations. These sectors, and the interconnected relationships between them, are shown in figure 1.1.

A similar set of industries has been identified by the United Nations Educational, Scientific and Cultural Organization (UNESCO) in its revised *Framework for Cultural Statistics* (UNESCO, 2009). In developing a revised Framework that recognized the expanded economic and social significance of culture and would allow for international comparative assessments, UNESCO has understood the cultural and creative industries as operating across *six direct domains and two related domains* (UNESCO, 2009: 22–32). The direct domains were:

1. Cultural and natural heritage: museums; archaeological and historical places; cultural landscapes; natural heritage;
2. Performance and celebration: performing arts; music; festivals, fairs and feasts;
3. Visual arts and crafts: fine arts; photography; crafts;
4. Books and print media: books; newspapers and magazines; other printed matter; virtual publishing; libraries; book fairs;
5. Audiovisual and interactive media: film and video; television and radio; Internet TV and podcasting; video games;

6. Design and creative services: fashion design; graphic design; interior design; landscape design; architectural services; advertising services.

In addition, there were two related domains:

7. Tourism, hospitality and accommodation;
8. Sports and recreation, including amusement parks, and theme parks and gambling.

The UNESCO and UNCTAD models have the advantage of having been developed from various national cultural statistics frameworks for the purpose of empirical data gathering to serve public policy purposes. The definition of creative industries used in this book works broadly with such frameworks, as they have evolved out of over a decade of debates, and have the potential to overcome the problem of 'competing definitions [which] make it difficult to evaluate the claims of individual scholars and to provide well-founded policy recommendations' (Boggs, 2009: 1484). At the same time, we need to recognize that the definition of an industry can never be set in stone. As the cultural economist David Throsby has observed, 'the difficulties in defining an industry . . . [include] whether the concept can be delineated according to groupings of producers, product classifications, factors of production, types of consumers, location etc.' (Throsby, 2001: 112).

Culture and Creativity

Defining the creative industries can be difficult as it brings forth two important yet contested terms: culture and creativity. David Throsby (2008b: 219) has argued that there cannot be a hard and fast line drawn between cultural and other goods and services, but rather there is a continuum over the full range of goods and services. This is partly because the concept of culture moves between a generalized anthropological understanding of the term as the way of life of a nation, people, community, etc., and a more specific association of the term with the creative and performing arts and some elements of the media (for competing definitions of culture, see Hartley et al., 2012: 73–7). Throsby proposed that cultural goods and services generally shared three characteristics:

1. Their production required some input of human creativity.
2. They were vehicles for symbolic messages to those who consume them, i.e. they serve a larger communicative purpose and their uses are not simply utilitarian.

3. They contained, at least potentially, some intellectual property that is attributable to the individual or group producing the good or service.

The concept of creativity was clarified by Mitchell et al. (2003), who made the point that the application of creativity rarely emerged by pure chance. Creative activity typically arises in the context of what Mihaly Csikszentmihalyi (1996) referred to as a *domain of application* (e.g., mathematics, music and cognitive science are domains, but humanity, culture and the human condition are not), as well as into a field into which new ideas are received, interpreted, critiqued and applied. Such fields are populated by people who can be understood as being creative individuals, who in the course of 'using the symbols of a given domain . . . have a new idea or see a new pattern' (Csikszentmihalyi, 1996: 28). Using this concept of creative domains, Mitchell et al. identified creative practices as being applied across three distinct but interconnected domains:

- *Cultural creativity,* that manifests itself in the production of original works of art, design and scholarship;
- *Scientific creativity,* that involves the undertaking of experiments that make new connections in problem solving; and
- *Economic creativity,* or the innovative application of ideas, talent and capital to create and make available new products and services.

All forms of creativity outlined here can be found in the creative industries, and Mitchell et al. point out that while the creative industries have a necessary relationship to cultural creativity, the two are by no means coterminous:

> Practices of cultural creativity . . . provide the foundation of the . . . creative industries that seek profits from production, distribution, and licensing . . . [but] there are some problems with the very idea of 'creative' industries. Creativity clearly is not confined to them, and much of what they engage in could hardly be called creative in any sense. Sometimes, as when they devote their efforts to churning out routine 'content', they even seem actively counter-creative. Still, the creative industries do ultimately depend on talented, original artists, designers, and performers to create the value that they add to and deliver, while many artists, designers, and performers depend on the infrastructure of the creative industries and are rewarded by their engagement with the creative industries. (Mitchell et al., 2003: 8)

As we have noted, there has been considerable debate about which industries can be said to constitute the creative industries. The original list prepared by the DCMS identified 13 sectors, ranging from the highly capital-intensive to ones that are highly labour-intensive, and sectors traditionally thought of as being a part of the arts sitting alongside those which are highly commercial in their nature. Table 1.1 shows the list of creative industries proposed in the UK DCMS model. It is a list that I have described elsewhere as *ad hoc* (Flew, 2002), as it brought together a highly heterogeneous set of industries that lacked a clear underlying thread. In relation to the original DCMS list, questions were asked about the inclusion of the software sector in the list, which was seen as artificially inflating the overall figures (Garnham, 2005), while excluding industries such as tourism, heritage and sports, and sectors such as the GLAM (galleries, libraries, archives and museums) sector (Hesmondhalgh, 2007a).

A second approach is that known as the *concentric circles* model of the creative industries. First developed by cultural economist David Throsby (2001, 2008a), the concentric circles model has been used in studies such as those undertaken for the European Union by KEA (2006), a report for the UK Government prepared by the Work Foundation (2007), and a National Cultural Policy Discussion Paper prepared through the Australian Department of Prime Minister and Cabinet (2011). This approach typically draws a distinction between:

1. *core* industries, sometimes referred to as the cultural industries or the creative arts;
2. *wider* industries, sometimes referred to as the creative industries; and
3. an outer sphere of *related* industries, which may range from marketing to tourism, which make use of creative inputs.

Table 1.1 shows this distinction as it was developed in Throsby (2008a). The distinction between 'core' and 'related' or 'wider' industries can be based on either the centrality of cultural value to the final product – what the Work Foundation termed 'expressive value' – or the centrality of 'creative inputs' to the production of a particular cultural product. In practice, both expressive value and creative inputs are very hard to establish empirically, and the model has been criticized for reinstating a *de facto* arts policy, where the levels and forms of public subsidy have drawn upon distinctions between high culture and popular culture that have been widely critiqued in fields such as cultural studies (Frow, 1995; Bennett et al., 1999) as well as arts and cultural management (Holden, 2009).

A third and very different approach has been taken by Hesmondhalgh (2007a) in his study of the cultural industries, which has been termed the *symbolic texts* model. Hesmondhalgh defined the core cultural industries as those which 'deal primarily with the industrial production and circulation of texts', and placed the media industries at the core, based on the proposition that their scale of production and distribution means that they are 'most

Table 1.1. Classification systems for the creative industries based upon four models

DCMS Model	Concentric Circles Model	Symbolic Texts Model	WIPO Copyright Model
Advertising	Core Creative Arts	Core Cultural Industries	Core Copyright Industries
Architecture	• Literature		
Arts and antiques	• Music	• Advertising	• Advertising
Crafts	• Performing arts	• Film	• Film and video
Design	• Visual arts	• Internet	• Music
Fashion		• Music	• Performing arts
Film and video	Other Core Cultural Industries	• Publishing	• Publishing
Music	• Film	• TV and radio	• Software
Performing arts	• Museums and libraries	• Video and computer games	• TV and radio
Publishing			• Visual and graphic arts
Software	Wider Cultural Industries	Peripheral Cultural Industries	Interdependent Copyright Industries
TV and radio	• Heritage services	• Creative arts	• Blank recording material
Video and computer games	• Publishing	Borderline Cultural Industries	• Consumer electronics
	• Sound recording	• Consumer electronics	• Musical instruments
	• TV and radio	• Fashion	• Photocopying and photographic equipment
	• Video and computer games	• Software	
	Related Industries	• Sport	Partial Copyright Industries
	• Advertising		• Architecture
	• Design		• Clothing and footwear
	• Fashion		• Design
			• Fashion
			• Household goods
			• Toys

directly involved in the production of social meaning' (Hesmondhalgh, 2007a: 12). This is in sharp contrast to Throsby and other 'concentric circles' analysts, who have placed the creative arts at the core on the basis of the importance of individual talent and creativity to their cultural products, and where those sectors where production is more industrially based are more peripheral. One could respond by questioning whether both approaches give a misplaced priority to distinguishing between core and periphery, particularly as these industries in practice tend to be quite interconnected. Just as placing the creative arts at the centre of the creative industries is open to question, it also seems odd to write off the contribution of the creative and performing arts as somehow peripheral to the media industries.

The fourth and final approach outlined in table 1.1 is that developed by the World Intellectual Property Organization (WIPO) in its model of the *copyright industries* (see, e.g., WIPO, 2012). The focus of the WIPO model is on 'intellectual property as the embodiment of the creativity that has gone into the making of the goods and services included in the classification' (UNCTAD, 2010: 6). It distinguishes between core copyright industries that are directly engaged in the production, broadcast and distribution of copyrighted works, and those industries that are connected to this production and distribution, and those where intellectual property is only a part of their overall operations. Studies of the copyright industries tend to see their size and significance as being greater than other models of the creative industries, in part because they include sectors such as transportation and manufacturing in their calculations, as the distributors of creative products. The problems with a classification based upon copyright and intellectual property are that it can be used as a retrospective justification of current intellectual property rights (IPR) regimes, and that it may also be impossible to differentiate 'cultural' forms of intellectual property from those associated with the sciences, information technology and engineering, except through introducing another means of defining cultural goods and services. Advocates of the STEM (Science, Technology, Engineering and Mathematics) sectors, such as the British industrial designer Sir James Dyson, have been critical of what they see as overstated claims about the uniqueness of the creative industries in generating new and innovative forms of intellectual property, and as 'rendering invisible the significant contribution of science and engineering to the economy' (quoted in Hartley et al., 2012: 93).

Case Study: Design Thinking

Design is an example of a creative industry sector whose impacts range well beyond the standard lists of the 'creative industries'. Perhaps more accurately, design can be described as a creative practice located in a diverse range of industries. Warren Berger (2009: 3) has described design as 'a way of looking at the world with an eye to changing it'. Noting that any challenge could be subject to design thinking, and that in principle anyone could do it, he adds:

> A designer must be able to see not just *what is*, but what *might be*. And seeing is only the beginning: designers are also makers. They sketch and build, giving form to ideas. They take that faint glimmer of possibility and make it visible and real to others. (Berger, 2009: 3)

Until quite recently, design was considered relatively marginal, and was a fragmented sector. Industrial designers primarily worked with engineers, interior designers with architects, and graphic designers with computer software developers. This industry-based fragmentation was mirrored in both education and public policy. A fashion design student would most likely be in a Fine Arts school, and an industrial designer in an engineering one; both would be some distance away from the business school. In business, design was commonly seen as a 'downstream' activity, where product developers brought designers into the process at a late stage, in order to advise on how to make a product more aesthetically pleasing, or how to develop a branding and marketing campaign. Design's standing in the arts was no less tenuous. Cunningham (2013) has identified the process whereby the creation of the Australia Council for the Arts in 1970 saw an Architecture and Design Committee established after protests from architects about its initial exclusion, but where various mergers of art form boards in the 1980s saw design folded into Visual Arts and Crafts, until it disappeared completely from the Australia Council's remit in 1989.

The 2000s saw a rapid transformation of the standing of the design field. With 'new economy' thinking giving a greater role to innovation as a primary driver of economic performance (Flew, 2003), designers were increasingly asked to create products and services that could better meet consumer needs and desires, rather than improve existing ones (Brown, 2008). With digital media technologies promoting greater convergence between the arts, science and business spheres, Mitchell et al. observed that 'innovative design is often situated precisely at the intersection of technologically and culturally creative practices', and that 'designers are frequently avid to exploit technological advances and to explore their human potential', while also 'having close intellectual alliances with visual and other artists' (Mitchell et al., 2003: 8). A range of government reports around the world in 2006 identified new possibilities for design to act as a facilitator of interaction between the creative industries and the business sector more generally, including the Cox Review of Creativity in Business in the UK (HM Treasury, 2006), the *Venturous Australia* innovation study (Cutler & Co., 2008), the Design Singapore Council report (DSC, 2010), and others (see Cunningham, 2013: ch. 2, for an overview of these reports).

From his study of over 100 leading designers, Berger (2009, 2010) has identified four key elements of design thinking:

1. *Question*: a preparedness to ask questions – even 'stupid' ones – is important to the development of new ideas and new solutions to existing problems. Asking 'why' things are done in a certain way enables a

challenge to be reframed, by opening up new connections and new creative possibilities. The Zen Buddhist concept of *shoshin*, or a 'beginner's mind', is one way of describing this way of thinking.

2. *Care*: an ethic of care, and a willingness to understand and empathize with the deep needs of people in their everyday lives, is central to designing more effective products and services. This is an ethically much deeper concept than that of 'customer care' as it is used in the corporate world, or the use of focus groups in market research. It requires a willingness to engage over time with people, in a manner influenced by ethnographic research methodologies.

3. *Connect*: finding new ways of recombining existing elements is central to design thinking, as is the willingness to 'think laterally', or search far and wide for influences. Associated with a desire to connect is a willingness to work collaboratively, and bring together people with diverse interests and skills, not as a functional team, but as divergent thinkers who provide the widest possible 'environmental scan' for new ideas.

4. *Commit*: giving ideas a tangible form is central to design thinking, so that the idea is made 'real'. Berger notes that sketching, model building and rough prototyping are all key elements of the design process.

These ways of thinking are not completely new, nor are they uniquely possessed by a specialist *caste* of designers. Historically, movements such as the nineteenth-century Arts and Crafts movement led by William Morris in the UK, or the German *Bauhaus* movement of the 1920s, have sought to disseminate design thinking widely and to have a real impact on society. There are debates today about the pros and cons of using the Internet to crowdsource design ideas through websites such as *99designs* and *DesignSpring* (Howe, 2009). Tim Brown, the CEO of design firm IDEO, has observed that 'you don't need weird shoes or a black turtleneck to be a design thinker, nor are design thinkers necessarily created only by design schools' (Brown, 2008: 93). Ways of thinking that are important include: a willingness to look at the world through the eyes of others; integrative thinking, rather than thinking in either/or terms; a willingness to experiment and a preparedness to accept failure, as a necessary condition of learning; and a desire to collaborate widely, and across existing institutional and intellectual boundaries.

Breadth and Depth Questions for Creative Industries

The question of what should be considered to be the creative industries is an example of what is known as the *breadth* question. It has two elements.

One is the issue of what industries are included, which is what has been discussed so far. The very fact of naming the creative industries created a new discursive object, and one that was very much of interest to policy makers. Aggregating arts, media, design and other cultural and related sectors into the creative industries provided new ways of collecting and aggregating data around these sectors that had been neglected under traditional Standard Industry Classifications (SIC) models, developed in the heyday of manufacturing industry, as well as giving new economic *cachet* to what had previously been termed the 'arts lobby'. As Andy Pratt observed when the DCMS discourse originally emerged:

> For policy makers, it is as if suddenly a successful new industry has arrived from nowhere. Although the constituent industries (film, television, advertising etc.) are widely recognized, previously they had been seen either as part of the state-supported sector, or viewed as somewhat peripheral to the 'real economy'. (Pratt, 2004: 19)

The debates discussed earlier draw out the extent to which questions of inclusion also raise those of exclusion. Inclusion of digital games potentially opens up the issue of whether or not to include all forms of software development, whether for gaming, word processing or managing financial accounts. Similarly, live performances, film, TV and radio, and cultural tourism are central parts of the entertainment industries, so should other aspects of entertainment be included in the creative industries, such as theme parks, casinos and sporting events? A conspicuous absence from the DCMS list was the GLAM sector, and we can only speculate as to why they were not included, given their centrality to British culture and its international reputation. Were they seen as too much a part of 'Old Britain', and not the 'Cool Britannia' that Tony Blair was fervently promoting in the late 1990s? If so, it would appear that London in the post-2012 Olympics period has achieved a better balance between the traditions embedded in its built environment and cultural heritage, and its aspirations to remain a leading global cultural centre.

The second element of the breadth question relates to the extent to which the creative industries are themselves prefiguring a wider shift towards a *creative economy*. An early version of this argument was developed by Scott Lash and John Urry in *Economies of Signs and Space* (1994), when they argued that contemporary capitalism was marked by a growing extent of what they termed 'reflexive accumulation' in economic life. This included a new degree of 'aesthetic reflexivity' in the spheres of both production and consumption, as capitalist production becomes increasingly design-intensive and oriented towards niche consumer markets, where commodities become increasingly expressive of a personal and social identity. For Lash and Urry, features of cultural production that were permeating the economy in a more general sense included:

- high and continuous levels of research and development;
- acceptance of a high rate of failure among the many 'prototypes' being developed;
- development of a 'star system' as a means of managing consumption and market demand;
- an economy increasingly driven by the production of new ideas rather than the reproduction of established commodities.

Jeremy Rifkin developed similar arguments in *The Age of Access* (2000), where he saw the rise of creative industries and services more generally mark out a new form of *cultural capitalism*, with the alignment of information and communication technologies (ICTs), cultural commerce and a knowledge-based economy meaning that 'cultural production is going to be the main playing field for high-end global commerce in the twenty-first century' (Rifkin, 2000: 167). Elements of the wider trends that Rifkin identified in the age of access and cultural capitalism that were transforming property and markets included shifts:

- from *markets* and discrete exchanges between buyers and sellers, to *networks* based around ongoing relationships between suppliers and users;
- from wealth based upon the *ownership of tangible assets* (plant, equipment, inventory, etc.), to the outsourcing of production, and wealth creation based upon *access to intangible assets*, such as goodwill, ideas, brand identities, copyrights, patents, talent and expertise;
- from the *ownership of goods* to the *accessing of services*;
- from *production and sales* to *customer relationship marketing*;
- from *production-line manufacturing* and long product cycles to what Rifkin terms *the Hollywood organizational model* of project-based collaborative teams brought together for a limited period of time.

Alongside the question of breadth in the creative industries, or the number of sectors that can be deemed to be within this domain, there is the question of *depth*, or the interconnectedness between different activities that are both 'cultural' and 'non-cultural'. For example, producing music clearly requires musical instruments, but to what extent is musical instrument production a part of the creative industries? Even if we were clear that both are a part of the creative industries, what then of the manufacture of consumer electronics, which are integral to both the production and the consumption of culture, but would be considered more as a part of manufacturing industry?

What we find is that the creative industries sit within a complex ecology of activities, which have elements that are connected and those that are profoundly different. Some aspects of what takes place in educational and training institutions (schools, universities, technical colleges, etc.) are connected to the creative industries, but many are not. Moreover, the most obvious links – such as courses that provide direct training for employment or creative practice in the creative industries – are not necessarily the most interesting ones. Andrew McNamara (2002) has made the point that many of the formative figures of 1960s British pop music – John Lennon, Pete Townshend, Keith Richards, Ronnie Wood, Jimmy Page and others – did not go to music colleges, but rather to art colleges. While none were to further a career in the visual arts, all were able to use art college as a base from which to begin their careers as musicians. This tradition has continued in Britain with institutions such as Goldsmiths, University of London (formerly Goldsmiths College) being formative to the careers of musicians as diverse as Malcolm McLaren, the members of Blur, and Placebo lead singer Brian Molko.

The UNESCO *Framework for Cultural Statistics* aims to capture and formalize these links through its notion of *transversal domains*. UNESCO proposes that all cultural domains are underpinned by the existence of four transversal domains that run across all of them:

1. *Intangible Cultural Heritage*, defined by UNESCO as the 'practices, representations, expressions, knowledge, skills – as well as the instruments, objects, artefacts and cultural spaces associated therewith – that communities, groups and, in some cases, individuals recognize as part of their cultural heritage' (UNESCO, 2009: 28).
2. *Education and Training*, particularly 'learning activities [that] support the development, understanding and reception of culture, including processes of critique' (UNESCO, 2009: 29).
3. *Archiving and Preserving*, or 'the collection and repository of cultural forms . . . for the purposes of preserving for posterity, exhibition and re-use (e.g. the preservation of historic sites and buildings, sound archives and picture libraries) . . . [and] the conservation or preservation and management of particular cultural and natural properties' (UNESCO, 2009: 29).
4. *Equipment and Supporting Materials*, or the 'tools of cultural products and activities' used in both production and consumption (UNESCO, 2009: 30), which can range from those with a single culturally related purpose, such as a musical instrument, to those which are used for many activities, of which some are cultural, such as computers.

In its framework for the development of cultural statistics, UNESCO represents this relationship in the manner shown in figure 1.2.

Case Study: Fashion as a Creative Industry

One example of a creative industry is that of fashion. Fashion has been central to cultural modernity, as observed by the German sociologist Georg Simmel in the early twentieth century (Simmel, 2003). It is also a global business, with the largest brands, such as LVHM (owners of Louis Vuitton, Donna Karan and other luxury labels), the Richemont Group (Cartier, Mont Blanc, Shanghai Tang and others) and Gucci, now earning the bulk of their revenues in fast-growing markets such as China (Ichikawa, 2008; Hartley and Montgomery, 2009). Craik (2009: 2) has observed that, historically, fashion has sought to strike a balance between being the product of a societal consensus about appropriate modes of appearance, behaviour and dress, while also being simultaneously driven by continuous change, movement and redefinition, as individuals use fashion to express a sense of social and cultural distinction and individuality.

Overlaid upon this balance between individual and society, mass and niche, tradition and transformation, is the nature of fashion as a business associated with high investments, considerable risk and short product lifecycles. Ichikawa (2008) and Craik (2009) observe that there are four interconnected stages to fashion as a creative industry:

1. *Creation/design*: the development of original products, often by 'star' designers (e.g., Marc Jacobs, Domenico Dolce and Stefano Gabbana, the late Alexander McQueen, Stella McCartney), that aim to reach new consumers while being consistent with a brand history and identity, as well as with consumer expectations concerning price, quality, social status and aspirational status.
2. *Manufacture/production*: features of the production process are the need for speed to market, short product lifecycles, risk linked to trends and obsolescence of last season's products (Ichikawa, 2008: 255). With production often occurring in high volumes at low retail prices, production has increasingly moved to developing nations such as China, India and Indonesia, with globalization and new technologies enabling the design and manufacturing processes to be separated. At the same time, there remain significant small and artisanal enterprises that are localized in their production, as with haute couture ('high fashion'), or products that retain a strong local identity (although this is in decline).

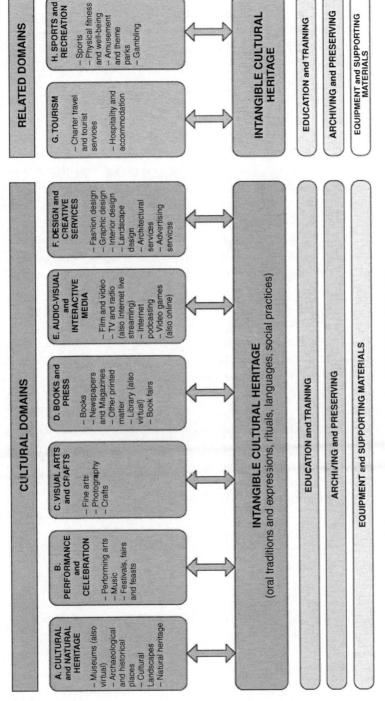

Figure 1.2. UNESCO framework for cultural statistics domains (UNESCO, 2009: 24)

3. *Distribution/marketing*: fashion distribution and marketing involves strategies for retailing, pricing, display, advertising and promotion that are similar to those for other products. At the same time, distribution and marketing are strongly tied to brand identity, which is in turn linked to product positioning in relation to the status and identity sought by its consumers.

4. *Communication*: fashion is always about more than the products themselves; it is about communicating an identity to consumers that connects to the product. Ichikawa observes that 'culture is present in the fashion process through product creation to communication and store design' (Ichikawa, 2008: 256), and there is a common message that is sought to be communicated through both the products themselves and the advertising and marketing associated with them. The French cultural theorist Roland Barthes described this as the *fashion system*, and he saw it as having a central role in the conveying of meaning in contemporary culture (Carter, 2003: 143–62). Celebrities such as pop stars, actors and fashion models play a critical role in fashion communication.

A number of key debates in the creative industries play themselves out in fashion, including:

- The relationship between aesthetics and industry, as fashion items can be designed products of great beauty, and fashion designers often have an 'art school' background, but they are also engaged in a global industry whose products are developed first and foremost to be sold in the marketplace.
- The challenge for fashion designers of working in an industry that is both highly glamorous and highly competitive, where passion and commitment are central elements of creative work, yet there is also a high level of career instability and 'creative destruction' of designers and brands (Neff et al., 2005; Arvidsson et al., 2010).
- The role of cities such as Paris, Milan, New York, London and Tokyo as centres of fashion design and communication (e.g., fashion shows) as well as clusters of interconnected fashion-related activities. Santagata (2004, 2010) has observed that creative forces in fashion have tended to cluster in certain locations in a series of 'waves' (the French wave, the Italian wave, etc.) that rise and decline, but that the role of these established metropolitan centres makes it difficult for other places to establish themselves as leading fashion cities.
- The challenges of globalization: the opening up of China and other countries as centres for low-cost manufacturing was welcomed in the fashion industry, as complex global production networks and digital technologies

allowed for 'fast fashion' and high product turnover while keeping the costs of production low (Doeringer and Crean, 2006). At the same time, China and other emergent economies aspire to be not only centres of production, but also leaders in fashion design – there is much investment in establishing cities such as Shanghai as new centres of global fashion and promoting a 'global aesthetic' in these cities (Montgomery, 2010: 82–92).

There are also increasingly important ethical issues arising for those working in the global fashion industries. An obvious issue is the contrast between the high prices charged for the products of the leading Western brands, and the low wages paid to many of those involved in their production, which has acted as a catalyst for consumer and labour movement activism (Korzeniewicz, 2000; Klein, 2001; Ross, 2006). This tension also manifests itself in the politics of copyright and intellectual property, where many in developing countries – particularly in those countries with a central role in global production networks, such as China – see copyright infringement as a rational response to the contradiction between high prices and low production costs, as testified by the plethora of fake designer-label goods available worldwide, and especially in the cities of the developing world (Ross, 2009; Montgomery, 2010). Finally, there is a growing number of people within the fashion industry who question the long-term environmental sustainability of the industry's practices: the flip side of 'fast fashion' and high product turnover is a substantial degree of waste, and some are asking whether an ethics of sustainable design and industry practice can supersede what is seen as the 'senseless destruction' endemic to the fashion system (Dunlop, 2012; Payne, 2012).

Global Creative Industries

One of the limitations of the discussion so far has been that the focus has been, perhaps implicitly, on creative industries at a national level. It has been typical to measure the size and significance of the creative industries at the national level, partly because much of the relevant data is collected at the national level, but also because much discussion of the creative industries has been focused on government policies that can advance a nation's creative industries in competitive global markets. Even where the focus is clearly international, as with the UNESCO and UNCTAD analyses, this is typically drawn from comparative national studies. While understandable, this national focus is inadequate, as the rise of the creative industries has occurred simultaneously with economic globalization, and it is vitally important to track these connections.

In their historical account of globalization, Held et al. (1999: 17) defined globalization in terms of 'the spatio-temporal and organizational attributes of global interconnectedness in discrete historical epochs'. They proposed three reasonably discrete stages in the history of globalization:

1. The *early modern* phase from the fourteenth to the late eighteenth centuries, marked by the emergence of the modern nation-state in Europe and the United States, and by European expansion across the globe to establish territorial empires. This is a period where the first major trading companies emerge, and colonialism is linked to trade, but where imported goods are largely luxury items, and most people consume goods that are produced in reasonable geographical proximity to where they live.
2. The *modern* phase, from the early nineteenth century to the end of the Second World War in 1945. This period was marked by a dramatic growth in foreign trade and investment, a massive increase in the international movement of people, as well as the expansion and consolidation of colonial empires. It is during this period that an integrated international division of labour begins to emerge, but it remains within colonial empires, with the colonies typically being providers of primary products to the industrializing core nations of Europe.
3. The *contemporary* phase from 1945 to the present, which sees the consolidation of a global system of states, particularly with the decolonization of much of Africa, Asia, the Middle East, Latin America and the Caribbean (and arguably Eastern Europe after the fall of Soviet communism in 1989–91), alongside a substantial intensification of economic globalization in all of its forms: trade, investment and production.

One of the most striking features of economic globalization in the post-1945 period has been the rise of the multinational corporation (MNC). While many companies operated outside the borders of their home country before the 1950s, it is from this period that the internationalization of production and sales activity take off. Defining an MNC – sometimes also referred to as a transnational corporation, or TNC – as 'a firm which has the power to coordinate and control operations in more than one country, even if it does not own them', Dicken (2007: 292) observes that there are about 61,000 MNCs worldwide, which currently carry out international production in over 900,000 foreign affiliates. These operations represent about 10 per cent of world production, and generate roughly one-third of world exports. Within this group, however, power is highly skewed, with

Table 1.2. Nation of origin of global Top 20 media, ICT, Internet and telecommunications companies (measured by revenue, 2009)

Firm	Sector	Revenue (US$m, 2009)	National headquarters	International revenue as % of total
AT&T	Telecoms	123.0	United States	0
Verizon	Telecoms	107.8	United States	0
NTT	Telecoms	104.1	Japan	0
Deutsche Telekom	Telecoms	90.1	Germany	56
Telefonica	Telecoms	79.1	Spain	65
Sony	Media/ICT	78.7	Japan	62
Vodafone	Telecoms	70.5	Great Britain	87
Nokia	ICT	57.1	Finland	57
Microsoft	ICT/Internet	46.6	United States	43
Telecom Italia	Telecoms	37.9	Italy	20
BT	Telecoms	36.8	Great Britain	22
Apple	ICT/Internet	36.5	United States	55
Cisco	ICT	36.1	United States	46
Disney	Media	36.1	United States	25
Comcast	Media	35.8	United States	0
Sprint Nextel	Telecoms	32.3	United States	0
News Corp	Media	30.4	United States/Australia	45
Viacom-CBS	Media	27.2	United States	28
Time-Warner	Media	25.8	United States	30
Google	Internet	23.7	United States	43

Source: Winseck, 2011: 8–9.

the top 100 non-financial MNCs accounting for 14 per cent of the sales of foreign affiliates worldwide, 12 per cent of their assets and 13 per cent of their employment. In other words, while there are a lot of companies that operate in more than one country, there is at the same time a 'super league' of global corporations whose names are recognizable to people throughout the world, and whose operations span multiple countries and indeed continents.

In the media and creative industries, the largest companies are in telecommunications, followed by the information and communications technology (ICT) sector, and then media, entertainment and Internet companies. Drawing upon data gathered by Winseck (2011), it can be observed that nine of the 20 largest firms in these sectors are telecommunications companies that have typically grown from a national base, and in the case of the largest companies (AT&T, Verizon, Japan's NTT) remain almost exclusively nationally based (see table 1.2). Moreover, while many of the world's largest companies are from the United States – or, in the case of News

Corporation, became US-based – there are significant companies based in Europe and Japan. In an updated study, Chinese companies such as Huawei and China Mobile would join such a list. As this is a revenue-based list, it tends to emphasize the more established media and telecommunications companies: a ranking based upon share market capitalization would give a far more prominent role to Internet companies such as Apple, Microsoft and Google, as well as companies such as Cisco and Oracle.

The first wave of post-Second World War transnational corporate expansion, from the 1950s to the 1970s, tended to be *market-oriented*. This meant that it was driven primarily by the search for profitable new international markets for products, which in many instances also created the need to develop new production facilities in the host country, due to transport costs, political or policy-related factors, or in order to better understand the new market. This was the age when the most famous global brands emerged, such as Coca-Cola, Marlboro, General Motors, Ford, IBM, Sony, Toyota, BP and Shell. Much of the literature on the MNC focused on the advantages it had compared to local producers in terms of this global reach, and there was considerable debate about whether MNCs now had more power than national governments (Barnet and Müller, 1974; Hymer, 1975).

In the cultural sphere, this was the high point of *cultural dependency* theories, which posited that the largest corporations – in what Herbert Schiller referred to as the 'entertainment, communications and information (ECI) complex' – were having a direct impact on culture and human consciousness. Schiller argued that 'multinational corporations are the global organizers of the world economy; and information and communications are vital components in the system of administration and control' (Schiller, 1976: 3). The result, for Schiller, was the perpetuation of *cultural imperialism*, defined as 'the sum of the processes by which a society is brought into the modern world system and how its dominating stratum is attracted, pressured, forced, and sometimes bribed into shaping social institutions to correspond to, or even promote, the values and structures of the dominating center of the system' (Schiller, 1976: 9). The cultural dependency thesis is considered in more detail in chapter 4 of this book.

The second wave of transnational corporate expansion, which began in the 1970s with the emergence of Export Processing Zones in developing economies, and really gained momentum after the opening up of China to the world economy from the 1980s onwards, is focused on the development of *global production networks*. Henderson et al. (2002: 445) define the global production network (GPN) as 'the nexus of interconnected functions and operations through which goods and services are produced, distributed and consumed [that] have become both organizationally more complex and also increasingly global in their geographic extent'. The origins of GPNs were in cost-driven relocation of less complex aspects of manufacturing to developing countries, to take advantage of lower wages for unskilled and semi-skilled workers.

This process was described as a 'new international division of labour' (NIDL) by the German political economists Fröbel et al. (1980), and this concept has been widely used by critics of corporate offshoring by companies such as Nike (Korzeniewicz, 2000). Miller et al. (2005) also drew upon this concept in their critique of what they termed the 'new international division of cultural labour' (NICL). The literature on GPNs indicates that this notion of purely cost-driven offshoring oversimplifies the diversity of what is actually occurring, as multinational corporations locate activities in a geographically dispersed manner for a range of reasons, including better access to local and regional markets, the ability to tap into local cultural and economic knowledge, favourable government policies, and a suitable business climate (Dunning, 2000). These GPNs involve *intra-firm networks*, or the geographical dispersal of activities among a company's international subsidiaries, and *inter-firm networks*, including subcontracting, strategic alliances with local producers, joint ventures and franchising arrangements (Coe et al., 2007: 228–47). Ernst and Kim have argued that GPNs are changing the nature of the multinational corporation itself, from 'stand-alone overseas investment projects, to "global network flagships" that integrate their dispersed supply, knowledge and customer bases into global (and regional) production networks', entailing a shift from top-down hierarchical models of corporate control to increasingly networked and collective forms of organization (Ernst and Kim, 2002: 1418).

The largest firms in media and media-related industries have a very high international profile. Companies such as Time-Warner and Disney, and individual media moguls such as Rupert Murdoch, the founder and CEO of News Corporation, are known worldwide for their media products, and in some cases – most notably that of Murdoch – their willingness to involve themselves in political affairs. As table 1.2 shows, the largest global media companies such as Disney, News Corporation, Time-Warner and Viacom-CBS now derive 25–45 per cent of their revenues outside of the United States, which is a significant change for most of these companies over the last two decades (Flew, 2007).

It is often argued that the global media are dominated by a small number of powerful media conglomerates. Herman and McChesney (1997: 1) argued that the global media were 'dominated by three or four dozen large transnational corporations (TNCs) with fewer than ten mostly US-based media conglomerates towering over the global market'. Similarly, Manfred Steger has observed that 'To a very large extent, the global cultural flows of our time are generated and directed by global media empires that rely on powerful communication technologies to spread their message . . . During the last two decades, a small group of very large TNCs have come to dominate the global market for entertainment, news, television, and film' (Steger, 2003: 76).

I have addressed these arguments at length elsewhere (Flew, 2007, 2009), but the major problems with the argument that a small number of multinational corporations dominate the world's media and creative industries markets are:

- They frequently conflate the presence of these media corporations in a large number of countries with the idea that they are dominant players in each of these national media markets.
- They overestimate the extent to which these media corporations are truly multinational in their operations, as distinct from companies that are primarily based in their home country but have overseas operations. On this criteria, for instance, it would be argued that while News Corporation has elements of being a truly multinational corporation, companies such as Disney, News Corporation and Viacom remain largely US companies that operate in other countries, even if there are important shifts towards globalization occurring.
- They underestimate the continuing significance of long-established national media corporations in their home markets, particularly in their understanding of how to produce content that appeals to local audiences, and their connections to national governments.
- To the extent that multinational media corporations do have success in multiple markets, they do so by developing content strategies designed to appeal to local audiences, rather than by pushing homogenized global media content. Examples of such 'localization' strategies include Rupert Murdoch's STAR TV in Asia and the many variants of MTV that exist around the world. As a chastened News Corporation executive put it after the failure to promote standardized media content throughout Asia with the STAR TV satellite TV service, 'We discovered there's no money to be made in cultural imperialism' (quoted in Flew, 2007: 90).

In referring to the global creative industries, then, we need to apply some caution. It should not be taken to mean that a small number of global media and entertainment conglomerates now dominate the world's cultural markets, even though a feature of the global creative industries is the presence of these media conglomerates around the world. It is also not synonymous with the increasing homogenization of cultures, although there is cultural and entertainment content that is recognizable around the world, particularly in the largest media industries such as film, television, news, popular music and games. Both cultural and policy factors continue to set limits to the globalization of creative industries, and it is important to recognize that the strategies of global media players themselves are highly fluid in how they engage with different local, national and regional media markets.

Case Study: Global Advertising

One area of the creative industries where the tensions surrounding the global and the local have played themselves out particularly strongly has been that of advertising. The relationship between advertising and globalization can be thought of at three interconnected levels:

1. The globalization of companies that engage in large-scale advertising, and who need to be able to market their products in multiple local and national markets.
2. Globalization of the major advertising agencies.
3. The global reach of the media platforms through which advertising occurs, including magazines, television channels and broadcast media services, particular programmes and 'global media events' (Kellner and Pierce, 2007), digital content delivery platforms (Google, Facebook, etc.), and so on.

John Sinclair (2012) has outlined global trends in the advertising industry, noting that the 1980s saw the rise of a globalization discourse within advertising. Management theorists such as Theodore Levitt argued that 'the emergence of global markets for standardised consumer products on a previously unimagined scale', overcoming 'accustomed differences of national or regional preference', necessitated 'the standardisation of products, manufacturing, and the institutions of trade and commerce' (Levitt, 1983: 92–3). The latter include, of course, the institutions of advertising and marketing, and Sinclair observes that this period saw the rise of global agencies such as Saatchi & Saatchi, who saw their role as being a global mega-agency capable of servicing global clients. This period also sees the consolidation of global holding companies such as WPP and Aegis (UK), Omnicon and Interpublic (US), Publicis and Havas (France), and Dentsu (Japan), which in turn had multiple agencies within their network (Sinclair, 2012: 32–7).

The development of global advertising agencies aiming to service global clients and create recognizable global brands – the holy grail of transnational advertising since the 1980s – has of course raised the question of whether such global branding strategies actually work. Sinclair observes that 'although the concept of "globalization" flags the territorial ambitions of the manufacturing/marketing/media complex and reflects the fact of their presence in ever more parts of the world, it remains very much a figure of speech, a strategic exaggeration in the ideological rhetoric of globalism' (Sinclair, 2012: 103). With the failure of various high-profile global brand campaigns in the 1980s and early 1990s, advertisers and their clients developed strategies that gave more significance to local cultural and other differences in developing a product marketing strategy for different countries and regions. Such strategies, which seek a 'practice compromise' (Sinclair, 2012: 119) between the global and the local, came to be referred to under the neologism of *glocalization*. Robertson and White explain this concept in relation to business marketing in the following terms:

> Rather than speaking of an inevitable tension between the global and the local, it might be possible to think of the two as not being opposites but rather as being different sides of the same coin . . . In order to produce goods for a market of diverse consumers, it is necessary for any producer, large or small, to adapt his/her product in some way to particular features of the envisaged set of consumers . . . real life producers as well as advertisers have simply *assumed* that coping 'globally' with 'local' circumstances is a necessary and an accomplishable project. (Robertson and White, 2007: 62)

It has been argued that advertising and marketing in the twenty-first century have shifted away from the 'global branding' models of the 1980s and 1990s, towards a more explicit incorporation of what de Mooij (2010) has termed 'national cultural value systems' into advertising content and campaigns. Critical to this has been the rise of the Asian economies as the fastest-growing markets worldwide, and the need for the global advertising agencies to develop distinctive strategies for countries such as China, India and Korea. As Thomas (2006) has observed, there is little point in pursuing pan-Asian advertising strategies, as the differences in national cultures, preferences, taboos, etc., throughout the region are simply too great. Satellite television channels such as STAR TV and the Asian divisions of Disney, Nickelodeon, MTV, etc., have needed to be alert to these important local differences, and differentiate their programming strategies accordingly.

It has also necessitated devolving decision making to the local level, even for global advertising agencies. Wang (2008) has observed that, in the case of China, advertising strategies may be developed at the sub-national and not just the national level: for instance, campaigns targeted at more middle-class consumers in Beijing and Shanghai are quite different from those focused upon rural China. Wang argues that what global advertising agencies have been doing in China has been not so much a response to local conditions as a 'production of the "local"' where 'each campaign takes a different approach to "local" aesthetics and to the notion of creativity itself' (Wang, 2008: 40).

Conclusion

This chapter has introduced the concept of creative industries, tracing its conceptual development from being a policy discourse arising in the UK in the late 1990s to its contemporary adoption by international agencies such as UNCTAD and UNESCO. It has noted that there are two recurring debates relating to creative industries: the breadth and depth of the concept, and the question of how important it is to distinguish creative industries from other economic sectors; and the question of whether there are 'core' creative industries, as identified through some measure of 'creative inputs', or by the extent to which the cultural forms produced in these industries circulate nationally and internationally. The question of whether creative industries operate on a global scale is one related to wider considerations of economic and cultural globalization, including the ability of multinational corporations to successfully promote cultural products across national cultures. The question of whether there are in fact global creative industries will bring us to consideration of the dynamics of production and consumption in these sectors, which is the subject of the next two chapters.

2   Production

It was observed in the previous chapter that the term 'creative industries' is often used as an umbrella concept, bringing together what are otherwise a heterogeneous group of firms and industries operating across the arts, media, design and cultural heritage. Four models of the creative industries were considered which defined the relevant industry sectors in terms of: (1) applications of creativity (the original DCMS model); (2) differing degrees of creative inputs (concentric circles models); (3) the industrial production of symbolic texts (Hesmondhalgh, 2007a); and (4) the generation of original forms of intellectual property (the WIPO model). All of these provide insights, but all equally present problems when applied across the board. In the next two chapters, consideration will be given to how creative industries may be understood in terms of particular dynamics of production and consumption. This will also involve elaboration of how globalization is shaping these dynamics, through the development of global production networks on the one hand, and global brands and the question of a global consumer culture on the other. Such developments also need to be understood as being shaped by rapid technological change and innovation, particularly as they relate to new forms of social media and the rise of user-created content (UCC).

Production and Consumption

In going beyond definitional and statistical questions to considering the dynamics of creative industries, we begin our analysis by considering the nature of production in the creative industries. There is a long history of analysis of firms, industries, work and labour, beginning with consideration of the field of production. This can be found in the classical and Marxist traditions of political economy, with their focus on labour as the primary source of value. Karl Marx argued in the *Grundrisse* that 'production produces consumption (1) by creating the material for it; (2) by determining the manner of consumption; and (3) by creating the products, initially posited by it as objects, in the form of a need felt by consumers. It thus produces the object of consumption, the manner of consumption and the motive of consumption' (Marx, 1973 [1857]: 92). Contemporary political economists such as Nicholas Garnham have claimed the pre-eminence of production in the study of culture, linking the study of production to the centrality they give to class relations, or 'the structure of access to the means of production and the structure of distribution of the economic surplus . . . as the key to the structure of domination' (Garnham, 1995: 70). Similarly, Miller et al. argued that the study of cultural production needs to start from the category of labour, since 'working backwards from the finished product, it is clear that objects and services obtain their surplus value as commodities through exploitation of the value derived from the combined labour generated by different kinds of work' (Miller et al., 2005: 50).

Yet the ontological certainties attached to production from such perspectives have been challenged, both analytically and with particular reference to the creative industries. An alternative tradition of political economy, which begins with Adam Smith's classic text *The Wealth of Nations*, identifies consumption as the driver of production, with his famous proposition that 'Consumption is the sole end and purpose of all production; and the interest of the producer ought to be attended to, only so far as it may be necessary for promoting that of the consumer' (Smith, 1991 [1776]: 444). In the context of global media culture, the French philosopher Jean Baudrillard proposed a new concept of *sign-value* that 'drew attention to the complex manner in which commodities function as signs and symbols in the sphere of consumption, as well as . . . regulating agents in the domain of culture . . . where, through advertising and marketing especially, commodities acquire certain cultural meanings' (Lee, 1993: 23). The sociologists Scott Lash and John Urry have argued that contemporary capitalism had become increasingly design-intensive and oriented towards niche consumer markets, meaning that 'ordinary manufacturing industry is becoming more and more like the production of culture' (Lash and Urry, 1994: 123).

One particular challenge that arises in considering production in the creative industries is that risk, novelty and innovation play central roles in the development of new creative industries' products and services. Those who have analysed the nature of cultural commodities (Collins et al., 1988; Ryan, 1992; Hesmondhalgh, 2007a) have identified a number of distinctive features when compared to traditional industrial or agricultural commodities:

- the *immateriality* of the product, where its use-value resides in the message conveyed rather than its material form;
- the need for continuous *innovation and novelty* in order to create new value and new demand;

- the *highly variable shelf-life* of cultural products, from those that lose almost all value after the initial distribution (e.g., live sports broadcasts), to those that maintain cultural value over decades and even centuries (e.g., the songs of The Beatles, the plays of William Shakespeare);
- the *quasi-public good* status of many cultural commodities, where consumption by one person does not preclude consumption by others, or what economists term 'non-rival' goods;
- *high costs of development* of the original product, combined with *near-zero costs of producing and distributing copies*, making it difficult to relate prices to costs of production.

Creative Industries, Technology and the Knowledge Economy

The rise of the creative industries has been seen as pointing to an increasingly important role for *intangibles* as sources of value (e.g., design, status, ease of use), and an increasing importance attached to new *ideas* as a primary source of new value. Both have been identified as central elements of the *knowledge economy*, which has been identified as superseding the idea of an industrial economy (David and Foray, 2002). The economist Geoff Hodgson has argued that the shift from an economy that is 'relatively less "machine-intensive"' to one that is 'more and more "knowledge-intensive"' (2000: 93) has the following features:

- both production and consumption are becoming increasingly complex and sophisticated;
- increasingly advanced knowledge and skills are being required in many processes of production;
- consumers also face increasingly complex decisions about evaluating the quality of goods and services that are on offer;
- there is an increasing reliance on specialist skills, that uniquely reside with particular individuals, who can in turn attach a premium to their services (as seen, for example, with the 'A-list' actor);
- the use and transfer of information is becoming increasingly important in a range of economic and social activities;
- uncertainty is increasingly central to all aspects of economic and social life.

It could be argued that a knowledge economy is best understood as a *learning economy* since, as Hodgson observes, the former implies a fixed stock of knowledge that is then distributed through the society, whereas 'in a complex and evolving knowledge-intensive system, agents not only have to learn, they have to learn how to learn, and to adapt and create anew' (Hodgson, 2000: 93).

The relationship of the creative industries to the knowledge economy alerts us to the importance of the Internet for the rise to economic prominence of these sectors, and the two are linked. Technological convergence brings together the arts, media and design industries in ever closer relationships, and (as was noted in the previous chapter) brings them into closer relationships with the sciences and the information technology sectors. At the same time, questions of culture and creativity move to the forefront of all industries, as economies become more service-based, design-led and ideas-driven (Giarini, 2002).

Technological convergence, and the blurring of distinctions between media platforms, mean that creative content now needs to be delivered across multiple platforms. Meikle and Young (2012) have described media convergence as having four elements:

1. *technological* – the combination of computing, communications and content around networked digital media platforms;
2. *industrial* – the engagement of established media institutions in the digital media space, and the rise of digitally based companies such as Google, Apple, Facebook, Microsoft and others as significant media content providers or enablers of access to user-created content;
3. *social* – the rise of social media such as Facebook, Twitter and YouTube, which promote content sharing and peer-to-peer communication and the large-scale distribution of user-created content; and
4. *textual* – the re-use and remixing of media into what has been termed a 'transmedia' model, where stories and media content (e.g., sounds, images, written text) are dispersed across multiple media platforms.

The *technological dimension* of convergence is the most readily understood. With the World Wide Web, smart phones, tablet devices, smart televisions and other digital media devices, billions of people are now able to access media content that was once tied to particular communications media (print, broadcast) or platforms (newspapers, magazines, radio, television, cinema). It also means that media organizations need to provide cross-platform media content, and that those working in these industries need skills to enable them to work across these multiple platforms. As Jane Singer has observed, with particular reference to journalism, 'the unmanaged and perhaps unmanageable nature of the network itself . . . creates an essentially infinite, unbounded product (Singer, 2011: 107). Another example of how media professionals are engaging with the challenges of convergence is through *transmedia storytelling*. Transmedia storytelling refers to the ways in which stories are told across multiple media platforms, and is both a way in which brands and franchises are being spread across media by corporate conglomerates (*Star Wars, The Matrix, Harry Potter*, various Disney franchises, etc.), and a form of fan engagement with particular media content, as they put together a richer and more complex narrative around it (Jenkins, 2006; Scolari, 2009).

There is a further layer to this relationship between creative industries and new technologies that is captured by the growing socio-economic significance of *networks*. Manuel Castells referred to the emergence of a *network society*, where 'networks constitute the new social morphology of our societies, and the diffusion of networking logic substantially modifies the operation and outcomes in processes of production, experience, power, and culture . . . the new information technology paradigm provides the material basis for its pervasive expansion throughout the entire social structure' (Castells, 1996: 469). Castells has also argued (2001, 2009) that, as the Internet has its roots – at least in part – in cultures of *networked individualism* that he associates with online design cultures and the ethos of hacking. Castells proposes that a network society is one that promotes both a culture of experimentation and a culture of sharing, that promotes both the fragmentation of mass media audiences that prevailed in twentieth-century mass communications, and the integration of dispersed Internet users across social media platforms. In relation to convergence, Castells concludes that:

> Convergence is fundamentally cultural and takes place, primarily, in the minds of the communicative subjects who integrate various modes and channels of communication in their practice and in their interaction with each other. (Castells, 2009: 135)

In *The Wealth of Networks*, Yochai Benkler argued that 'the removal of the physical constraints on effective information production has made human creativity and the economics of information . . . core structuring factors in the new networked information economy' (Benkler, 2006: 4). Benkler argued that the rise of the Internet and networked ICTs were a necessary but not a sufficient condition for the rise of a networked information economy. In particular, Benkler argued that even when information, knowledge and creative industries were at their most industrialized, as in the mid twentieth century, the inherent riskiness of investments in cultural products, the need for originality and creativity in their products, the importance of non-market motivations to many who choose to pursue their craft in these fields, and the unpredictability of what would prove popular with audiences and consumers; all made these sectors different from traditional large-scale industries. With the radical dispersal of creative capabilities and the ability to distribute creative products enabled by digital media technologies and the networked infrastructure of the Internet, it is the information, knowledge and creative industries that are the harbingers of what Benkler refers to as a new era of *social production* in the twenty-first century. Social production entails the rise of models of production that are loosely collaborative, not typically 'owned' by a single individual or group, and often not primarily driven by pecuniary motivations. The rise of Wikipedia is, for Benkler, most emblematic of this new age of social production, but its logics increasingly pervade the information, knowledge and creative industries, and indeed the wider economy, society and culture.

One important feature of the creative industries, whose logic is becoming pervasive throughout all sectors, is the blurring of lines between producers and consumers. At one level, the success of creative producers has always been contingent upon the reactions of an unpredictable and sometimes fickle public. The performers of a stage play will be able to sense whether an audience is enjoying their show or not; the live concert circuit tests the *bona fides* of musicians; pleasure in the cinema is often derived from the degree to which audiences have the sense of a real experience from watching the action taking place on screen. But this is nonetheless premised upon the idea that there is a group (the writers, producers, performers, artists, etc.) who possess a combination of unique talents, professional skills and access to distribution and/or performance outlets, who are able to distribute cultural products to a wider section of the community that constitutes audiences, readers, attendees, users of online services, etc. The concept of social production points to the ways in which these lines are increasingly blurring, as consumers themselves become cultural producers, commentators and content co-creators, and as the distribution technologies that enable this through networked ICTs become more globally ubiquitous. In developing its revised *Framework for Cultural Statistics*, UNESCO explicitly acknowledged this shift in its change of focus from a relatively linear and stable cultural production chain to the idea of a *culture cycle* (see figure 2.1), a non-linear, networked form that draws attention to the interconnections between creation, production, distribution, exhibition/reception and consumption/participation, and 'the interconnections across these activities, including the feedback processes by which activities (consumption) inspire the creation of new cultural products and artefacts' (UNESCO, 2009: 20).

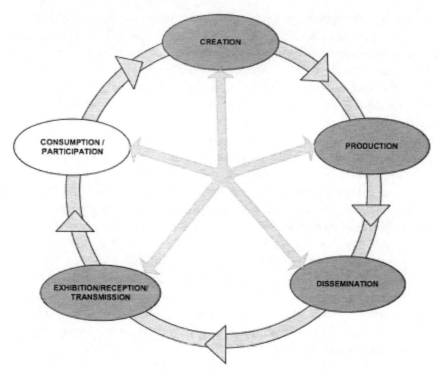

Figure 2.1. UNESCO model of the culture cycle

Source: UNESCO, 2009: 20.

Innovation in the Creative Industries

In identifying what it is that distinguishes the creative industries from other industries, much attention has been given to the distinctive role played by *innovation* in the creative industries. Collins et al. observed that while the need for product innovation is a feature of all consumer industries as a form of competitive strategy, it is only in the creative industries that 'extremely rapid product innovation is a central condition of existence' (Collins et al., 1988: 9). Pratt and Jeffcutt (2009: 7) identified very rapid turnover of innovation, fashion and the product cycle as a common feature of cultural and creative industries, along with market uncertainty, a high risk of failure, and a preponderance of short-life, project-based companies with freelance workers. The rise of creative industries has been linked to what has been termed 'new competition' (Best, 1990), where it is the complementary relationship between the generation of novelty in the form of new products and services, and the capacity of organizations to be flexible and committed to continuous improvement, that forms the basis of sustainable competitive advantage. This is distinct from so-called 'old' competition, based on reduced prices and/or productivity improvements for established products and services, although in reality the two will always work in tandem.

In such an environment, as Pratt and Jeffcutt observe, 'it is creativity (or invention) that stimulates and supports the achievement of innovative outputs. Organisations may thus become configured to value creativity and innovation as sources of competitive advantage rather than as additional costs' (Pratt and Jeffcutt, 2009: 3). Shalini Venturelli has referred to creativity as 'the "gold" of the information economy', arguing that in a global information society, the most significant source of wealth and power for both firms and nations has become 'intellectual and creative ideas packaged and distributed in different forms over information networks' (Venturelli, 2005: 396).

Such analyses of innovation and creativity as the central and defining features of the rise of the creative industries raise as many questions as they answer. First, there are a diverse range of industry forms and creative practices associated with the creative industries, and the same pressures and expectations will not apply to all of them. For instance, the expectation of continuous innovation is less apparent in some forms of arts practice than in, say, the global games industry. Second, we need to be aware of the distinction made in innovation theories between *incremental innovation*, or small variations to established products, processes and services, and *radical innovations* (also termed *disruptive innovation*) where a new product, process or service fundamentally transforms an industry or market (Christensen, 2003). In industries such as film and television, for example, a large array of cultural products are produced and distributed in any given year, but many of them bear similarities to one another that can be understood through the concept of *genres* – sitcoms, horror movies, romantic comedies, action films, reality programmes, game shows, etc. Genres serve both as coordinating devices for the multiple stakeholders engaged in the production, distribution and promotion of films and TV programmes, and as 'taken-for-granted categories that guide thought and action, serving to rationalize and legitimate decisions made in a context that is characterized by a high degree of ambiguity and uncertainty . . . providing an immediate frame of reference for the new and unknown cultural product' (Bielby and Bielby, 1994: 1293).

Moreover, claims about the distinctiveness of creativity in some industries, and in the current historical context, raise a similar question to that observed in the previous chapter about setting boundaries around the creative industries. If trends towards greater levels of innovation, and new applications of creativity, are being identified as becoming more general features of the creative economy, can a case continue to be made for distinguishing creative industries from other industries? If we think about how the car industry has evolved over the last 30 years, there has been little change in the number of major car firms around the world – it may in fact have diminished – but there has been a proliferation of models and types, major innovations in design as well as production and vehicle operation, and innovative measures to distinctively brand different models. In other words, what has been going on in the car industry sounds not dissimilar to the claims for continuous innovation that are identified as hallmarks of the creative industries.

Paul Stoneman has proposed one way of addressing this duality through his concept of *soft innovation*, defined as 'innovation in goods and services that primarily impacts upon aesthetic or intellectual appeal rather than functional performance' (Stoneman, 2010: 22). Stoneman argues that there are two main forms of soft innovation. The first type of soft innovation involves innovation in products that are generally not considered to be functional in nature, but instead offer aesthetic appeal, that is, they appeal primarily to the sense or the intellect. The products of the creative industries typically arise out of such innovative practices, as seen in the development of new titles and products in the arts, media and culture, including fashion, books, music, film, television, video games, etc. The second type of soft innovation involves aesthetic innovations in industries whose output is typically understood to be functional rather than aesthetic *per se*. This includes innovation in marketing and designing products that may or may not also be undergoing forms of functional innovation. Functional innovation is understood through the traditional focus, as outlined in the *Oslo Manual* used by the Organisation for Economic Co-operation and Development (OECD), on: product innovation (a new or significantly improved good or service); process innovation (a new or significantly improved production technique or delivery method); and organizational innovation (the implementation of a new organizational or business method by a firm).

Introducing the concept of soft innovation provides an important way of better valuing the contribution of the creative industries to the overall economy. Stoneman makes the point that despite their high sales and other impacts, J.K. Rowling's *Harry Potter* novels or the subsequent films do not count as innovation, as currently defined in economic measures such as the *Oslo Manual*. In considering the wider impact of innovations in the creative industries, there is often a blurring of the lines between the aesthetic and the functional. For example, the fashion creations that appear on the catwalks of New York, Milan, Paris and elsewhere do not typically appear on the streets or in department stores, but the creativity embodied in them creates symbolic value that is sought much more widely in the more functional form of clothing that is available in retail stores more generally, through a process of idea diffusion. Walter Santagata describes the process in these terms:

> For fashion goods, creativity is actually at the core of the production value chain. The convention of originality – i.e. the quest for novelty which characterizes this sector's dynamics – implies the formation of a sense of social belonging: people like a particular piece of apparel which is original and allows them to develop a sense of distinction, but at the same time also allows them to develop a sense of social belonging. (Santagata, 2004: 87)

The creative industries can have innovation impacts beyond their own domains. An example would be the 2009 James Cameron-produced movie blockbuster *Avatar*, which not only grossed over US$2 billion in box office and other revenues, but also brought onto the market a range of 3D-enabled home electronics devices. This interaction between soft innovation in the creative industries and other industries can work in the other direction. The classic example from the 2000s was the transformative impact of the Apple iPod on how music was purchased, distributed and consumed: the digitization of music was a necessary condition for this, but the design properties of the iPod saw it maintain market dominance over other MP3 players, and it in turn dramatically changed the music industry, as seen with the decline of album sales relative to single songs, to take one of many examples. There can be soft innovation that has no relationship to the creative industries at all. Stoneman (2010: 131) gives the example of financial innovation, with Barclays Bank marketing at least 12 credit cards in 2007, that included such distinctive features as: the ability to use the card to board London buses and trains; zero interest on football ticket purchases; donations to nominated charities based on transactions; donations to projects that tackled climate change based on transactions; and return flights for university students. All of these could be termed innovations, none of them have a direct relationship to the original function of the credit card, and they come from the banking industry, which would not characteristically be thought of as a creative industry.

The four forms of soft innovation discussed here can be mapped as shown in figure 2.2, through illustration of the examples discussed above.

The proposition that creative industries are defined by their propensity for continuous innovation is a highly suggestive one, linking the rise of the creative industries to wider transformations in twenty-first-century economies. It has been proposed, for example, that an innovation-based approach

Sector of impact

		Creative industries	Other industries
Sector of original innovation	**Creative industries**	Harry Potter books and films; Designer fashion impact on clothing	*Avatar*'s promotion of 3D home electronics
	Other industries	Apple iPod's impact on the music industry	Financial innovation through new credit card products

Figure 2.2. Forms of soft innovation

to defining creative industries is superior to the models based on industrial aggregation that were discussed in chapter 1. Potts and Cunningham (2008: 239) have argued that 'the creative industries are part of the innovation system driving and coordinating the growth of knowledge process that underpins economic evolution'. The idea that creative industries are best understood as part of the innovation system rather than as sectors defined by a distinct cultural remit or the need for public support has been argued elsewhere, drawing upon the concept of *creative destruction* as an endemic feature of capitalist economies, as originally argued by Joseph Schumpeter (e.g., Cunningham et al., 2008a; Potts et al., 2008). Such a proposition has its critics. For example, Galloway and Dunlop (2007: 25) argued that the turn from cultural to creative industries runs the risk that 'the distinctive aspects of the cultural sector have been subsumed within the wider creative industries agenda – culture is now viewed as just one more "knowledge economy asset"'.

Further consideration of innovation as a defining feature of creative industries production certainly requires some conceptual ground clearing, around two areas in particular. The first is the relationship between innovation and novelty. Creative industries sectors such as fashion, film, television and music certainly have the continuous production of new products built into their *modus operandi*, but as analysts of these industries have pointed out, they operate in the context of a range of conventions that allow new products to be understood within established framing devices. The role that is played by generic conventions in the film and television industries is an example of this.

Second, there are important differences between notions of creativity as they are understood in the business context and as they are understood in the cultural sectors. To give an example, the Harvard Business School defines creativity as 'a process for developing and expressing novel ideas for solving problems or satisfying needs . . . creativity is not so much a talent as it is a goal-oriented process for producing innovations' (Harvard Business Essentials, 2003: 82). By contrast, in his analysis of the fashion industry, Santagata (2004) rejects such an instrumentalist understanding of creativity as the process of generating ideas for producing innovations, arguing that by its inherent nature the creative process must be driven by self-fulfilment, self-realization and intrinsic motivations, and is thus the opposite of the innovation process, which is utilitarian, incremental and cumulative. We are still some way from addressing the different ways in which concepts such as creativity and innovation are approached in business and economics as compared to the arts, media and design, and there are many conversations yet to be had on such questions.

Work in the Creative Industries

The nature of work in the creative industries has been the subject of accounts that are both highly utopian and radically dystopian. An example of a utopian account can be found in the publication *Your Creative Future*, issued by the UK Department of Media, Culture and Sport, the Design Council, and the Arts Council of England, when it proposes:

> Just imagine how good it feels to wake up every morning and really look forward to work. Imagine how good it feels to use your creativity, your skills, your talent to produce a film . . . or to edit a magazine . . . Are you there? Does it feel good? (Cited in Hesmondhalgh and Baker, 2011: 5)

At the same time, there are those who see work in the creative industries as exemplifying the dystopian future of capitalism in the twenty-first century. The Marxist cultural theorist Stefano Harney, to take one example, finds in the creative industries unique forms of exploitation 'deriving from the artistic life but bred with the precarious life, the migrant life, life in the reserve army of labour at the sharp end of responsibility for survival, a responsibility for reproduction almost entirely abdicated by state and capital' (Harney, 2010: 432). Such accounts raise the spectre of precarious labour, of work that is never properly paid and which exploits the enthusiasm of young people in particular for participation in the glamorous worlds of the arts, the media and digital culture. Many critics present this as a critical counterpoint to those accounts of the creative industries which associate them with what Hesmondhalgh and Baker observe as being 'a number of desirable features of work: flexibility, safety, autonomy, intrinsic interest, skill, the blending of conception and execution, recognition' (Hesmondhalgh and Baker, 2011: 5).

There are four angles from which we can approach work in the creative industries:

1. the features of artistic and creative labour markets;
2. empirical findings on average incomes in the creative industries sectors;
3. creative labour as understood from the perspective of management;
4. the experience of work among workers in the creative industries themselves.

In relation to creativity and the arts, there is an interesting mix of contemporary arguments with long-established claims. The contemporary valuing of creativity in the modern workplace can be seen with authors such as Daniel Pink (2006) arguing that 'the MFA (Master of Fine Arts) is the new MBA (Master of Business Administration)', as well as in the 'New Humanism' in management discourse, that values the sorts of 'soft skills' associated with the arts, such as reflexivity, intuition, valuing intrinsic motivations and 'emotional literacy' (McWilliam and Hatcher, 2004; cf. Flew, 2004). The older tradition that such discourses draw upon is the European Romantic tradition, which identified artistic creativity and 'the free, wakeful play of the imagination' as a vital counterpoint to 'the cold, clinical fetters of rationalism and instrumental approaches to knowledge' in enabling the full development of the human subject (Negus and Pickering, 2004: 7).

From the point of view of labour market theories, the market for artists and creative workers presents some interesting anomalies. It is well known that in many areas of the arts there is an oversupply of professionally trained people relative to the opportunities available for paid work. Caves (2000: 35) observed that American music schools turned out about 14,000 graduates per year, while 250–300 positions became available in symphony orchestras. A study of Australian visual artists undertaken for the National Association of Visual Artists (NAVA) found that only 17 per cent of NAVA members who responded were able to rely upon sales of their art works as a primary source of income (Callus and Cole, 2002). There are many such examples.

Institutional economics explains such income inequalities in terms of *dual labour markets*, where a divide is observed between *primary* labour markets, characterized by jobs with higher wages, relative security, decision-making autonomy and opportunities for career advancement through internal promotion and workplace training, and *secondary* labour markets, characterized by low pay, job insecurity and work that is often menial and/or repetitive (Bulow and Summers, 1986). The reasons these two labour markets remain relatively distinct are, on the one hand, the willingness of larger firms to offer employees a premium in order to retain and motivate them, and, on the other, that workers in the secondary labour market often have fewer marketable skills and lower average levels of education.

When applied to the arts, however, the paradox is, as Menger (1999) observed, that much employment in the artistic and cultural sectors tends to be based upon short-term, contingent contracts, thereby having the characteristics of secondary labour markets, but at the same time those working in these sectors are among the most educated and highly trained workers in the whole economy. In seeking to address this paradox, which manifests itself in comparatively low wages and a chronic oversupply of artistic and creative labour, three possible explanations have emerged:

1. Intrinsic motivations are so powerful for those choosing to pursue artistic and creative careers that they are prepared to forgo better-paying alternatives in order to achieve the personal satisfaction and peer group recognition that arise from successfully pursuing their art or craft practice.
2. The highly skewed and seemingly random distribution of incomes and other rewards (e.g., awards, celebrity status) that can be achieved by the most successful artists and creative workers (the 'A-list') leads to systematic overestimating of the prospects of success, and to responding to endemic uncertainty by investing more in developing creative skills than their probability of success would suggest, as the allure of success is so personally appealing.
3. The mix of monetary and non-monetary rewards is a complex one, and the non-monetary rewards ('psychic income') that pursuit of an artistic and creative career can provide has its own appeals, although not necessarily in opposition to the pursuit of financial gain through such creative work. Menger has observed that 'self actualization through work, which makes artistic activity so appealing, occurs only if the outcome is unpredictable . . . [and] the possibilities of personal invention wide open' (Menger, 1999: 558).

It is important at this point to note that, by definition, the creative industries are broader than the arts. Studies of creative industries employment in Australia (Higgs et al., 2007; CIE, 2009) have found that average wages in the creative industries are higher than those for the economy as a whole, and that more people in the creative industries are high-income earners than in Australian industries as a whole. At the same time, the distribution of incomes is more unequal in the creative industries than in the economy as a whole, and in the arts and arts-related occupations, average incomes are significantly below those for the Australian economy as a whole (Cunningham, 2011).

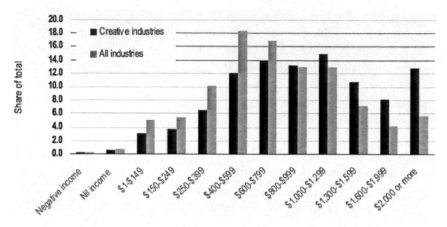

Figure 2.3. Weekly income distribution for Australian creative industries workers compared to the workforce overall, 2006

Source: CIE, 2009: 29.

The Australian data on income distribution for creative industries workers as compared to the Australian workforce as a whole is shown in figure 2.3.

In considering such apparently anomalous outcomes, we need to be aware that these analyses of the creative industries include typically high-income sectors of the economy such as software development and interactive content and advertising and marketing, as well as occupations within an industry segment that typically have quite different employment structures and average incomes, e.g. journalists compared to creative writers, and architects compared to visual artists. In the Australian study, those working in the software development and interactive content industries accounted for 39 per cent of the total creative industries workforce, and as table 2.1

Table 2.1. Average wages in the creative industries in Australia, 2006

	2004–05 '000	2005–06 '000	2006–07 '000	2007–08 '000
Music and performing arts	31,914	32,888	33,435	34,389
Film, television & radio	48,850	52,402	52,127	53,920
Advertising & marketing	70,578	74,304	78,117	81,481
Software development & interactive content	69,137	73,657	77,601	80,491
Writing, publishing & print media	56,014	58,705	61,542	63,824
Architecture, design & visual arts	29,125	31,011	32,836	33,554
Total creative industries	52,025	55,259	57,955	60,078

Source: CIE, 2009: 29.

indicates, their average incomes were considerably above other sections of the creative industries, most notably music and performing arts and architecture, design and visual arts.

Case Study: Gathering Data on Work in Creative Occupations

Another major issue arising in any consideration of creative industries work is that many people engaged in creative industries work are doing so in sectors outside of the creative industries. At the same time, many of those working in the creative industries are in occupations that are not typically considered to be in the suite of creative industries occupations. In other words, there are many in creative occupations outside of the creative industries, working in manufacturing, mining, education, health, public sector occupations, finance and other industry sectors.

Higgs et al. (2007) addressed this question with the concept of a 'creative trident' where a distinction is made between:

- *specialist creatives*: those employed in creative occupations in creative industries (e.g., a camera operator at a television station);
- *support workers*: those employed in creative industries, but in non-creative occupations (e.g., an accounts manager for a theatre company);
- *embedded creatives*: those employed in creative occupations, but in industries that do not produce creative products (e.g., a Web designer for a bank or an airline).

The result is a breakdown of the creative workforce that takes the form shown in table 2.2.

Table 2.2. The creative trident

	Employment in creative industries	Employment in other industries	Total
Employment in creative occupations	Specialist creatives	Embedded creatives	Total employment in creative occupations
Employment in other occupations	Support workers		
Total	Total employment in creative industries		Total creative workforce

Source: Cunningham, 2011: 28.

Table 2.3. Comparison of Australian, New Zealand (NZ) and United Kingdom creative share of workforce

Country	Year	Specialist	Support	Subtotal creative industries	Embedded	Subtotal creative occupations	Creative employment
Australia	1996	1.3%	1.9%	3.2%	1.5%	2.7%	4.6%
	2001	1.7%	2.0%	3.7%	1.7%	3.3%	5.4%
	2006	1.5%	1.9%	3.4%	1.8%	3.3%	5.2%
NZ	2001	1.4%	2.3%	3.7%	1.7%	3.1%	5.4%
	2006	1.5%	2.5%	4.0%	1.8%	3.2%	5.7%
UK	1991	1.2%	1.3%	2.6%	2.2%	3.5%	4.8%
	2001	2.1%	2.6%	4.7%	2.4%	4.5%	7.1%
	2006	2.5%	2.1%	4.6%	2.5%	5.0%	7.0%

Source: Cunningham, 2011: 30.

This framework provides significant insights into the diverse range of industries into which people with creative industries-related qualifications go, as well as enabling a better understanding of the contribution of 'embedded creatives' in industries such as design, health and education, in addition to their experiences in the more conventionally defined creative industries (Cunningham, 2011). The study by Higgs et al. (2007) for Australia, as well as complementary studies for countries such as the United Kingdom (Higgs et al., 2008) and New Zealand (Andrews et al., 2009), found that in all countries, 'specialist creatives' are a minority of those employed in creative employment as a whole, as shown in table 2.3.

There are further complexities involved in calculating the size of the creative workforce. In relation to the Australian study, the Centre for International Economics (2009) argued that the 'creative trident' methodology of Higgs et al. ran the risk of double counting if applied to the Australian economy as a whole: they therefore estimated the total Australian creative industries workforce at 4.8 per cent of total employment in 2001 rather than 5.4 per cent.

Some of these difficulties are indicative of what is in terms of employment statistics a new sector, but some are also reflective of the longstanding problems of adapting service industry occupations to industrial classification data developed in the heyday of manufacturing industry (Castells and Aoyama, 1994). But there are additional anomalies to be considered in the creative industries as compared to traditional industries:

1. People working in the creative industries are often 'hidden' in other industries. For example, over 50 per cent of those working in Music and

Performing Arts occupations in Australia are 'embedded' in other industries, of which education is the largest (Higgs et al., 2007).

2. Many people working in the creative industries have more than one occupation, and they tend to list the occupation that pays most as their primary occupation, meaning that their creative industries activity may not be counted in census data.

3. A large number of those who contribute to creative activities do so as volunteers or in an unpaid capacity. This is particularly common in the creative and performing arts and in music.

4. The creative industries operate on long timelines, and many people may identify with creative occupations even if their participation is more sporadic.

5. There are high levels of self-employment in the creative industries. A study of cultural workers in the European Union found that the rate of self-employment of cultural workers in 1999 was 40.4 per cent, which was three times the average EU level of self-employment (14.4 per cent) (KEA, 2006).

6. Industry and occupational categories are changing quickly, particularly in those industries associated with digital content, where distinctions between 'creative' and other activities can be shifting quickly.

7. Many of the fastest-growing activities related to the creative industries are pursued on a non-market, non-paid basis (e.g., contributing videos to YouTube and other online file-sharing services), and discovering the motivations for activity in these fast-growing 'social economy' sectors remains an ongoing challenge for those seeking to measure their value and significance (Benkler, 2006; Quiggan and Potts, 2008).

Contracts and Soft Control

Economists and management theorists have developed important insights into the nature of work in the creative industries. From an economic perspective, Richard Caves has argued that a core feature of employment in the creative industries is the existence of *incomplete contracts*:

> Most contracts that we find in the creative industries have strong though incomplete incentive provisions. The contracts are commonly simple, and they evade a complete contract's need to describe every input or action *ex ante* and monitor it *ex post*. (Caves, 2000: 13)

For Caves, the need for such incomplete contracts arises from the uncertainty of demand for each creative product or service on the one hand,

and on the other from the complex nature of production processes, which 'require the collaboration of several parties, each providing different but complementary inputs or resources . . . Each might be necessary for the project to create any value, which makes it impossible to identify and reward the contribution of each one individually' (Caves, 2000: 12–13).

From a management perspective, the corollary of incomplete contracts is *soft control*. Accounts of soft control argue that detailed descriptions of the process through which things are done give way to a framework where contracts provide the binding context for things getting done on time and within budget, but considerable autonomy is granted in terms of how to realize these outcomes. Davis and Scase (2000: 19–21) identified the three central features of creative organizations as being:

1. *autonomy*: individuals occupy broadly defined work roles which allow them to experiment and to exercise relatively independent judgement as to how tasks are executed and organizational goals are met;
2. *nonconformity*: work processes need to be constructed in such a way as to promote creative problem solving and innovative, non-standardized approaches to achieving goals; this tends to be accompanied by 'vaguely defined patterns of work, relaxed dress codes and informal patterns of personal relations and communication' (Davis and Scase, 2000: 20);
3. *indeterminacy*: the shaping of organizational goals comes in this instance, not from top-down management, but from more organic processes shaped by the relatively autonomous employees and work teams themselves.

The central message here is that top-down management practices based upon the enforcement of hierarchical relations of authority are less likely to work in the creative industries than may be the case in other industries. As a parallel, creative industries are very likely to operate according to a *networking logic*, where loose coordination, horizontal connections and informal arrangements become the norm, as distinct from hierarchical models based on governance through rules that inform the process as well as outcomes, on the basis of vertical 'chains of command', and where formal lines of authority, decision making and appeal are the norm (Thompson, 2003: 28–52).

In this respect, work in the creative industries can appear liberating when compared to hierarchical and bureaucratic models of work organization. Not only can the work be personally satisfying, as it enables the realization of individual creativity, but non-hierarchical workplaces come to be seen as the norm and the best way to align creative people to management and organizations. Chris Bilton describes the new principles of creative management in the following terms:

> In pursuit of creativity, today's managers are encouraged to reject control and hierarchy in favour of release and individualism. According to the new orthodoxy, the role of management is to enable the individual autonomy and self-actualization of the employee, not to control the workforce by setting limits and deadlines. Hierarchies are flatter, organizational cultures are self-consciously 'casual' and managers have removed their neckties. In this system of creative management or 'soft control', managers seek to remove constraints in order to free individual workers to express themselves, to take risks and to challenge conventional thinking. Consequently, the employees will, of course, be more productive and inventive. (Bilton, 2007: 66)

There are a variety of accounts of the so-called 'no-collar' workplace, ranging from the highly supportive account of Richard Florida (2002) to the more critical perspective of Andrew Ross (2003). One risk in such accounts is a propensity to consider both creative industries and the motivations and drives of creative workers independently of associated changes in the wider economy (Christopherson, 2011a). There is an extensive literature on the nature of 'soft control' in the workplace that couches it within the wider framework of debates about the sociology of work and employment and the nature of the labour process, or the transformation of labour power into the production of commodities through the combination of labour, purpose, raw materials and technology (Smith and McKinlay, 2009; Gregg, 2011).

Networked Organizations

There is an extensive literature on the nature of networks as a core feature, not only of the creative industries, but of twenty-first-century capitalist economies more generally (Thompson, 2003; Barney, 2004). In the most famous account of the network society, Manuel Castells associates its rise with the pervasive role played by ICTs in modern societies, rather than with the creative industries as such:

> Networks constitute the new social morphology of our societies, and the diffusion of networking logic substantially modifies the operation and outcomes in processes of production, experience, power and culture. While the networking form of social organisation has existed in other times and spaces, the new information technology paradigm provides the material basis for its pervasive expansion throughout the entire social structure. (Castells, 1996: 469)

The extent of the change from hierarchical management to soft control and creative autonomy has been questioned by authors such as Chris Bilton (2007). Bilton has rejected the dichotomy between 'wild' creativity and bureaucratic control implicit in some of these accounts, observing that in practice the application of creative thinking and practice is typically *bounded*: 'creative thinking takes place within a bounded conceptual space or a specific artistic domain combining expertise, tradition and experience (Bilton, 2007: 77).[1]

While it may indeed be the case that 'rules were made to be broken', it is the existence of such rules in the first place that makes this possible. In relation to networks, Thompson (2003: 8–9) makes the point that 'it might be informative to think of networks through the work of a limited kind of social deconstructionism; through a kind of unmasking, an "unsettling", and as a refutation of other coordinative devices. But this should not by any means be taken as a "rage against reason"'.

In practical terms, Bilton argues that creative industries must by their very nature be strongly reliant upon *intrinsic motivation* (motivation driven by personal self-fulfilment) as a starting point, it is very often the case that *extrinsic motivation* (motivation driven by the need to deliver the final product on time, on budget and according to design specifications or market expectations) is central in the later stages of a creative project:

> If intrinsic motivation provides a starting point for creativity, extrinsic motivation provides an exit strategy, a reason for seeking closure even if it means sacrificing the possibility of perfection. And whereas the constraints around starting a project are often self-imposed and self-generated, the constraints around closure are more likely to come from outside, from cold commercial realities or from a third party's assessment. The outside eye may provide a judgment which the creator, blindly caught up in the process, can no longer make. (Bilton, 2007: 85–6)

In reflecting on what holds together teams and projects in the creative industries in the context of soft control, three factors stand out. The first is the centrality of *reputation* to ongoing work in the creative industries. The flip side of the importance of tacit knowledge and particular skills is that, where contract-governed projects are subject to delays, a distinction will be made within that creative community between factors that were unavoidable and those that resulted from the damaging actions of a particular individual, whose transgression will make it subsequently difficult for them to get work within that community (Caves, 2000). This is indicative of the more general emphasis upon trust, co-operation and reciprocity as central to the functioning of networks that are typically built upon 'weak ties' between individuals (Granovetter, 1985). Second, managers frequently use *organizational culture* as a way to 'create an *esprit de corps* within which to limit human recalcitrance at work . . . constituting culture management projects that seek to create culture as a mechanism of soft control' (Clegg et al., 2005: 293).

The significance of organizational culture can be seen in many contexts: an example would be Apple shops, where one is met by a plethora of young, highly motivated and culturally diverse workers in Apple uniforms, who present a sense of enthusiasm for their products that is intended to be conveyed back to the potential purchaser, who is often paying a price premium to own Apple products. At the same time, appeals to organizational culture have limits in the creative industries, as they are more likely to be based upon freelance workers, short-term projects and the entrepreneurship of small firms and sole traders. A third and less desirable driver is of course *economic necessity*. A seemingly endemic oversupply of talented creative workers, combined with rapid technological and market changes that undercut established organizational and work practices, promotes a degree of compliance with managerial requirements among creative workers that cuts across the rhetoric of autonomy and creative drives that are so central to the folk wisdom surrounding these sectors (Christopherson, 2011b; Deuze and Fortunati, 2011).

The Flexible Workplace and its Critics

There is now an extensive literature on the downsides of this flexible workplace. Neff et al. argued that the motivations for working in industries such as fashion and digital media had 'less to do with material rewards than with qualities of cultural work: the work is "cool", "creative" and "autonomous"' (Neff et al., 2005: 330). As a result, what tended to be celebrated were the elements of risk associated with highly flexible and unequal work environments, creating a 'structural disincentive to exit during difficult economic times' (Neff et al. 2005: 331), as well as a high personal degree of tolerance towards poorly paid and/or problematic work environments and working conditions. In their study of creative industries workers in the UK, Hesmondhalgh and Baker (2011) identified the appeal of work environments that appear to go beyond the experience of alienated labour, such as lack of autonomy and flexibility, lack of meaning attached to the final product, and isolation from others. They observe, however, that this is often achieved at a subjective cost of endemic uncertainty about work from one project to the next, as well the disappearance of a distinction between work time and free time, a resulting sense of being perpetually overworked, and the need to commit to a culture of serial networking. McRobbie (2005: 386) observed that such work environments have a tendency to reproduce existing hierarchies of income and career opportunity, so that 'age, gender, ethnicity, region and family income re-emerge like phantoms . . . from the disguised hinterland of the new soft capitalism and add their own weight to the life chances of those who are attempting to make a living in these fields'.

Gill (2011) and Gregg (2011) have undertaken grounded ethnographies of workers in flexible employment arrangements in the creative industries. Gill identified ten elements of the 'work biographies' of new media workers in Amsterdam:

1. a love of their work;
2. an entrepreneurial mindset;
3. work being short-term and intermittent in the sector;
4. relatively low pay;
5. a work culture where long hours (60–80 hours per week) are expected;
6. the need for continual reskilling in order to 'keep up' with industry developments;
7. an interest in 'DIY learning', and often an experience of disappointment with formal learning environments;
8. a culture of informality and 'work as play', as well as the importance of networking;
9. concerns about the informal nature of hiring practices, and whether these may be discriminatory, e.g. a reluctance to hire women with young children;
10. a sense that current employment does not offer a future pathway. (Gill, 2011: 252–9)

Gregg's case studies made similar findings, although some of her respondents were in more highly paid and occupationally structured positions. Her work identified the extent to which access to digital technologies enhanced the mobility of work, and with that an associated degree of autonomy and flexibility, but can do so in ways that promote an 'always on' culture, where people continue to be engaged with work at all hours of the day and night, and where personal and professional lives have become fundamentally blurred.

Such developments have been theorized around the concept of *precarious labour*. While the experience of precarity has long been characteristic of those in secondary labour markets identified earlier, authors such as Ross (2007, 2009) have argued that 'the precariousness of work in [creative industries] . . . reflects the infiltration of non-standard employment from low-wage service sectors' (Ross, 2007: 34). Ross has further argued that:

> Though they occupy opposite ends of the labour market hierarchy, workers in low-end services, both formal and informal, and members of the 'creative class', who are temping in high-end knowledge sectors, appear to share certain experiential characteristics. These include the radical uncertainty of their futures, the temporary or intermittent nature of their work contracts, and their isolation from any protective framework of social insurance. (Ross, 2009: 6)

The critique of precarious labour has been associated with radical critiques of so-called 'cognitive capitalism' and the 'social factory' (Harney, 2010; Boutang, 2011). Boltanski and Chiapello have argued that a *new spirit of capitalism* emerged from the late 1960s onwards, whereby a commitment to work is internalized by workers themselves on the basis of its being creative, seemingly empowering and enabling high degrees of autonomy and flexibility. This apparent co-opting of counter-cultural values by a more bohemian form of capitalism – which Steve Jobs may well have been an exemplar of – is seen as a new form of work discipline, since 'everyone knows what they must do without having to be told . . . nothing is imposed on them since they subscribe to the project' (Boltanski and Chiapello, 2005: 76). This commitment to 'passionate work' (Arvidsson et al., 2010) is the flip side of a form of cognitive capitalism whose 'mode of production . . . is based on the cooperative labour of human brains joined together in networks by means of computers' (Moulier Boutang, 2011: 57). In other words, this represents a fusion of digital technologies and human creativity. Some have therefore identified a coalition of low-wage workers and those at the higher ends of the creative industries as sharing a common cause around opposition to the flexibilization of work, so that 'the vanguard of the precariat is perceived to lie with the high-wage brainworkers, whose conscientious core consists of creative workers for whom irregular employment has long been a customary way of life' (Ross, 2009: 35).

There is much to engage with in the critiques of flexible employment and cautionary tales about over-investing in the 'passionate work' of the creative industries. At the same time there are concerns, expressed by Hesmondhalgh (2007b), Flew (2012a), Cunningham (2013) and others, that a degree of over-claiming has taken place in equating the critique of work in the creative industries with a wider experience of precarious labour said to be characteristic of capitalism in its most contemporary forms. Five points can be made in this regard:

1. While there are wide variations in average incomes among those who work in the creative industries, available data would suggest that, on average, those working in these industries are better paid than many other economic sectors. To take the Australian data discussed earlier in this chapter, 58 per cent of those working in the creative industries earned over AUS$800 a week in 2006 (with the AUS$ roughly comparable in value to the US$), as compared to 43 per cent of those in the workforce overall, with 15 per cent earning over AUS$2,000 a week, as compared to 5.8 per cent overall (CIE, 2009).

2. Even allowing for the wide variations within the creative industries, this is consistent with the proposition that those with higher degrees earn higher incomes and have lower unemployment rates than those without higher degrees. In spite of substantial growth in the number of people undertaking university degrees since the 1990s, the wage differential in OECD countries was over 60 per cent by the mid-2000s (Machin and McNally, 2007). An Australian study found the wage differentials between the tertiary educated and the non-tertiary educated to be 65 per cent for males and 80 per cent for females in 2012, although it did note that the differentials were lower in the arts and humanities than in degrees such as architecture and building, commerce, law and medicine (Norton, 2012).

3. This data would suggest that forms of class solidarity that may exist between high-end creative workers and those in low-skilled jobs and the secondary labour markets are likely to be undercut by the large, and growing, wage differentials between the two groups. While authors such as Scott (2008) have identified that the two sectors have grown in tandem, and tend to coexist most strongly in so-called 'creative cities' (to be discussed in chapter 5), there would appear to be significant material barriers to a sense of common interest that constitute real class divides between these groups of workers.

4. Much of the critical literature on creative work identifies people as being 'seduced' into such work, particularly by the advertising industry (e.g., Gregg, 2011: 32–8). This arguably underestimates the extent to which such people have made conscious decisions to pursue careers in the creative industries with a clear awareness of the potential downsides of such a choice. Cunningham (2013) makes the point that many choose to mitigate the risks of such work by having other forms of employment that are more stable and ongoing, such as teaching and public sector employment.

5. The political desire for a common cause between cultural and informational workers, intellectuals and others involved with the education and

training of this workforce, and the full range of marginalized workers operating at the edges of the secondary labour market (as cleaners, construction workers, domestic labourers, etc.), has simply run ahead of the available evidence on the experience of work in the creative industries. This is in spite of the highly sympathetic readings of such work that have come from those who associate such ethnographic work with a wider critique of creative industries and cognitive capitalism. As David Hesmondhalgh – himself hardly an uncritical advocate of these sectors – has concluded, 'too many different kinds of work are being lumped together in the same category . . . [and] this may well undermine the coherence of the critique being presented' (Hesmondhalgh, 2007b: 62).

Conclusion

This chapter has identified production in the creative industries as being defined by, among other features, the continuous search for innovation in products and processes. In a context of technological convergence, this generates considerable instability for those working in these sectors, and challenges in terms of how work is organized. Creative industries have been pioneers in developing networked innovation models, but this can be seen as having downsides as well as upsides – it enables greater flexibility and informality in work arrangements, which is appealing to many who identify personal opportunities for creative self-fulfilment, but this can be accompanied by forms of 'soft control' as well as ongoing risk and uncertainty, and the experience of what critics have termed precarity. At the same time, the available empirical evidence suggests that, in many instances, those working in the creative industries are among the better-paid and most in-demand segments of the workforce. Much can depend upon in which areas one works, as well as more general economic conditions. This ongoing relationship between opportunities for work in the creative industries and the uncertainties of technological change and market fluctuations draws attention to the need to consider consumption as the couplet of production in the creative industries, and the cultural economy more generally.

3   Consumption

Consumption plays a central role in modern economies and societies. The classical political economists gave it a central role in their accounts of the rise of capitalism. The eighteenth-century political economist and moral philosopher Adam Smith, in *The Wealth of Nations*, made the point that 'consumption is the sole end and purpose of all production and the interest of the producer ought to be attended to, only in so far as it may be necessary for promoting that of the consumer' (quoted in Appleby, 2003: 36). Karl Marx developed his theory of the commodity-form, which he saw as being at the core of capitalist economies, around the relationship between use-value, or the human needs met by particular products, and exchange-value, or the prices at which they are bought and sold in markets. He observed 'without production, no consumption; but also, without consumption, no production' (Marx, 1973 [1857]: 91).

Sociologists have also given consumption a key role in their accounts of modernity. One example is Zygmunt Bauman's concept of 'liquid modernity', and the manner in which the shift from industrial production to post-industrial consumption is implicated in new forms of identity and self-formation (Blackshaw, 2010). Another is Ulrich Beck's concept of a 'second modernity' or 'risk society' characterized by globalization, the crisis of the work society and identities being increasingly derived from the practice of consumption as distinct from that of production (Beck and Lau, 2005).

Consumption has long been a subject of particular interest in cultural studies research. One prominent example was du Gay et al.'s (1997) cultural analysis of the Sony Walkman, which was the leading device of its time for portable music consumption. Du Gay et al. proposed that consumption of the Walkman needed to be understood not only alongside its production, but as part of a *circuit of culture*, which also entailed critically analysing 'how it is represented, what social identities are associated with it . . . and what mechanisms regulate its distribution and use' (du Gay et al., 1997: 3). In other words, the Sony Walkman – along with comparable current products such as the Apple iPod and iPad, and the Samsung Galaxy – are not just electronic devices for doing things, like listening to music: they also possess cultural meanings through how they are advertised, how they are used by consumers in everyday life, and how they are associated with other social traits, such as mobility.

Potts et al. (2008) have argued that the creative industries are best understood as arising out of the continuous interaction among agents in complex social networks, as distinct from the degree to which creativity is applied in their production. The decisions made by individuals to both produce and consume particular creative industries products and services are profoundly shaped by the decisions of others within their social networks. As a result, the products of the creative industries are seen to uniquely rely upon 'word of mouth, taste, cultures, and popularity, such that individual choices are dominated by information feedback over social networks rather than innate preferences and price signals . . . Other people's preferences have commodity status over a social network because novelty by definition carries uncertainty and other people's choices, therefore, carry information' (Potts et al., 2008: 169–70). Potts et al. thus argue that the creative industries emerge at 'the liminal zone between the social and the market' (Potts et al., 2008: 179), and are therefore particularly likely to be driven by consumption dynamics.

This chapter will begin with an overview of some of the key theorists of consumption. It will discuss the contributions made by Karl Marx, Georg Simmel, Thorstein Veblen, Pierre Bourdieu and Jean Baudrillard to our understanding of the relationship between culture, commodities and consumption. It will then discuss the question of whether we are seeing the rise of a global culture as a corollary of the spread of capitalist modernity, and whether this is leading to greater cultural homogenization worldwide. Finally, it will consider the implications of digital technologies for consumption, and particularly the question of whether the rise of user-created content is blurring the lines between production and consumption to the point where consumers are now becoming what Alvin Toffler termed 'prosumers', and what Axel Bruns (2008) has described as 'produsers'.

Karl Marx

The critical political economy of Karl Marx continues to be a key influence upon theories of consumption to the present day, even if his account was developed in the historical environment of nineteenth-century capitalism. It is difficult to present a Marxist theory of consumption, partly because Marxist political economy approaches questions of production, distribution and consumption in a holistic manner, but also due to the diversity of 'Marxisms' that have existed in the twentieth and twenty-first centuries.

Nonetheless, there are core elements of Marxist political economy that continue to inform theories of consumption to this day.

The first concerns the *dual nature of the commodity*, as possessing both *use-value* and *exchange-value*. All human societies have been engaged in production of their means of daily existence, or products with *use-value*. For Marx, it is through material production that humans develop 'a definite mode of *life* . . . what they are . . . coincides with their production, with *what* they produce and with *how* they produce it', so that 'what individuals are, therefore, depends upon their material conditions of production' (Marx, 1976 [1867]: 69–70). Under the capitalist mode of production, such products are neither directly consumed by the producers, nor exchanged in simple barter relations; all products are bought and sold in markets in exchange for money. As such, they also possess *exchange-value*, or a set of relative prices that appear to be determined in the market. Where Marx differed from other economists of his age, however, was in his view that the wealth of capitalist societies could not simply be explained by these exchange values, or the laws of supply and demand: 'the real inner laws of capitalist production cannot be explained by the interaction of supply and demand' (Marx, 1976 [1867]: 189).

Marx believed that the wealth of capitalism appeared as a collection of commodities, but was in fact based upon 'the exploitation of living labour by capital as the generalised condition necessary for the production of surplus-value, and therefore for the reproduction of the capitalist mode of production as a whole' (Lee, 1993: 13). All hitherto existing class societies – which for Marx included slavery and feudalism as well as capitalism – were founded upon the relationship between control over the means of production and the surplus product, i.e. that produced over and above what is required for direct consumption by its producers. As Marx put it, 'The specific economic form in which unpaid surplus labour is pumped out of the direct producers, determines the relations of domination and servitude, as it emerges directly out of production itself and in its turn reacts upon production. Upon this basis . . . is founded the entire structure of the economic community' (Marx, 1979 [1867]: 112). In contrast to these earlier class societies, Marx proposed that the substantive exploitation of labour by capital was hidden in capitalist societies behind the formal appearance of equality between individual workers and employers in the wage contract, so that labour appears as a 'factor of production' like resources, technology and other inputs; in reality, however, collective labour is seen as producing all value, including the surplus-value appropriated by capitalists through the production and sale of commodities.

Two very important concepts flow from this analysis. The first is that of *alienation*. Alienation has been defined as 'a condition in which human creations escape conscious control and instead become forces which govern their creators' (Howard and King, 1985: 18). In Marx's account, individuals in capitalist societies are alienated: (1) from the products of their own labour, which they do not own or use themselves, and which are produced through an increasingly complex division of labour; (2) from nature, as modern societies become more industrialized, urbanized and mechanized; (3) from other human beings, particularly their fellow workers, with whom relations become increasingly competitive rather than collaborative; and (4) from their 'species-being' and human possibilities (Petrovic, 1983). The consequence is that, under capitalism, alienation takes a specific form of arising within and through market society:

> Since any society is nothing more than a matrix of human interactions, social phenomena are not actually independent of human actions. They are in fact nothing more than expressions of the structure of social relationships. However, commodity production in all its forms generates perceptions in which social relations are seen as relations between things. (Howard and King, 1985: 19)

Marx referred to this propensity to view relations between people as relations between things, akin to the apparently equal status of commodities in the market, as *commodity fetishism*, which 'disguises the essential social reality of the production of commodities, and makes it impossible to penetrate down beneath this appearance and to identify the real conditions and social relations from which the commodity emerges' (Lee, 1993: 14).

The commodity-form, use-value and exchange-value, alienation and commodity fetishism remain vital elements of any critical theory of consumption. Two further elements are worth noting. The first is the *social production of needs*. For Marx, human needs are never simply given, but are relative to historical circumstances and to one's social status vis-à-vis others in a society; for example, capitalists may seek conspicuous wealth in order to mark their own class status. The presumed 'average' needs of a person or household are likely to increase with the development of capitalism, not least because capitalist growth requires the constant expansion of production and therefore consumption, thus entailing 'a constantly expanding and constantly enriched system of needs' (Marx, quoted in Harvey, 1982: 49). The second issue is that of *underconsumption*, or the question of whether capitalism is prone to recurring economic crises arising from 'the poverty and restricted consumption of the masses as compared to the tendency of capitalist production to develop the productive forces' (Howard and King, 2004: 417). In the work of later neo-Marxists such as Paul Sweezy, this propensity towards underconsumption would be seen as a core driver of the advertising industry and the 'sales effort', as well as prodigious wasteful-ness, in twentieth-century monopoly capitalism (Baran and Sweezy, 1968; Sweezy, 1968; Howard and King, 2004).

Thorstein Veblen

Thorstein Veblen was a late nineteenth-century American economist who has been described as the intellectual founder of institutional econom-ics (Stilwell, 2002). Veblen argued that an evolutionary perspective was required in order to understand modern industrial economies, rather than the more mechanistic, equilibrium-based approach of the neoclassical school. In particular, he sought to understand the social bases of consump-tion, and how these interacted with questions of social class and status iden-tities. Like Karl Marx, he was a critic of the capitalism of his time, but, as John Kenneth Galbraith observed, 'That Marx was an enemy whose venom was to be returned in kind, capitalists did not doubt. But not Veblen. The American rich never quite understood what he was about – or what he was doing to them' (quoted in Sackrey et al., 2005: 84).

Veblen proposed the concept of *conspicuous consumption*, in order to understand the dynamics of consumption among the upper classes of society. Observing that the mere possession of wealth does not in itself generate social status, Veblen emphasized how the rich sought to engage in highly visible consumption of high-status goods to display not only their wealth, but also their acquired taste, to others. He saw this as a particular characteristic of those he termed the *leisure class*, whose wealth increasingly exempted them from the need to directly engage in the production process. Describing the economic process as 'a struggle between men *[sic]* for the possession of goods' (Veblen, 1970 [1899]: 34), Veblen saw this struggle as having both economic and symbolic dimensions. As a result, consumption could never simply be understood as an economic process, since the display of material wealth was a vitally important source of symbolic power and social status. As Veblen colourfully observed:

> The quasi-peaceable gentleman of leisure, then, not only consumes of the staff of life beyond the minimum required for subsistence and physical efficiency . . . He consumes freely and of the best, in food, drink, narcotics, shelter, services, ornaments, apparel, weapons and accouterments, amuse-ments, amulets, and idols or divinities . . . Since the consumption of these most excellent goods is an evidence of wealth, it becomes honorific; and con-versely, the failure to consume in due quantity and quality becomes a mark of inferiority and demerit. (Veblen, 2000: 104)

The consumption habits of the rich are by no means a socially isolated phenomenon. Through what Veblen referred to as *pecuniary emulation*, consumption benchmarks were established that came to be held more widely throughout the society, as the middle and working classes sought to imitate and emulate their wealthier peers by consuming the goods and services that they had been seen to favour. A variety of concepts have spun off from Veblen's pioneering analysis of consumption, including what economists term the 'Veblen effect', where a product may become more highly demanded when its price goes up, as ownership of it is seen as a demonstration of social status. There is also the concept of *conspicuous waste*, or excessive product obsolescence, where:

> The styles of the leisure class this season are eventually incorporated into the standards of the next class down the social ladder. Through this trickledown effect, objects lose their distinction as markers of particular status levels. Particular patterns of ceremonial consumption have a high obsolescence rate, implying the constant generation of new needs. (McIntyre, 1992: 46)

Georg Simmel

The German sociologist Georg Simmel has been described as 'the first sociologist of modernity' (Featherstone, 1991: 4), and his work on culture, society and the urban experience has played a key role in theories of consumption. Writing in the context of late nineteenth/early twentieth-century Berlin, Simmel understood society as a 'web of interactions' among individuals, and was particularly interested in how the modern city intensified such social interactions, as well as how the experience of living in a market economy shaped social behaviour and attitudes.

For Simmel, the rise of both the city and the market economy promoted what he referred to as 'objective culture' over the subjective. By this, he meant that as more and more relations between individuals took the form of commodity relations (the exchange of things, and people, for money), it promoted what he referred to as a 'blasé attitude' (Simmel, 1950 [1902]: 414). This blasé attitude meant an increased focus upon valuing things in terms of their material worth, or what economists termed utility or exchange-value, over concerns for ethics, tradition and more subjective forms of appreciation. As cities represent the places where the market economy is most advanced, it is in cities that 'the individualisation of mental and psychic traits' (Simmel, 1950 [1902]: 420) is most advanced.

Simmel's 1902 essay 'The metropolis and mental life' drew out most systematically this connection between a modern economy characterized by universal systems of money exchange, the densely populated modern city, and the individualization of experience. Simmel emphasized the speed, variety, quality and quantity of sensory and social experiences and interactions in modern urban life, arguing that the sheer size of the city and the numbers of people who live in it mean that individuals develop psychological defence mechanisms against this intensification of mental and nervous stimulation (Simmel, 1950 [1902]). Among these defence mechanisms are the greater use of reason as against emotion in interactions with others, and the greater use of formal, logical criteria in decision making. It has been observed that, for Simmel:

> [t]he increased rhythm of life . . . that is the everyday experience of life in the modern metropolis . . . leads concomitantly to the creation of a self-preserving blasé, urban–metropolitan personality. The blasé personality is an attempt to preserve identity, integrity, and individuality in the face of such an assault on the senses, on experience, and on the increased opportunities offered in the city. This sensual experience is, in part, a consequence of the potential and possibility that we have come to understand as being characteristic of the city in modernity. (Zieleniac, 2010: 719)

One area of consumption theory where Simmel's work has been highly influential has been in relation to *fashion*. Simmel observed that, by its nature, fashion can never be universally accepted, since 'as soon as a fashion has been universally adopted . . . we can no longer characterize it as fashion' (Simmel, 2003: 238). He proposed that the modern city was a natural incubator for fashion, since it depends upon the interplay between fleeting expressions of individual identity and more widespread adoption through the society, to the point where it moves from fashion to a commodity status. Simmel observed that 'fashion is the genuine playground for individuals with dependent natures, but whose self-consciousness . . . at the same time requires a certain amount of prominence, attention, and singularity' (Simmel, 2003: 239). As a result, such figures as the 'slave to fashion' appear, who craved the distinctiveness associated with being 'in fashion', but who also seek the recognition and approval of their peers. There is thus, for Simmel, a dialectic of sameness and difference at play in the cycles of fashion, as they develop in modern cities.

Jean Baudrillard

One of the most influential interpretations of Marx's theory of the commodity-form, and consumption in capitalist societies, was developed by the

French philosopher Jean Baudrillard. Baudrillard observed that whereas the concept of exchange-value had been subject to rigorous appraisal in Marxist political economy, the concept of use-value had been treated as synonymous with that of need, understood in an a-historical sense as part of humanity's common species-being. By contrast, the realm of exchange-value has been understood, following Marx, as one of alienation and commodity fetishism, where the apparent equality of exchange in the market hides the structural inequalities of social class. This had meant that use-value was understood as something that both pre-dates and post-dates capitalism, as people discover their 'true' needs independently of the manipulations of capitalist society, striving to live an unalienated existence.

Baudrillard rejected this formulation, arguing that use-value was 'every bit as socially produced as exchange-value' (McIntyre, 2002: 51). The proposition that needs themselves are socially produced meant that what he referred to as the 'system of needs' was itself an ideology that 'describes . . . the relation of the subject to the economic system' (Baudrillard, 1988: 67). In developing this argument, Baudrillard identified a parallel between Marx's theory of the commodity-form and structuralist semiotics (Barthes, 1973; Eco, 1976). While, for Marx, the commodity was defined by the relationship between use-value and exchange-value, in semiotics the sign or message is constituted through the relationship between the object itself (the signified) and its means of representation (the signifier). In order for signs to be meaningful, and for messages to be effectively communicated, there is a need for a general social understanding of representational codes, so that knowledge about the relationship between the objects and their social referents can be shared.

It is Baudrillard's contention that in modern capitalist societies both use-value and exchange-value have become subsumed within a wider logic of sign values, whereby exchanges are never simply the buying and selling of commodities themselves, but include the exchange of social meanings. When we view advertisements, for example, we are not simply, or even primarily, receiving information about the product or service in terms of its use-value; we are instead consuming a series of signs that give the commodity social meaning. Baudrillard's work would become central to theories of postmodernism, with its proposition that the consumption of sign-value entailed the commodification of culture in all of its forms. It pointed, for instance, to a collapse in the distinction between high culture and popular culture that had been the basis of modernist theories of art; art works 'are evaluated in a relative manner within the same system of objects as, for example, Levi's jeans or McDonald's hamburgers' (Ritzer, 1998: 15–16). It also pointed towards the complexities of distinguishing social reality from its forms of representation in media-saturated societies that would be a theme of Baudrillard's later work on simulation.

Pierre Bourdieu

The French sociologist Pierre Bourdieu produced an enormous volume of work across such diverse fields as education, art, philosophy, literature, language, the media, and methods of social research (for a summary, see Webb et al., 2002). This discussion focuses on his analysis of cultural production and reception, particularly the relationship between how art and culture are understood by different social groups and the reproduction of cultural power in various forms. In his major work *Distinction* (Bourdieu, 1984), Bourdieu sought to understand how the capacity to interpret the qualities of various forms of art and culture, or what is often termed aesthetics, is in fact distributed among the general population in ways that reinforce and reproduce class-based inequalities of access to symbolic power and cultural capital.

Bourdieu understood individuals as being located within *fields of interaction* in a society. The social context is a combination of social structures (relations of class, gender, race and other forms of social inequality), social institutions (relatively stable clusters of rules, resources and relations located within particular entities, such as cultural institutions, political parties, government departments, corporations, etc.), and fields of interaction, which are the structured combination of particular forms of capital on the one hand, and rules, conventions and everyday practices on the other (Thompson, 1991: 149–51). The term 'capital' is used broadly by Bourdieu, referring to both the ownership of material objects – economic capital – and culturally significant attributes such as prestige, status and authority, or what he refers to as *symbolic capital*. In the cultural field, the ability to combine economic and symbolic capital entails the possession of *cultural capital*, or the resources that can enable one to both understand and shape the 'rules of the game' that are central to positioning for advantage within that field.

In relation to art as a field of cultural production, two features stand out. The first is that the ability to define what is 'good' art is itself a product of the distribution of cultural capital within the field of cultural production, even though aesthetic judgements are frequently taken to be 'above the fray' of material interests. As Webb et al. put it:

> Aesthetic judgements are not made on the basis of an abstract or universal standard. Rather, something becomes 'culture' because it is in someone's (or some institution's) interests for this to be so. And the 'someones' able to promote their personal interest include the government, the education system,

major cultural institutions, and important gatekeepers – or, in Bourdieu-speak, the dominant. (Webb et al., 2002: 155)

The second point to be made is that there are uneven distributions of different forms of capital in the cultural field, which generates its own dynamics. For instance, it is not uncommon for artists, musicians and others engaged in cultural production to have high levels of symbolic capital, but to not have much economic capital. At the same time, those who have economic capital often seek to acquire prestige and status, which can require them to cultivate 'taste' in relation to the arts. In this respect, *cultural intermediaries* become particularly important, as those who broker and manage relations in the cultural field, acquiring key gatekeeper roles in relation to the production and circulation of symbolic goods and services. Some key roles in the creative industries for cultural intermediaries include advertisers and marketers, media critics and cultural commentators, lifestyle journalists, managers of cultural institutions, and spotters of 'talent' in the creative and performing arts as well as music (Bourdieu, 1984: 358–9; Hesmondhalgh, 2007b: 66–7).

Consumption, Capitalism and Modernity

Classical political economists such as Adam Smith and Karl Marx readily observed that the capitalist society that was coming into being in eighteenth- and nineteenth-century Europe was not only one of smokestack factories. Other features of the Industrial Revolution included the development of high-speed rail transport, and the creation of large, densely populated cities, as large numbers of people moved from farms and small towns to become the industrial wage-labourers of modern capitalism (Hobsbawm, 1996). It was also a society where individual consumption was becoming more and more prominent, as economic historians of the period have observed. McKendrick has observed that 'there was a consumer boom in England in the eighteenth century . . . Men, and in particular women, bought as never before . . . the later eighteenth century saw such a convulsion of getting and spending . . . that a greater proportion of the population than in any previous society in human history was able to enjoy the pleasures of buying consumer goods' (McKendrick, 2003: 40). Bermingham has traced the catalytic role of consumption back even further, arguing that 'since the seventeenth century . . . consumption has been the primary means through which individuals have participated in culture and transformed it' (quoted in Storey, 1999: 3).

The relationship between consumption and production varied between the competing traditions of political economy. For Adam Smith, it was the desires of individuals that brought forth the products, and hence the producers, that would meet those desires. As a result, the neoclassical economic tradition followed Smith in identifying the consumer as a rational actor, whose changing desires and demands prompt profit-seeking entrepreneurs to develop means through which such wants can be met, meaning that market economies are ultimately driven by *consumer sovereignty* (Friedman and Friedman, 1980; cf. Aldridge, 2003: 17–19).

By contrast, Karl Marx presented the *accumulation of capital* as being at the core of modern capitalist economies, forcing individual capitalists to strive to ever increase the production and realization of surplus-value, and hence profit, through the production and sale of commodities, in order to survive in the competitive struggle with other capitalists. From this perspective, where 'capital is driven to an imperative which forces it to undertake the continual search for those economic conditions which may be the most immediately propitious for growth' (Lee, 1993: 63), strategies to promote greater consumption of individual products, or the creation of new needs and desires, become a key means through which individuals can maintain and bolster their individual profits. Writers in the Marxist tradition tend to view theories of the sovereign consumer as at best naïve, and as complying more as part of the dominant ideology of the capitalist system itself (Mohun, 2003). Political economists who followed Marx, such as Paul Baran and Paul Sweezy (1968), have placed great stress upon the role played by the 'sales effort' associated with advertising, marketing and the techniques of persuasion in maintaining high and growing rates of consumption, and hence staving off tendencies towards the over-accumulation of capital and economic crisis.

The discussion above makes clear that, in analysing consumption, its economic dimensions are not the only consideration. The first concerns the relationship between *consumption and class*, or *consumption and status*. Marx observed the social nature of needs, arguing that 'our wants and pleasures have their origins in society; we therefore measure them in relation to society . . . [and] since they are of a social nature, they are of a relative nature' (quoted in McIntyre, 1992: 44). Thorstein Veblen more fully developed the concept that consumption was one of the central means by which wealthy elites differentiated themselves from the broader population through conspicuous consumption. Veblen proposed that being seen not only to possess material wealth, but also to have the personal capacities to differentiate and thus acquire goods of the highest quality, was a marker of social status commensurate with economic wealth. In so far as others aspired to the status of what Veblen termed the leisure class, this set off society-wide consumption effects, including:

- pecuniary emulation, or the tendency towards consuming particular items because of their social status;
- the 'Veblen effect' on the prices of goods, whereby more expensive versions of a product are sought because they are more expensive;
- conspicuous waste, where product obsolescence is accelerated in order to artificially stimulate the demand for 'new' products.

The work of Pierre Bourdieu finds complex articulations between class and culture through consideration of the relationship of 'taste' to cultural value. While Bourdieu proposed that cultural capital was unequally distributed through society, its distribution was not synonymous with that of economic capital. In particular, it was seen as possible to acquire symbolic capital through specialist knowledge of the arts and culture, which may then be sought after by others with economic capital in order to acquire 'taste'. Such cultural capital can also be used by cultural intermediaries to promote particular cultural forms and products to the wider population through key gatekeeper roles in cultural distribution.

A second issue to be considered is that of *consumption-as-manipulation*. Many followers of Marx have seen consumption as a key means through which capitalists manipulate the working population to hold beliefs that are contrary to their own material interests, both in order to sell commodities and to maintain social order in the face of contradictory class-based social relations. Mandel (1983: 93) argued that the development of capitalism inevitably entails 'a broadening of the sphere of consumption . . . [and] implies a growing manipulation of the consumer by capitalist firms, in the production, distribution and publicity spheres'. Similarly, Bocock (1993: 50–1) defined consumerism as 'the active ideology that the meaning of life is to be found in buying things and pre-packaged experiences', and that it 'has become the major ideology that legitimates modern capitalism'. As noted in chapter 1, theorists of the culture industry such as Adorno and Horkheimer (1979) saw modern capitalism as being engaged in systematic degradation of the cultural sphere, in order to promote mass-produced and commodified cultural products as generating the semblance of freedom and choice. In such a vein, Herbert Marcuse proposed, in *One-Dimensional Man* (Marcuse, 1964), that capitalist industrial society integrated individuals into the economic system of production and consumption by promoting false needs, and redirecting intellectual and libidinal energies away from critique and the consideration of social alternatives, thereby creating a 'one-dimensional' universe of thought and behaviour. This meshes with the analysis of institutional economists such as John Kenneth Galbraith, who argued that the requirements of corporations to plan growth and technological change led to a 'revised sequence', whereby new product and services are developed and then techniques of persuasion are used in order to create a demand for them among consumers (Stilwell, 2002: 233–4).

The consumption-as-manipulation thesis is an important one to consider in relation to the global creative industries for two reasons. First, with the global spread of capitalist modernity, many argue that Western consumer society – or, more particularly, American consumer capitalism – has been presented as a global ideal for developing nations, in a manner akin to how the leisure class display their conspicuous wealth to the lower classes. Second, the concern about 'Americanization' relates to the idea that globalization leads to a more homogeneous global culture, dominated by a small number of global multinationals and their commercial products. The latter concern is widely held outside of the developing world, particularly in parts of Europe as well as countries such as Canada.

It is important to note the criticisms of the consumption-as-manipulation thesis. Daniel Miller (2010) refers to the 'poverty of moralism' in critiques of consumption, positing that much of the academic literature is reflective of assumptions that the desire to consume commodities is evidence of a shallow materialism, undertaken by deluded individuals in thrall to commodity culture, and losing touch with 'authentic culture' by virtue of the blandishments of the capitalist culture industries. Against this, Miller argues that there are historical continuities in how people have used consumption, and the products of material culture, in expressive ways and in the maintenance of social relations. Moreover, there can be a politics of consumption that is not simply expressed through anti-consumerism, as seen with movements such as consumer boycotts, ethical consumption and green consumerism (cf. Aldridge, 2003: 132–46). The consumption-as-manipulation thesis also presumes that use-value is in some sense authentic, whereas exchange-value is the product of consumer manipulation. As was noted above, this position was extensively critiqued by Baudrillard with his notion of sign-value as the contemporary state of capitalist consumer societies.

A third element of consumption theories to be considered is the relationship between *consumption and identity*. Consumption has been generally linked to the rise of modernity. Zukin and Maguire define the relationship between consumption and modernity in the following way:

> Accounts of modernity trace the development of this new self to the process of individualization . . . in which identity shifts from a fixed set of characteristics determined by birth and ascription to a reflexive, ongoing, individual project shaped by appearance and performance. The roots of this shift lie

in urbanisation and industrialisation, which open access to an array of new goods and experiences, while at the same time permeating the core of the family and extending interdependencies . . . The individual is then free to choose his or her path towards self-realisation, taking on an opportunity and obligation once reserved for the elite. This freedom, however, comes at the cost of security; without fixed rules, the individual is constantly at risk of getting it wrong, and anxiety attends each choice. Simply put, modernity's legacy is a mass crisis of identity. (Zukin and Maguire, 2004: 180–1)

Simmel's account of the modern city as a driver of individualization associated urbanization and the rise of a market economy with the decline of deeply held beliefs, and an increasingly blasé attitude towards underlying values and commitments. At the same time, he saw the city as a natural incubator of fashion, as the desire to express difference and individuality through one's consumption choices could have a more immediate social and cultural impact. A similar ambivalence can be found in Baudrillard's account of sign-value. He argues that use-value is no less socially produced than exchange-value, meaning that there is no longer the possibility of transcending the alienation of commodity society: as McIntyre (1992: 55) observes, 'needs, which are complex and vague, cannot be disentangled from products, which have greater coherence'. Paradoxically, as the sign-value associated with branded commodities becomes universalized, individuals comprehend the nature of the manipulation that underlies them, and in turn use commodities as signifiers of cultural difference. The extensive academic literature on postmodernism referred to this 'semiotics of excess', whereby cultural products become self-referential and intertextual in their nature, and their consumers critically engage with this play of signs (Collins, 1993). While Baudrillard's account has been critiqued for being overly pessimistic, seeing no way out of the endless reproduction of signs (e.g., Lury, 2011: 67–72), it nonetheless raises the point that a moral critique of consumption-as-manipulation runs the risk of not only critiquing capitalism, but of rejecting modernity itself. As Zukin and Maguire conclude their overview of the literature on consumption, 'the point . . . is neither to praise nor to condemn consumers, but to understand how, and why, people learn to consume, over time, in different ways' (Zukin and Maguire, 2004: 193).

Consumption and the Question of Global Culture

Understanding the nature and significance of the global creative industries is not possible without giving considerable attention to consumption.

As Goodman (2007: 344) has observed, 'Globalisation cannot be understood without the category of consumption'. Indeed, one of the most visible manifestations of globalization is the proliferation of global cultural products, including the films and television series produced by 'Global Hollywood' (Miller et al., 2005), the 24-hour news channels that have proliferated across satellite and cable services (Volkmer, 1999; El-Nawawy and Iskander, 2002), and the global brands with which we are so familiar – McDonald's, Disney, Coca-Cola, Nike, Starbucks, Apple, Hello Kitty, etc. (Klein, 2001; Kornberger, 2010; Lury, 2011). The proliferation of global media and cultural products, and the demand to consume them that seems to exist worldwide, have raised the question of whether we now need to speak of a *global culture*. Goodman (2007: 330, 331) makes the point that 'Globalisation undoubtedly has cultural effects . . . [and] modern culture can only be understood within a global setting', but that 'the question still remains open as to whether this constitutes a global culture'.

Early attempts to theorize global culture include Marshall McLuhan's concept of a 'global village', and theories of cultural imperialism. Writing in the 1960s, McLuhan understood media technologies as 'extensions of man' (McLuhan, 1964). Observing the capacity of broadcast media technologies to bridge both time and space, McLuhan proposed that modern humanity now found itself in a *global village*, where 'electric circuitry has overthrown the regime of "time" and "space" and pours upon us instantly and continuously the concerns of all other men *[sic]*' (McLuhan and Fiore, 1967: 16).

While McLuhan saw global media culture as moving us closer to better understanding our common humanity, more critical accounts pointed to the overwhelming dominance of Western commercial media interests in these technologies and the cultural products they distributed. These critical theorists identified global media culture as instruments of Western cultural domination over the non-Western world. One of the most influential accounts of such cultural domination was that of Herbert Schiller (1969, 1976, 1996), who argued that the US-dominated global media were at the core of a capitalist world system that promoted *cultural imperialism*. Schiller defined cultural imperialism in the following terms:

> The concept of cultural imperialism . . . describes the sum of processes by which a society is brought into the modern world system and how its dominating stratum is attracted, pressured, forced, and sometimes bribed into shaping social institutions to correspond to, or even promote, the values and structures of the dominant centre of the system. (Schiller, 1976: 9)

For Schiller, the processes associated with cultural imperialism had three dimensions. First, there was an economic dimension, as multinational corporations spread their worldwide operations, and the global brands discussed above were marketed and promoted in the developing world, displacing local companies and products. Schiller (1969) outlined the rise to ascendancy of what he termed the 'Entertainment, Communication and Information (ECI) industries' in the US economy, and saw these as being at the advance guard of global corporate expansion. Second, the context of the Cold War with the Soviet Union saw the United States drawing upon academic and diplomatic as well as military and intelligence resources to acquire political hegemony in what had come to be known as the 'Third World'. Development communications became an important component of such geo-political strategies, identifying North American consumer society as the archetype of modernity, and seeking to promote transformations in attitudes, beliefs and values away from what was termed 'traditionalism' towards cultural modernization, through the use of mass communications media (Sparks, 2007; Melkote, 2010).

Finally, ongoing exposure to the products of Western consumer culture, and to associated advertising, marketing and branding techniques, was seen as generating psychological displacement, particularly among elites and the middle classes, who identified more with the culture and lifestyles of global elites than with the culture of their own peoples. Schiller (1996: 115, 125) argued that the influence of global creative industries, or what he terms the ECIs, was never simply economic. These industries differed from others on the basis of their 'direct, though immeasurable impact on human consciousness', as well as their capacity 'to define and present their own role to the public'. The broader consequence has been the global circulation of 'American pop culture product', which has become the cultural ideal to which others around the world aspire, resulting in 'the phenomenally successful extension of marketing and consumerism in the world community' (Schiller, 1996: 115).

A number of variants of Schiller's cultural imperialism thesis can be found in the critical academic literature. Herman and McChesney argued that the global media system was central to the global market economy as a whole, not only because of the size and significance of the media corporations in question, but also because 'the global media provide a vital forum for advertisers and the promotion of demand and *consumerist values* that grease the wheels of the global market' (Herman and McChesney, 1997: 189; emphasis added). Sklair (2000) argued that the global system is characterized not only by the dominance of capitalism in the economic sphere, but also by *consumerism as its dominant culture-ideology*, promoted by global mass media through their 'systematic blurring of the lines between information, entertainment, and promotion of products' (Sklair, 2000: 68), and by a transnational capitalist class who share cosmopolitan lifestyles and values. Barber (2000) argued that global brands are 'pressing nations into one homogeneous global culture, one McWorld tied together by communications, information, entertainment, and commerce' (Barber, 2000: 21), challenged primarily by reassertions of local and particularist identities – what he provocatively terms 'Jihad' – in a particularly stark account of democratic values being subverted by the global market on the one hand, and pre-modern communitarianism on the other.

The claim that globalization has led to greater cultural homogeneity, and a more uniform global culture, has been disputed from several directions. Smith (1990) disputes the central premise that people around the world are coming to have more in common culturally, arguing that it confuses global communications with global culture. Tomlinson (1991, 1999, 2007) has also argued culture never simply consists of products and media images, but is bound up with systems of social meaning. He asserts that theories of cultural imperialism (and related concepts such as 'Americanization', 'Westernization' and 'McWorld') explicitly assume the primacy of economic relations, and 'a tacit assumption that globalization is a process that somehow has its sources and its terrain of operation *outside* of culture' (Tomlinson, 2007: 353).

Tomlinson's argument that, for Schiller, 'capitalism *is* culture; that the "effects" of the spread of the system are evident in the immersion of individuals within it' (Tomlinson, 1991: 40), draws attention to the assumptions about media effects that underpin theories of cultural imperialism. From an audience and reception studies perspective, it was argued that the cultural imperialism thesis was overly reliant upon the 'media effects' theory, losing sight of the degree to which the consumption of 'global' media programmes in different countries and the manner in which they are interpreted and given meaning by local audiences varies considerably (Ang, 1996). At the same time, Schiller questioned arguments derived from the reception of single media texts such as a film or a television programme, arguing that the relationship of audiences to media content needed to be considered at the level of what he termed the 'total cultural package' of programmes, advertisements and services, rather than at the level of individual TV programmes or other forms of media content (Schiller, 1991).

A more substantive question for the media/cultural imperialism thesis lies in the empirical evidence of local audiences continuing to demonstrate a consistent preference for nationally based media as it is available. Tunstall (2008) estimates that 80 per cent of television content consumed globally is produced and consumed on a national basis, and only 10 per cent is imported or 'global' content, while Straubhaar (2007) has made the point that national television systems have often become more local, not less, in the face of competition from global product. Such *glocalization*, or the refinement of cultural products for local markets as global brands become more widely available, is reflective of a more general tendency, identified by Waters (2001), towards a two-way relationship between the arrival of global brands and the development of local variants; for example, specialist Asian restaurant chains emerging as an alternative to McDonald's arriving in Asian countries.

This is not to downplay the significance of global trade in cultural products, but even here it needs to be noted that this is far more de-centred than the cultural imperialism thesis has presumed. Sinclair et al. (1996) identified the importance of *geo-linguistic regions* and *geo-cultural regions* as sites of audiovisual trade. The success of Latin American *telenovelas* with audiences in the Spanish- and Portuguese-speaking worlds, Hong Kong-produced 'Canto-pop' and action/martial arts films in Chinese-speaking media markets, and Australian serial dramas or 'soaps' in English-speaking markets, are commonly cited examples of 'indigenization' or 'hybridization' of global cultural forms, that have considerable appeal in regional sub-markets. In his work on *media capitals*, Curtin (2007, 2010) observed that while Hollywood remains the global exemplar, very significant sites of film and television production aimed at international markets can be identified in cities as diverse as Mumbai, Hong Kong, Seoul, Cairo, Beijing, Miami and Lagos (cf. Sinclair, 2003; Huang, 2012).

Case Study: What Do We Mean by 'Global Culture'?

A discussion about whether a common global culture is emerging presents the question of what we mean by 'culture'. Raymond Williams famously described culture as 'one of the two or three most complicated words in the English language' (Williams, 1976: 87). At the root of these difficulties are two distinct but related understandings of culture. First, there is the *social* or *anthropological* definition of culture, defined by Raymond Williams as 'a particular way of life, whether of a people, a period [or] a group' (Williams, 1976: 87), and where culture itself refers to 'meanings and values not only in art and learning but also in institutions and ordinary behaviour' (Williams, 1965: 57). In this definition, culture is associated with the everyday practices of people and social groups, and is regarded as a lived and shared experience that is grounded in history, beliefs and shared values.

The second sense in which culture can be understood is as *mediated symbolic communication*, or the processes of imagining and meaning-making, and the associated forms of communication, interaction and symbolic representation through which such processes are developed. In this second sense, it is *media* that is central to culture, the more so that a society has developed advanced communications technologies. Douglas Kellner (1995: 5) has observed that 'the products of media culture provide materials out of which we forge our very identities, our sense of selfhood', and that 'media images help shape our view of the world and our deepest moral values . . . media stories provide the symbols, myths and resources through which we constitute a common culture'. John Thompson (1995: 46) has situated this rise of media culture historically, observing that:

> With the advent of modern societies . . . a systematic cultural transformation began to take hold. By virtue of a series of technical innovations . . . symbolic forms were produced, reproduced and circulated on a scale that was unprecedented. Patterns of communication and interaction began to change in profound and irreversible ways. The changes . . . comprise what can loosely be called the 'mediatisation of culture'. (Thompson, 1995: 46)

These two definitions are not mutually exclusive: both are central to fully understanding culture. But they pull in different directions when applied in the context of globalization. For Anthony Smith, culture is a form of 'collective identity . . . [that] is always historically specific because it is based on shared memories and a sense of continuity between generations'. As such, the concept of global culture appears as a form of technological determinism: 'Given the plurality of such experiences and identities, and given the historical depth of such memories, the project of a global culture, as opposed to global communication, must appear premature for some time to come' (Smith, 1990: 180). Daniel Miller has argued against moralizing about the negative impact of global brands, since 'we have to allow culture to be the product of the subsequent localisation of global forms, rather than only that which has some deep historical and local tradition' (Miller, 2010: 255).

By contrast, it is through conceptualizing culture in this second sense, as symbolic or signifying systems through which social identities are formed, that the concept of a global culture can make sense. It is the concept of a mediated culture, with an increasingly common global repertoire of images, stories, information, events and myths, that authors as otherwise diverse as McLuhan, Baudrillard and Schiller are making reference to.

It is in this latter sense that we can see how consumption, particularly as it pertains to media and communications technologies, can point towards common experiences of something akin to a global culture, even if it does not mean that people in one location are becoming more like people in another. John Tomlinson has referred to this phenomenon as *deterritoriali-zation*, where:

> The vast majority of us live local lives, but globalization is rapidly changing our experience of this 'locality' . . . Deterritorialization . . . means that the significance of the geographical location of a culture – not only the physi-cal, environmental and climatic location, but all the self-definitions, ethnic boundaries and delimiting practices that have accrued around this – is erod-ing. No longer is culture so tied to the constraints of local circumstances. (Tomlinson, 2007: 360)

In this definition, deterritorialization is not the same as cultural imperial-ism or cultural domination. Indeed, as Appadurai (1990) and Tomlinson (2007) have observed, globalization may be associated with greater cultural diversity, rather than cultural homogenization. A global media culture can, however, be one of the forces that destabilize traditional cultural forms and practices, while never eliminating cultural specificities and forms of cultural difference.

Productive Consumption

In considering consumption in relation to the creative industries, in both a historical and contemporary sense, two propositions are apparent:

1. Culture needs to be conceived of in dynamic rather than in static terms. Concepts such as needs, wants, quality, taste and identity need to be understood as both highly fluid and changeable over time. The glo-balization of culture cannot therefore simply be seen as the imposition of Western culture on the developing world, or the emergence of an increasingly homogeneous global culture, or 'McWorld'.
2. As we think of culture as increasingly constituted through mediated symbolic forms, with the means of global communication such as broadcasting and the Internet becoming ubiquitous, there is a need to be aware of the growing diversity of locations from which cultural forms are being produced and traded, as well as the increasingly diverse and heterogeneous sites in which they are consumed. This means that meta-phors of either a 'global village' or 'cultural imperialism' are insufficient for understanding the dynamics of global media culture.

To this we can add a third proposition, that culture and consumption have become increasingly important to the dynamics of contemporary global capitalism. This can be understood from a few angles. At a purely economic level, there is what is known as 'Engel's Law', after the nineteenth-century German economist and statistician Ernst Engel, which posits that the proportion of personal incomes devoted to cultural goods and services, as non-necessities, increases more than proportionately to increases in income (Zweimuller, 2000). A corollary of Engel's law is that cultural consumption in all of its forms – including audiences for the arts – is positively correlated with economic growth and development, as barriers to participation arising from economic subsistence are gradually lifted. Such a finding would also be consistent with the *hierarchy of needs* concept, first proposed by social psychologist Abraham Maslow (1943). Maslow argued that, as humans had greater security in terms of physiological and safety needs, they could pursue higher-order goals associated with self-actualization, including artistic, creative and intellectual pursuits.

From a sociological perspective, Featherstone (2007) has argued that there is a growing prominence of culture and consumption in contemporary economies and societies. Factors underpinning this *culturalization of the economy* include: the greater application of design aesthetics to the products of everyday culture; the rise of cultural intermediaries; growing employment in the creative industries; and the challenging of established cultural and symbolic hierarchies associated with postmodern culture. The rise of service industries can also be identified as promoting the culturalization of the economy, as there is a more significant interpersonal dimension attached to the sale of services, often accompanied by much work on the internal culture of self-presentation of those engaged in the direct sale of products (du Gay and Pryke, 2002; Lury, 2011).

It was noted earlier in this chapter that historians have begun to see consumption as playing a more active role in economic development than has been commonly assumed. It has been argued, for example, that the Industrial Revolution in eighteenth-century Britain was as much about a revolution in consumption and consumer expectations as it was about new technologies and the factory system (McKendrick, 2003). Hartley (1996) has argued that the origins of modern journalism lie in the creation of a *reading public* in eighteenth- and nineteenth-century Europe, as a form of popular culture brought together by urbanization, industrialization, the growth of print literacy, and the intellectual culture of the Enlightenment, and the French Revolution. Such an account does not deny the importance of technological changes such as printing presses to enabling the mass distribution of newspapers and magazines. Rather, it proposes that production-centred accounts of socio-economic and technological change are insufficient, and that an appropriate weighting needs to be given to the cultural changes that were also occurring, as expressed in changing patterns of media consumption. For Hartley, these trends in media consumption are also expressive of a popular demand for representation, which in the nineteenth and twentieth centuries took the form of national citizens seeking out media which best expressed their personal and political interests. He argues that in the twenty-first century, as the capacity to produce and distribute media digitally has become far more widely available, this is transforming into a demand for self-representation, making use of platforms such as YouTube and personal blogs to seek out online communities with shared interests, on a global rather than primarily a national scale (Hartley, 2012).

The Latin American scholar Nestor Garcia Canclini (2001) has argued that emergent forms of transnational citizen identity can be identified in trends towards cultural globalization, even if they are also deeply corrosive to the traditional cultures of nation-states. Canclini argued that globalization weakened the links between culture and territory, so that 'objects . . . lose any necessary tie to territories of origins', meaning that 'culture becomes a process of multinational assemblage, a flexible articulation of parts, a montage of features that any citizen in any country, of whatever religion or ideology, can read and use' (Canclini, 2001: 17–18). He distinguishes globalization from internationalization on the basis of this deterritorialization of culture:

> What distinguishes internationalization from globalization that . . . the majority of messages and commodities that we consumed were made in our own societies, with strict policing of customs offices and laws that protected what each country produced. Nowadays, what is produced in the entire world is right here and it is difficult to know what is our own. Internationalization was an opening of the geographic boundaries of each society for the purpose of bringing in the material and symbolic commodities of all the other societies. Globalization operates according to a functional interaction of dispersed economic and cultural activities, and a multicentric system of production of commodities and services, in which the speed of circulation round the globe is much more important than the geographic sites where decisions are made. (Canclini, 2001: 18)

Part of the process of globalization in Latin America involved transnational elites uncoupling their own affairs and cultural practices from the nation-state, which was one factor in a crisis of national governments and national cultural policies felt throughout Latin America since the 1980s. But the 'rearrangement of the institutions and circuits for the exercise of public life' that sees 'local and national institutions decline in importance as transnational corporate conglomerates benefit' (Canclini, 2001: 24) impacts far more widely than does elite culture. The cultural impacts of globalization are felt throughout society with 'the predominance of goods and messages emitted by a globalized economy and culture over goods and messages based in the cities and nations in which one lives . . . [and] the sense of belonging and identity, ever less shaped by local and national loyalties and more and more by participation in transnational or deterritorialized communities of consumers' (Canclini, 2001: 24).

Canclini does not see greater cultural homogenization as the result of this economic and cultural globalization, but rather fragmentation and recomposition into *hybrid* cultural forms. These hybrid cultures undermine established cultural dichotomies between local/imported, high/popular, arts and crafts/media and digital culture, and traditional/modern. He identifies these new modes of consumption as prefiguring new forms of public participation and citizen formation, seeing consumption not as an alternative to active citizenship, but as an alternative way of expressing citizen identities. For Canclini, this means that the political effects of global consumer culture are not yet determined; it may mark disengagement from citizenship and the public sphere, or it may mark the emergence of new, more transnational forms of citizen identity formation and participation in public life.

> When we recognize that when we consume we also think, select, and re-elaborate social meaning, it becomes necessary to analyze how this mode of appropriation of goods and signs conditions more active forms of participation . . . we should ask ourselves if consumption does not entail doing something that sustains, nourishes, and to a certain extent constitutes a new mode of being citizens. (Canclini, 2001: 26)

The question of the productive agency of consumers is also a theme of Henry Jenkins' work, particularly *Convergence Culture: When New and Old Media Collide* (Jenkins, 2006). Jenkins argued that new media and media convergence need to be understood not only in terms of technological development or changing industry structures, but also through the active engagement and participation of consumers. This meant that convergence is 'both a top-down corporate-driven process and a bottom-up consumer-driven process', where:

> Media companies are learning how to accelerate the flow of media content across delivery channels to expand revenue opportunities, broaden markets, and reinforce viewer commitments. Consumers are learning how to use these different media technologies to bring the flow of media more fully under their control and to interact with other consumers. The promises of this new media environment raise expectations of a freer flow of ideas and content. Inspired by those ideals, consumers are fighting for the right to participate more fully in their culture. (Jenkins, 2006: 18)

Understanding *media convergence* as 'the flow of content across multiple media platforms' (Jenkins, 2006: 2), Jenkins understands convergence as not simply the merging of media forms through digital technologies, but rather as a new level of engagement with media by its users, as 'consumers are encouraged to seek out new information and make connections among dispersed media content' (Jenkins, 2006: 3). Out of this merging of digital media and active users come new forms of *participatory culture*, and the transformation of media communication in the early twenty-first century from a system of mass communication, based around one-to-many message transmission and a structural separation between the producers and consumers of media, to one where both now constitute 'participants who interact with each other according to a new set of rules that none of us fully understands' (Jenkins, 2006: 3). New media forms such as multi-player online games, blogging, YouTube videos and *connect.tv* may all be instances of participatory media culture, but it is not simply a 'new media' phenomenon: reality television programmes such as *Big Brother* and *Survivor* were powerfully driven by the intersection between media convergence and participatory culture, even if they were appearing on the 'old' media of broadcast television.

Wikipedia may be the most powerful application of collective intelligence, and Jenkins' account of such collectively authored and collaborative media has parallels in the work of Benkler (2006) on networks and social production. It also draws attention to the final element of productive consumption to be considered, which is when the consumers themselves become creative producers. Both Bruns' (2008) account of *produsers*, who are both users and content producers in the digital media space, and Gauntlett's (2011) account of *Media Studies 2.0*, where students of the media no longer only expect critical media literacy but also hands-on skills to express their own digital creativity, remind us of the extent to which consumption can no longer be thought of as the passive 'other' to production in contemporary global and digital cultures.

Conclusion

This chapter has sought to understand the significance of consumption to the shaping of the creative industries. It has undertaken this analysis in a historical and conceptual sense, noting the contributions of theorists as diverse as Karl Marx, Thorstein Veblen, Georg Simmel, Jean Baudrillard and Pierre Bourdieu to enabling us to think about the relationship between consumption, culture and identity in contemporary capitalist modernity.

It has considered the relationship between consumption and globalization, particularly in relation to debates about whether we now live in a global consumer culture and, if so, whether it is indicative of cultural imperialism. Noting that the question of a global culture is itself a complex one that does not simply point in the direction of one-way flows of cultural product and patterns of cultural domination, it was also noted that the lines between production and consumption themselves are increasingly blurred in an age of digital networks and social media. With consideration of creative industries from the perspectives of industry forms and structures, production and labour, and consumption and culture now having taken place, the next chapter will undertake an analysis of creative industries markets.

4   Markets

Introduction

The products and services of the creative industries and the consumption preferences of individuals are typically brought together through markets. At its simplest, 'a market for something exists if there are people who want to buy it and people who want to sell it' (McMillan, 2002: 5). While it was historically the case that market transactions took place in a physical location – what we refer to metaphorically as 'the marketplace' – buyers and sellers can now be quite geographically separate from one another, and the process through which a product is brought to market has become subject to ever more complex global production chains, as discussed in chapter 2. Clearly, the rise of Internet commerce marks a further geographical and structural separation of buyers and sellers.

But whether it is second-hand books, CDs and DVDs for sale at a flea market, or the same items being downloaded onto an iPad, a Kindle or some other electronic device, there are some general features of markets that can be identified. These include:

- buyers and sellers participating voluntarily, and independently of one another;
- demand for the product or service being inversely related to its price (i.e., as the price falls, demand increases – this is known as the price elasticity of demand);
- as prices rise, the willingness to supply the product or service increases, as the profitability of supplying it increases;
- if the product or service is increasingly in demand, competition will increase, and – other things being equal – the number of those prepared to participate in the market as suppliers or consumers is likely to increase;
- resources can be shifted from areas where market demand is in decline to those where it is increasing.

While these are identifiable general features of markets and of market economies, questions arise as to their general applicability. In particular, they draw upon neoclassical microeconomic models that have assumed perfect competition, where all firms in a market are price takers, where there is ease of entry and exit in the industry in question, and where individual firms lack the capacity to manipulate market outcomes to their own ends. From the 1920s onwards, there was growing criticism of the model of perfect competition, in 'real-world' industry environments characterized by: increasing returns to scale (i.e., average costs continue to fall for firms as they get larger); barriers to entry deriving from control over technology; high start-up costs for prospective new entrants; government controls over entry, exit and prices in particular industries; and the ability to compete on the basis of product differentiation and the deployment of advertising and marketing strategies rather than on the basis of price. The theories of imperfect competition and oligopoly aim to capture the dynamics of such markets, which typically feature a small number of big industry players (Zamagni, 1987). From outside of the neoclassical tradition, the institutionalist, post-Keynesian and Marxist schools of political economy have focused on the implications of competition leading to monopoly and oligopoly, and questions of market power, in modern capitalist economies (Sweezy, 1968; Veblen, 1970 [1899]; Galbraith, 1973; Stilwell, 2002). Such market structures are considered later in this chapter.

Media and Cultural Economics

Alan Albarran (2010) has observed that in relation to media economics, three traditions have evolved – theoretical, applied and critical – and similar observations have been made about the field of cultural economics (Throsby, 2001; Towse, 2010). First, at the *theoretical* level, media and cultural economics has involved the application of conventional economic concepts and tools – such as markets, price, supply and demand, theories of the firm, and macroeconomic theories – to understanding media, cultural and creative industries.

Second, there is the *applied* level, where there is closer consideration of some of the specificities of the media and cultural sectors, and how these may act to qualify 'textbook' economic approaches. In cultural economics, for instance, the point is commonly made that cultural value is by no means synonymous with economic value as measured in terms of market prices and consumer demand (Throsby, 2001: 26–9). As a result, cultural economics often identifies instances of 'market failure' such as imperfect information, imperfect competition and externality effects. The latter is used as a general term to capture third-party effects of particular forms of production and consumption that are not adequately captured by the price mechanism. Examples of externality effects may include noise or pollution generated by particular activities (negative), or the benefits of education in generating a more skilled or culturally aware workforce (positive). Applied media and cultural economics often has a strong policy orientation, as it has been connected to government decisions around matters such as appropriate forms and levels of funding for the arts and culture, the role of public broadcasters, or questions of competition and monopoly in media markets.

Third, there are *critical* approaches, most commonly associated with the political economy traditions in media, communications and cultural studies. The political economy perspective will be considered below, but it is worth noting that even those who apply conventional economic tools to the media and cultural sectors often have a degree of scepticism towards the dominant economic methodologies. The cultural economist David Throsby has argued that 'neoclassical economics is in fact quite restrictive in its assumptions, highly constrained in its mechanics and ultimately limited in its explanatory power', and notes that 'its supremacy can be challenged if a broader view of the discourse of economics is taken' (Throsby, 2001: 2).

Media and cultural economists harbour periodic doubts about the influence of their discipline on cultural matters, with some cultural economists seeing their primary role as being one of protecting the arts from the influence of economics (e.g., Caust, 2003). Authors from the critical humanities perspective have been highly critical of the influence of neoclassical economics on media and culture, associating this with the rise of free market or neoliberal ideologies (e.g., Hesmondhalgh, 2007a: 30–1). Media and cultural economists often qualify the findings of conventional economics significantly when they apply it to the media and cultural spheres. Contrary to the assumption that media and cultural economists uncritically promote markets as the preferred means of addressing cultural questions, the literature often draws attention to the limits of markets in the provision of cultural goods and services.

Of particular importance here is the question of whether the market will tend to *undersupply* cultural goods and services, as this provides a basis for public subsidy and an interventionist approach to media and cultural policy. Throsby (2001: 23–9) observed that individual consumption of private cultural goods and services, where individual preferences are expressed through their willingness to consume particular cultural commodities at a set price, is only one of nine possible forms of value relevant to the cultural sector. Others include:

- *Public value.* Cultural goods such as broadcast television programmes are freely available to all, and are non-rival and non-excludable in their consumption, i.e. one person's consumption has no impact on the availability of such programmes to others.

- *Aesthetic value.* The unique attributes of creative works may lead relevant taste communities to attribute a high cultural value to them. Some cultural goods are also termed *merit goods*, as it is presumed that more members of the community should have access to such creative works.
- *Spiritual value.* A cultural artefact may have particular value to those of a religious faith, tribe or other cultural grouping, or it may have beneficial effects in a more secular sense of enabling greater understanding, enlightenment or insight.
- *Option value.* People may not wish to consume a cultural good or service at present, but wish to maintain the option of either consuming the good or service themselves in the future, or ensuring its availability for future generations – this concept is commonly used in environmental economics.
- *Social value.* Cultural works are sometimes seen as providing a society with a better understanding of itself and its place in the world, and a shared sense of identity and place. For example, the promotion of feature film production in Australia through government support has been justified on the basis that locally produced films 'had an important function in maintaining and refining a progressive sense of national pride' (O'Regan, 1996: 31).
- *Historical value.* A cultural product or creative work may have ongoing historic significance to a society or community, or to humanity as a whole.
- *Symbolic value.* Art works and other cultural artefacts exist as repositories and conveyors of symbolic meanings, but the precise nature of such meanings, and their value and significance, is very much a property of individual experience, and is therefore difficult to objectively determine. In economics, this also refers to *experience goods*, where 'you need to experience the good in order to have information about it and judge its quality' (Towse, 2010: 151–2).
- *Authenticity value.* Value that a cultural artefact derives from its being the real and original product of a particular time, place or community. One example would be the importance of authenticity in relation to indigenous arts and culture.

For cultural economists such as Throsby, the point is not simply that cultural value is complicated. It is related to a more significant divergence between economic and cultural value, deriving from the proposition that 'the economic impulse is individualistic [but] the cultural impulse is collective' (Throsby, 2001: 13). As a result, 'the cultural impulse can be seen as a desire for group experience or for collective production or consumption that cannot be fully factored out of the individuals comprising the group' (Throsby, 2001: 13).

The analytical consequence of such a divergence between economic and cultural value is that the allocation of cultural resources exclusively or primarily through the price mechanism will not produce the most socially desirable amount, or composition, of cultural goods and services, or distribute such resources in ways that are the most socially desirable. Cultural activities will therefore require some form of public support in order that higher-order cultural goals can be achieved. Such cultural goals may include: preservation of cultural heritage; promotion of cultural identity; the promotion of cultural diversity and intercultural dialogue; promotion of creativity and new forms of cultural production; equitable access to culture in all of its forms; broadening opportunities for cultural participation; and promoting cultural education in order to maintain sustainable cultural development (Throsby, 2010: 34–45). It can also generate positive externalities, or third-party benefits of particular forms of cultural consumption, such as a more culturally aware and better-educated population.

In the discussion so far, the question of what is a 'socially desirable' allocation of resources to cultural activities has been left deliberately vague. A lot of cultural activity is primarily supported through the market, and cultural economists have typically not had a lot to say about this. The undersupply of cultural goods and services in modern capitalist economies does not refer, for instance, to rappers, boy bands, heavy metal, reality TV programmes, celebrity chefs, *Fifty Shades of Grey* or *Alvin and the Chipmunks*. Such cultural forms live or die in the market. Rather, it refers primarily to those cultural activities that are deemed to have *intrinsic cultural value* by key decision makers, be they arts bureaucrats, governments, or those with cultural capital and political influence, along the lines discussed by Pierre Bourdieu, and discussed in chapter 3. Moreover, the undersupply of particular 'socially desirable' cultural products coexists with an endemic oversupply of creative workers in most fields, relative to the demand for their works (Menger, 1999; Caves, 2000).

The general case made for public subsidy of cultural activity by cultural economists does not in itself answer questions of how much subsidy should be provided, or to whom. Towse (2003: 1) has observed that cultural economics has had a generic bias towards the study of the creative and performing arts and publicly subsidized culture – what is sometimes referred to as 'high culture' – rather than, say, the mass media, entertainment or commercial culture. For many leading cultural economists, this was simply an expression of what they considered to be most important. Lord Robbins, a key figure in both twentieth-century neoclassical economics and arts policy, argued that the question of taxpayer support for the arts could never simply be one of economics, but of political philosophy, and his personal view was that he 'never had any difficulty in regarding some cultivation of the arts and higher learning as part of my conception of the state obligation' (quoted in Towse, 2010: 172). The general point, as Ruth Towse has concluded, is that:

> Welfare economics makes its case through the recognition of market failure in the arts due to external benefits; the great weakness of this approach for practical purposes, however, is that it cannot tell the government the value of the external benefits so that subsidy can be gauged accordingly. It is then open to people to argue how great these benefits are – some say a lot and some say a little – and so the matter has to be decided in the political rather than the economic arena. (Towse, 2010: 287)

Political Economy

There is a strong critical tradition in the study of media and culture that arises from the political economy perspective. In his overview of political economy approaches to media and communication, Mosco (2009: 50–60) observed that the term 'political economy' can incorporate a diverse range of approaches, including public choice theory, institutionalism, Marxism, and feminist and environmental perspectives. It is, however, most commonly associated with the critical and Marxist traditions in media, communications and cultural studies. Mosco defined political economy as involving 'the study of the social relations, particularly the power relations, that mutually constitute the production, distribution, and consumption of resources' (Mosco, 2009: 24). He also noted that some approaches extend this framework to understanding political economy as being about 'the study of control and survival in social life' (Mosco, 2009: 25). The political economy approach is most commonly concerned with the structural nature and consequences of capitalism as a class-based society. Garnham (1995: 70) observed that 'political economy sees class – namely, the structure of access to the means of production and the structure of the distribution of the economic surplus – as the key to the structure of domination'.

Mosco (2009), Murdock and Golding (2005) and Wasko (2004) have identified the following four central characteristics of a critical political economy approach to media, as points of contrast to mainstream media and cultural economics:

1. *Focus on social change and history.* Following in the tradition of the classical economists such as Adam Smith, David Ricardo and Karl Marx, there is an interest in the dynamics of both continuity and change in capitalist economics and societies over time.
2. *Holistic approach.* A distinction between 'the economic' and other areas of social, political and cultural life is rejected, in favour of an interdisciplinary approach to understanding the relationships between commodities, institutions, social relations, media and culture, as they exist in particular social and historical contexts.
3. *Social relations and power.* In contrast to methodological individualism, political economists focus upon 'sets of social relations and the play of power' (Murdock and Golding, 2005: 62). One particular area of interest is in the shifting balance of power relations between 'capitalist enterprise and public intervention' (Murdock and Golding, 2005: 61), or between market dynamics and state regulations.
4. *Ethics and praxis.* Political economists do not view their academic work as being neutral in terms of values, ethics or politics. Instead, they stress the need 'to clarify and make explicit the moral positions of economic and political economic perspectives' (Mosco, 2009: 32). The concept of 'praxis' is critical to this, as it identifies the need for political economists to develop their work in dialogue with other non-corporate actors seeking social change in the media and cultural spheres, including activists, trade unions and policy agencies.

A fifth element can be added to these core features of critical political economy:

5. *Global perspective.* Critical political economy insists upon understanding the development of media institutions, markets and practices from a global perspective, observing the ongoing interaction between developments in media and culture at a local and national level, and the global dynamics of capitalism as a world system (Schiller, 1976; Herman and McChesney, 1997; Schiller, 1999; cf. Flew, 2007: 31–2).

A characteristic feature of critical political economy is scepticism towards the role played by markets for media and culture. This includes both scepticism about the ability to understand the relevant industries by focusing on markets, and a critical view of the impact of markets on media and culture. Critical political economists typically question the explanatory capacity of those forms of media and cultural economics that take the market and the forces of supply and demand as their starting point. In their study of 'Global Hollywood', Miller et al. (2005) argue that 'the neo-classical vision of

Hollywood asserts that the supposedly neutral mechanisms of market competition exchange materials at costs that ensure the most efficient people are producing, and their customers are content', but that such a model lacks realism since 'the rhythms of supply and demand, operating unfettered by states, religions, unions, superstitions and fashion, have never existed as such' (Miller et al., 2005: 48). The bracketing off of economics from other areas of social analysis, as well as the lack of an explicit moral framework, has also generated criticism from political economists. Hesmondhalgh argued that 'neoclassical economics is not concerned with determining human needs and rights, nor with intervening in questions of social justice. Instead, it focuses on how human wants might be most efficiently satisfied'; he observed that 'such a bracketing off of questions concerning power and justice is limiting' (Hesmondhalgh, 2007a: 30).

The second concern is that, to the extent that market dynamics do in fact shape media and culture in capitalist societies, this leads, on the one hand, to greater corporate control over media and culture and, on the other, to the commodification of culture. In relation to media industries, Murdock and Golding have argued that 'media production has been increasingly commandeered by large corporations', and that corporate power has been extended in recent years through 'the sale of public assets to private investors (privatization), the introduction of competition into markets that were previously commanded by public monopolies (liberalization), and the continuing squeeze on publicly funded cultural institutions' (Murdock and Golding, 2005: 64). Such arguments have also been made in relation to global media industries by Herman and McChesney (1997), McChesney and Schiller (2003), Miller et al. (2005) and others. The question of whether media industries have become more monopolistic, and what this may entail for theories of markets and competition, is considered in more detail below.

As discussed in chapter 3, *commodification* is a term used in Marxist political economy to describe 'the process of transforming things valued for their use into marketable products that are valued for what they can bring in exchange' (Mosco, 2009: 127). Political economists associate the rise of corporate power and influence with the commodification of culture (Murdock and Golding, 2005: 64–5; Mosco, 2009: 133–43). For critical political economists, adverse consequences of the commodification of culture include:

- greater control over cultural production by a small number of private corporations, more accountable to shareholders and financiers than to the public interest or the public good;

- greater corporate influence over media and cultural production through advertising and sponsorship;
- access to media and cultural products being increasingly dependent upon capacity to pay, thereby accentuating the cultural dimensions of social and economic inequalities;
- the potential to reduce risk and innovation in favour of familiar and well-tested genres and formats, in order to maximize audience share;
- the ability to use economic power to influence public debates, and to exclude alternative viewpoints which dissent from the views of dominant corporate interests.

The political economy approach to culture and communication has been subject to significant critiques from within its own paradigm in recent years. Winseck (2011) has argued that, in its focus upon the dominant power of monopoly capital, there is a tendency to view the media industries 'as a giant pyramid, with power concentrated at the top, and not enough attention paid to the details of key players, markets, and the dynamics and diversity that exist among all the elements that make up the media' (Winseck, 2011: 23). He argues that there is a pervasive tendency to overstate the extent to which market concentration has eliminated competition in and differences between media industries. Winseck also argues that, in terms of cultural analysis, the political economy approach 'overplays the ineluctable colonization of the lifeworld by market forces and the one-dimensional commodification of all cultural forms, even oppositional ones' (Winseck, 2011: 24).

As one of the pioneers of the political economy approach to culture and communications, Nicholas Garnham's critiques are even more far-reaching. His argument is that 'the term "political economy" . . . has become a euphemism for a vague, crude and un-self-questioning form of Marxism, linked to a gestural and self-satisfied, if often paranoid, radicalism', which he considers to be 'both empirically questionable and theoretically and politically dubious' (Garnham, 2011: 42). Garnham has argued that 'a crude and unexamined romantic Marxist rejection of the market *per se* . . . has blocked analysis of how actual markets work and with what effects', meaning that 'it has not taken the economics in PE [political economy] with the seriousness it deserves and requires' (Garnham, 2011: 42).

In contrast to a simple political economy which says that power is becoming more concentrated in fewer hands, Garnham asks whether the media and cultural policy environment is in fact far more complex than simple market/state dichotomies would suggest. In particular, he questions whether one can make any general claims about the ideological content of commercial media, given that the rise of capitalist modernity sees societies become more internally complex and heterogeneous, and that cultural producers seeking to make a profit will always have an economic interest in producing for more diverse cultural markets. For Garnham, cultural production under capitalism is not characterized by ideologically driven censorship or insufficient diversity of content. Instead, he has proposed that capitalism has made more cultural product available, and 'has clearly widened cultural diversity on both a national and international scale, even if it continues to be unevenly spread' (Garnham, 2011: 45).

Case Study: Monopoly and Competition in Media Markets

One of the recurring dilemmas of economics relates to the question of monopolies. In addition to so-called 'natural monopolies', such as roads or water provision, there are also those monopolies that arise out of the process of competition itself. This occurs when the largest supplier in an industry acquires cost advantages over its competitors, so that it can drive them out of the industry, and where barriers to the entry of new competitors are substantial, typically due to high start-up costs. Michel Foucault observed that monopoly presented itself as a 'semi-natural, semi-necessary consequence of competition in a capitalist regime', so that 'the paradox of monopoly . . . raises the problem . . . that monopoly is actually part of the logic of competition' (Foucault, 2008: 134). The problem of monopoly is that, from an economic perspective, markets that are monopolistic are seen as generating higher prices, lower output and less innovation than more competitive markets, leading to above-average profits for the monopolist (Ferguson, 1988: 61–4). Moreover, firms with monopoly power may also be able to 'game' the regulatory process in order to ensure that political decision makers and regulators act in ways that continue to protect their monopolistic status and the extra profits that accrue from it, to the detriment of consumer welfare and the public interest (Horwitz, 1989: 34–8).

In mainstream economic theory, the relationship between monopoly and competition is addressed through *industrial organization theory*. Observing that relatively few industries are either perfectly competitive or purely monopolistic, industrial organization theory instead proposes that industries sit on a spectrum between the two poles of perfect competition and monopoly, with monopolistic competition and oligopoly (few sellers) being two variants within this continuum. Using the *structure-conduct-performance* (SCP) model, the structure of an industry shapes the conduct of firms within that industry, with relevant variables including pricing behaviour, product development strategy, advertising levels in the industry, investment and research and development strategies, and the likelihood of co-operation among industry participants (Hoskins et al., 2004). This conduct can then in turn be empirically assessed in terms of the industry's overall performance, and whether the exercise of market power has led to higher prices, lower output and less innovation than a more competitive market would.

In order to measure the degree of concentration in an industry, or the extent to which a small number of firms account for the majority of market share, industry economists use concentration ratios, such as the percentage of total market share accounted for by the four largest firms (CR4) and that of the eight largest firms (CR8); another measure used is the Hirschman-Herfindahl Index (HHI) (Ferguson, 1988: 24–6). Using such measures, Albarran and Dimmick (1996) argued that most US media industries were highly concentrated. They found that the broadcast television, advertising, publishing and recorded music industries had CR4 ratios of over 80 per cent (the four largest firms accounting for over 80 per cent of total market share), and all industries surveyed except for the newspaper and magazine industries had CR8 ratios of over 70 per cent. Similar findings have been made in virtually all other countries.[2]

The critical political economists also understand the media industries to be highly concentrated in terms of ownership and control. With the industrialization of the print industries in the late nineteenth to early twentieth centuries, the dominance of the 'Big Six' Hollywood film studios, and the high barriers to entry for new entrants into broadcast television, monopolistic or oligopolistic control is seen as the norm for 'Big Media'. The existence of such market power, and the ability to transform economic power into political power or the ability to influence the 'marketplace of ideas', is characteristic of the broader shift from competitive to *monopoly capitalism*, where power relations have largely displaced market competition. John Bellamy Foster argued that 'with the rise of the giant firm, price competition ceased to take place in any significant sense within mature monopolistic industries . . . the giant corporations that dominate the contemporary economy engage primarily in struggles over market share . . . but the goal is always the creation or perpetuation of monopoly power' (Foster, 2000: 6–7).

From the point of view of government, ways of responding to concentration of media ownership include:

- setting maximum ownership limits (e.g., one media company can only control X per cent of a particular market);
- forced divestiture, as with the 1948 *Paramount* case, where the major

Hollywood studios were required to relinquish control over theatre chains, or the US Justice Department's 1982 ruling that AT&T divest itself of local telephony services;
* selective government funding of alternative media, as with the press subsidy schemes developed in countries such as Austria and Sweden.

An alternative approach may not see the lack of market competition as the problem, but rather the distribution of monopoly profits. In Australia, restrictions on the issuance of new commercial broadcasting licences have been seen as a *quid pro quo* for the commercial television industry's obligations in terms of meeting programming quotas for locally produced drama, documentaries and children's television (Flew, 2006). Alternatively, if lack of content diversity is seen as the problem, alternative forms of public service media have been developed with specific programming remits for 'minority' audiences: examples include Channel 4 in the UK and the Special Broadcasting Service in Australia (Flew, 2011a).

One of the major debates in media economics in recent years has been whether the concentration of media ownership has been increasing or decreasing. Political economists have consistently argued that media concentration is increasing, and that, moreover, media ownership is increasingly concentrated on a global scale. Authors such as Herman and McChesney (1997), McChesney and Schiller (2005) and McChesney (2008) would argue that concentration indexes such as those discussed above consistently understate the degree of monopoly power that a small number of media companies have over the world's information and entertainment industries. In particular, they point to three powerful trends in media ownership that move discussion beyond consideration of particular industries in national markets:

* *Conglomeration*: most of the world's largest media companies operate businesses across multiple media platforms, including film, broadcasting, print media and the Internet.
* *Globalization*: the largest media companies now operate on a global scale, with the four largest US media companies (Time-Warner, Disney, News Corporation and Viacom) earning between 20 and 45 per cent of their revenues outside of North America in 2005 (Flew, 2007: 87).
* *Mergers, acquisitions and strategic alliances*: as well as major formal mergers such as the Time-Warner/AOL merger in 2001, there have been strategic alliances between traditional media companies, telecommunications and information technology companies, and Internet businesses.

There have been a series of counter-arguments to the media monopoly thesis, where it is argued that the Internet is reducing the scope for concentration in media markets by substantially reducing the barriers to entry for new players, and that the current period is one of crisis rather than consolidation for traditional mass media (Compaine and Gomery, 2000; Compaine, 2001). It is also argued that even if aggregate concentration shares are not substantially changing, evidence of competition can be found in movement within the 'league table' of companies that occupy the dominant places. For example, Apple and Google would not have featured prominently in discussions of media control a decade ago and they now do, and others may take their place in the near future.

Against the 'digital optimist' strand of thinking, the detailed empirical work on US media industries by Eli Noam (2009) has found that mass media industries have become more concentrated from the 1980s to the present, albeit to a less dramatic degree than the 'media pessimists' have assumed. Importantly, he finds growing concentration in Internet-related industries, debunking the claim that the Internet is a new digital frontier, free of the constraints that scale economies presented in traditional capital-intensive media businesses. He also notes the growing importance of the 'integrator firms', which include Apple, Google, Yahoo! and Microsoft, who operate globally and 'whose main function is to conceive the basic product, implement it through specialists, and distribute it to the world in branded bundles' (Noam, 2009: 39).

I have also observed elsewhere (Flew, 2011b) that bigness *per se* does not provide evidence of market dominance: there are many examples of media merger and conglomeration strategies not working out in practice, including the Time-Warner/AOL merger in 2001 – the world's biggest corporate merger ever in its day – and the takeover of MySpace by News Corporation. One of the problems is that, because corporate histories tend to focus on successes rather than failures, a gap exists between what favourable outcomes were proposed at the time when big mergers and acquisitions took place – 'synergies' being a particularly popular buzzword – and the actual outcomes of such attempts to merge creative functions. If Noam's analysis of the rise of the media integrators is correct, we will also need different analytical tools through which to measure market power and market dominance from those which could be used when the mass media was dominated by vertically integrated but industry-specific media corporations.

New Institutional Economics and the Creative Industries

Critiques of conventional media and cultural economics have come not only from the critical political economy perspective, but also from approaches that have been influenced by *new institutional economics*. It was noted in chapter 3 that conventional neoclassical economics had been subject to robust critique from authors such as Thorstein Veblen and John Kenneth Galbraith, who argued that the focus on rational, maximizing individuals consistently ignored the importance of habits, customs and beliefs in shaping economic behaviour, as well as the importance of historical factors and the desire for power and status as drivers of social behaviour. For Veblen in particular, neoclassical economics also failed to address the challenge of theories of *evolution* to scientific modelling. The institutionalist perspective has long sought to reclaim economics as an interdisciplinary field 'concerned with studying the interactions between social values, technology, and economic institutions' (Stilwell, 2002: 210). It has been influenced by insights from history, politics and sociology, and by social theorists such as Karl Marx, Karl Polanyi and Max Weber. Institutional economics has typically developed as an element within critical political economy, or what is sometimes referred to as heterodox economics (Dugger and Sherman, 1994; Stilwell, 2002; Lee, 2009).

The new institutional economics differs in its stronger connection to the economic mainstream. Authors such as Oliver Williamson (1975, 1985, 2000) proposed that, while institutions matter, they are nonetheless understandable using conventional economic concepts. In particular, and drawing upon the earlier conception of the firm developed by Ronald Coase, it was argued that the problem of *transaction costs*, or how to manage the costs to firms of engaging with markets, generated a series of institutions of capitalism. Economic institutions of capitalism include: (1) the market itself as an embedded institutional form; (2) institutional arrangements such as laws governing property rights; (3) the corporation as an institutional form with its own legal identity; and (4) what are referred to as *hybrid forms*, including subcontracting, partnerships and other forms of 'relational contracting' (Chavance, 2009: 46). Richard Caves' *Creative Industries* (2000) is an extended mediation on such questions in the creative industries, which he sees as particularly innovative in terms of the relational contracts they develop. This is due to factors such as: the inherently unpredictable relationship between individual creativity and market demand; the often team-based nature of cultural production; and the importance of personal reputation as a guarantor of income and status, in what tend to be highly skewed income distribution outcomes in the arts and creative industries.

Work on alternative forms of economic organization now draws attention to the role of *networks* as a third form existing alongside markets and internal corporate hierarchies, and the particular roles that informal coordination mechanisms play within network forms of organization, including consensus seeking, reciprocity, trust and the role played by 'weak ties' (Granovetter, 1985; Thompson, 2003). Yochai Benkler has argued that the shift he traces from an industrial economy to a networked information economy is associated with both a radical decentralization of production, and a 'shift from an information environment dominated by proprietary, market-oriented action to a world where nonproprietary, nonmarket transactional frameworks play a large role alongside market production' (Benkler, 2006: 18). In the sphere of cultural production, Benkler associates such trends with greater transparency, participation and critical self-reflection, as the networked information economy 'adds to the centralized, market-oriented production system a new framework of radically decentralized individual and cooperative nonmarket production' (Benkler, 2006: 275).

While the literature on transaction costs is relevant to understanding the balance between markets, contracts, informal relations and industrial organization, or what are referred to as 'institutional arrangements', it has less to say about the broader role played by customs, ideas, beliefs, law, politics, etc., or what are referred to as the 'institutional environment' (Chavance, 2009). Williamson (2000) presented the new institutional economics as having four levels, from that of embedded institutions (customs, norms, beliefs and traditions as expressed through formal and informal institutions), through the institutional environment, governance arrangements (around which transaction cost economics apply), to the market system itself (see table 4.1).

The distinction between formal and informal institutions has been proposed by the economic historian Douglass North, who defines institutions in the following manner:

> Institutions are the humanly devised constraints that structure human interaction. They are made up of formal constraints (rules, laws, conventions), informal constraints (norms of behaviour, conventions, and self imposed codes of conduct), and their enforcement characteristics. (North, 1994: 361)

As Chavance (2009: 50) observes, North's definition of institutions recalls the earlier institutionalism of authors such as Veblen, who saw institutions and ideologies as being linked in terms of 'shared habits of thought'. Work on the comparative performance of national economies, and the importance of the 'institutional matrix' to the resulting development of markets and governance structures, also recalls the evolutionary orientation of authors such as Veblen, as well as more recent work in the field of *evolutionary economics* (Beinhocker, 2006; Hodgson and Knudsen, 2010). A critical bridging concept here is that of *creative destruction*, first developed by the Austrian economist Joseph Schumpeter, who was also highly critical

Table 4.1. Levels of institutional economics

Level of theory	Level of analysis	Frequency of change	Purpose
Level 1 Social theory	Embeddedness; informal institutions, customs, traditions, norms, religion	100–1000 years	Often non-calculative; spontaneous
Level 2 Economics of property rights/law and politics	Institutional environment; formal rules of the games – esp. property (polity, judiciary, bureaucracy)	10–100 years	Getting institutional environment right; first-order economizing
Level 3 Transaction cost economics	Governance; play of the game – esp. contract (aligning governance structures with transactions)	1–10 years	Getting governance structures right; second-order economizing
Level 4 Neo-classical economics/agency theory	Resource allocation and employment (prices and quantities; incentive alignment)	Continuous	Getting marginal conditions right; third-order economizing

Source: Williamson, 2000: 597.

of the static nature of neoclassical economics, and its failure to adequately capture the dynamic and quasi-Darwinian nature of capitalist development. Schumpeter described creative destruction in the following terms:

> The opening up of new markets, foreign or domestic, and the organizational development from the craft shop and factory . . . illustrate the same process of industrial mutation . . . that incessantly revolutionizes the economic structure *from within*, incessantly destroying the old one, incessantly creating a new one. The process of Creative Destruction is . . . what capitalism consists in and what every capitalist concern has got to live with. (Schumpeter, 1950: 83)

A clear statement of such an evolutionary approach as applied to the creative industries is provided by Potts (2011). Potts understands the creative industries as 'deal[ing] with the human interface, with new ways of being and thinking and interacting, and with . . . the human side of change', thereby contributing to the innovation process on the demand side of economic evolution (Potts, 2011: 2). He contrasts this to what he sees as the 'protectionist instinct in cultural policy', driven by cultural economics and other perspectives that view these sectors as 'somehow special, possibly separate, sometimes ineffable; too important in any case to be left to the market' (Potts, 2011: 3). He distinguishes what he refers to as the 'economics of creative industries (ECI)' approach from that of cultural economics according to the distinctions shown in table 4.2.

Table 4.2. Distinctions between cultural economics and the economics of creative industries

	Cultural economics	Economics of the creative industries
1. Analytic foundations	Applied neoclassical economics; static equilibrium models; focus on market failure in 'closed system' models	Evolutionary and new institutional economics; dynamic, 'open systems' perspective
2. Agents and preferences	Problem is lack of demand for particular cultural products; need for policy makers to 'educate' the public	Artists and entrepreneurs work together to generate new cultural forms that are sought after in the market
3. Markets	Markets produce the 'wrong prices' for culture due to information imperfections, imperfect competition, and externalities	Markets provide the 'institutional infrastructure' for the testing of new ideas by artists and entrepreneurs
4. Coordinating institutions	Focus on market failure, but not on problems of public provision, including rent seeking – deals primarily with established culture industries and institutions	Focus on new forms of organization that can emerge in response to new problems/opportunities – focus is on emergent industries and new cultural forms
5. Technology	Pessimistic about ability of technology to solve cost problems in the arts	Optimistic about digital ICTs as enabling new forms of production, distribution and coordination
6. Income, culture and progress	Tends to focus on threats to incomes and opportunities for artists and creative workers from new technologies, globalization, etc.	Sees a dynamic relationship between economic growth and development of the arts, media and culture; positive about cultural impact of globalization

Source: Potts, 2011: 20–9.

Social Network Markets

The work of Potts et al. (2008) on social network markets marks an application of new institutional and evolutionary economics, along with cultural and media studies, to defining the nature of the creative industries. The authors observe a familiar paradox that arises in defining the creative industries, namely that there is simultaneously an attempt to mark out particular sectors of production as being 'creative', and a claim that the importance of creativity is manifesting itself across all spheres of economic life, and into social life and public policy. This paradox was discussed in chapter 1. In line with the move proposed by Hartley (2009), the argument is that the definition question in relation to creative industries needs to shift from *production and outputs* to *markets and knowledge.* Such a 'market-based interpretation of the creative industries' (Potts et al., 2008: 168) bypasses the seemingly perpetual debates about what is in or out of an output-based definition (why are software and crafts included but not sport or tourism?), or an input-based one (why is it deemed creative to write a poem or a song, but not to design a bridge or land a spaceship on Mars?).

Potts et al. propose a definition of creative industries as 'the set of agents in a market characterized by adoption of novel ideas within social networks for production and consumption' (Potts et al., 2008: 171). Critical to this definition are the concepts of social networks and novelty and adoption. While the rise of social networks has become a general feature of twenty-first-century Internet-enabled institutions and practices (Benkler, 2006), it is argued that they are particularly significant in the creative industries because these are domains of social life where the consumption choices of individuals are inherently shaped by the decisions and choices of others: 'because of inherent novelty and uncertainty, decisions both to produce and to consume are determined by the choice of others in a social network' (Potts et al., 2008: 169). The focus upon demand-side novelty can be seen as the corollary of innovation in products and services that was identified in chapter 2 as a key feature of the creative industries.

The ability to demonstrate choices and inform others of such decisions requires forms of social signalling, which may now be performed through socio-technical networks themselves (e.g., information circulated on Facebook or Twitter), but has also been flagged through fashion, subcultures, fads, trends, etc. As discussed in chapter 3, it was Georg Simmel who first observed in 1890s Berlin how the 'slave to fashion' was simultaneously never in fashion (because they inherently followed others) or out of fashion (no longer being prepared to play the 'fashion game'). Whether enabled by digital technologies, by the concentrated spaces of modern cities, or through news or entertainment media, the creative industries are thus very much reliant upon the social circulation of information:

> The CIs rely, to a greater extent than other socio-economic activity, on word of mouth, taste, cultures, and popularity, such that individual choices are dominated by information feedback over social networks rather than innate preferences and price signals . . . other people's preferences have commodity status over a social network because novelty by definition carries uncertainty and other people's choices, therefore, carry information. (Potts et al., 2008: 170)

Critical to the conception of creative industries in terms of social network markets, then, is the concept of *novelty*. What distinguishes creative industries from agriculture, manufacturing or professional services, in this definition, is not that they produce intangibles, or are digital, or have more creative inputs; it is that their markets are always emergent, whereas these other sectors rely upon relatively mature markets and technologies (Potts et al., 2008: 173). This is not to say that innovations from the creative industries do not spin off into these sectors, but that they typically do not have their origins in these sectors. A TV programme such as the BBC's *Top Gear*, for instance, would be a CI input to the automobile industry, as it marked out a novel way of conveying information relevant to consumers' decisions to purchase cars, as well as being a form of entertainment television.

Markets are critical here in that they constitute the institutional framework through which evolutionary processes can occur. Markets do not in themselves create novelty – novelty comes from those who choose to engage in such spaces with new ideas, concepts, products or services – but they do provide the content in which such novelty is tested through its uptake in the wider population, with the adoption and adaptation of successful new ideas, products, etc., and the retention and replication of that which is successful, which may in turn be superseded in time by something else. Potts (2011: 162–83) has referred to *novelty bundling markets* as sites where this filtering occurs, which may include festivals, trade fairs, online information sites, the media, and so on. Competition is particularly important in this regard as it 'underpins the operation and advance of the creative industries because, more than many industries, it depends upon the creation of continuous flows of novelty to meet consumer demand' (Hartley et al., 2012: 26).

Models of the Creative Industries

The work on social network markets has important public policy implications. Most significantly, *it identifies the creative industries as sites of innovation in knowledge-based economies, rather than as sectors where market failure is endemic but culture is undervalued and therefore requires public subsidy.* Potts and Cunningham (2008) elaborate upon this proposition in their discussion of four models of the creative industries (cf. Cunningham et al., 2008a). They argue that traditional arts and cultural policy has worked with a *welfare model* (Model 1), where the relevant industries are subject to endemic market failure, but where their full cultural value can never be fully captured by measures of market value. This is the typical position of cultural economics as discussed above, and justifies the transfer of income from other parts of the economy to these industries on the basis of their high cultural value.

They note a second model, the *competition model* (Model 2), which approaches the creative industries as being effectively just like other industries. As a result, they will benefit from the sorts of policies that governments apply to other industries, all of which may have 'special features'. Such an approach is consistent with the US government's negotiating position in debates surrounding the General Agreement on Trade in Services (GATS), where they argue that cultural sectors should not be exempt from the general free trade provisions of the GATS, and that inequalities in cultural trade are reflective of consumer preferences; i.e., cultural trade inequalities between the US and the European Union, for instance, reflect the preference of European audiences for US-produced films and entertainment products, and cultural protectionism cannot eliminate this problem.

It is the growth model and the innovation model of the creative industries that particularly follow from the concept of creative industries as embedded in social network markets. The *growth model* (Model 3) posits that the creative industries are growing faster than other segments of the economy because of broader shifts in post-industrial, knowledge-based economies, including rising consumer incomes, a more educated workforce, the global growth in ICT access, and economic and cultural globalization. Such thinking was behind the work of the DCMS in the UK, as well as other creative industries policy models developed in Europe, East Asia, Australia and New Zealand, as well as the creative economy analyses developed by UNCTAD (Flew, 2012a: 34–6, 42–5, 52–8). While Potts and Cunningham are sympathetic to this argument, they nonetheless note that it is premised upon the idea that one can clearly identify types of industries and differentiate them on the basis of what they produce, which possesses the definitional problems discussed in Potts et al. (2008). Such policies also run the risks associated with government policies that aim to 'pick winners' for specialist industry attention, given that such decisions are often made as much for political as for economic reasons.

Finally, Potts and Cunningham propose an *innovation model* (Model 4), where 'rather than thinking of the creative industries as an economic subset "driving" growth in the whole economy . . . the creative industries may not be well characterized as an industry *per se*, but rather as an element in the *innovation system* of the whole economy' (Potts and Cunningham, 2008: 238). In this view, the significance of the creative industries, and of culture more generally, is not that it may drive an economic boom akin to how investment in mining or housing or building a new airport may, but rather that they are at the leading edge of connecting innovative ideas, information product and services to consumers who are seeking novelty. They therefore both generate and embed new forms of knowledge that is acquired through social network markets, and their rise to prominence is associated with the greater speed through which both knowledge and novelty are being produced and circulated, with ICTs as a major new enabler of such evolutionary processes. In line with the new institutional economics discussed earlier, the major policy implication is that governance arrangements, institutional practices and policy settings in areas such as innovation, intellectual property and education are likely to be the keys to generating further development of the creative industries as direct public subsidy or interventionist industry policies.

The Limits of Markets: Exit and Voice

Not surprisingly, this analysis – some would say advocacy – of markets as the primary drivers of cultural development in the creative industries has its critics. Some question the realism of the assumptions about competitive markets in a world of giant corporate media-cultural conglomerates. Winseck (2011) has questioned whether the rise of social network markets and innovative small firms has reduced the dominance of global media conglomerates, noting that 'there is nothing about digital networks that renders them immune from concentration' (Winseck, 2011: 39). For others, such as Couldry (2010) and Turner (2012), the concern is about what they see as an apparent endorsement of the values of market society. Couldry has argued that 'markets do not . . . function to provide voice' (Couldry, 2010: 11), while Turner has questioned what he sees as a turn away from 'cultural studies' longstanding commitment to the applied critique of the social and political effects of . . . the operations of the market', arguing the continuing need for 'a structural, politics and ethical critique of business' (Turner, 2012: 106). As noted above, even cultural economists such as David Throsby have expressed concerns about the 'intellectual imperialism' of neoclassical economics, and a propensity to subordinate all other discourses of value (particularly cultural value) to the hegemony of economic measures of value.

Such debates recall the work of the famous sociologist Karl Polanyi, who argued in *The Great Transformation* that market society generated its own 'double movement', whereby critics of market liberalism would seek to use the state to safeguard social and cultural values and institutions (Polanyi, 1945; Dale, 2010). Couldry's reference to the concept of 'voice' also recalls Albert Hirschman's analysis of the limits of the market as a means of addressing socio-economic problems. In *Exit, Voice and Loyalty* (Hirschman, 1970), Hirschman used the concepts of 'exit' and 'voice' in the first instance to discuss the potential and limits of market-based solutions to economic problems. Hirschman argued that the problem of under-utilized economic resources, or a slack economy, is a pervasive feature of all economies. It has a multitude of causes, including poor management practices, public or private monopoly, inefficient uses of technologies or resources, regulatory failures or government mismanagement, and is often experienced in terms of poor quality products and services, or a decline in their quality relative to price.

In economic analysis, the most obvious response to such a situation on the part of consumers is that of exit, which in turn will set in train the self-correcting forces of the market and Adam Smith's 'Invisible Hand', either through firms adjusting their operations in response to such market signals, or their disappearance through loss of market share to more efficient and responsive competitors. The impersonal and indirect nature of such corrective mechanisms is seen as the cardinal virtue of the market system, and in so far as there are hindrances to the effective operation of markets and competition – as in the case of public or private monopolies, or inefficiencies that result from inappropriate public regulation of markets – the role of economists as policy advisors was seen as one of recommending to governments means by which a more competitive and responsive market situation can be established.

The counterpoint to exit is voice, defined as 'any attempt at all to change, rather than to escape from, an objectionable state of affairs, whether through individual or collective petition to the management directly in charge, through appeal to a higher authority with intention of forcing a change in management, or through various types of actions or protests, including those that are meant to mobilize public opinion' (Hirschman, 1970: 30). As Hirschman observed, voice has been a central concept to political theory, yet a marginal one to economic theory, although strong counter-tendencies have emerged including the rise of the consumer rights movement, environmental activism and shareholder activism, while notions of countervailing institutional power have been central to industrial law since the rise of the trade union movement.

Voice achieves its most concrete expression in the political sphere through the concept of citizenship. The right to participate in public life and to use one's voice to influence the affairs of state is a cardinal tenet of liberal democratic societies, and the development of institutional frameworks that enable extended participation in public and political decision-making processes is central to ensuring that 'rights . . . are practically enacted and realised through actual participation in the community' (Hall and Held, 1989: 175). As Jürgen Habermas put it, 'the institutions of constitutional freedom are only worth as much as a population makes of them' (Habermas, 1992: 7). Hirschman captured the importance of voice in conceiving of citizenship in liberal democracies by observing that 'it has long been an article of faith of political theory that the proper functioning of democracy requires a maximally alert, active, and vocal public' (Hirschman, 1970: 31–2).

Hirschman drew attention to the limits of exit in economic theory, as well as those of voice in political theory. He observed that if exit was too readily acted upon by consumers, then firms would lose the capacity to respond to market signals, as they would experience rapid decline in revenues before they could respond; firms rely on a certain level of stickiness, or loyalty, on the part of consumers towards their product or service. Hirschman also observed instances where consumer exit has little impact on firms in a market as they pick up new customers while losing other ones, so that there is little corrective mechanism in operation. Consumers face the danger of 'diverting their energies to the hunting for inexistent improved products that might possibly have been turned out by the competition' (Hirschman, 1970: 27), rather than 'bring[ing] more effective pressure upon management towards product improvement . . . in a futile search for the "ideal" product' (Hirschman, 1970: 28).

This raised for Hirschman a wider issue of the consequences of situations where 'the presence of the exit alternative can therefore tend to atrophy the development of the art of voice' (Hirschman, 1970: 43). Whereas the exit decision is one that requires little more than the existence of effective competition, the exercise of voice 'depends also on the general readiness of a population to complain and on the *invention* of such institutions and mechanisms as can communicate complaints cheaply and effectively . . . while exit requires nothing but a clear cut either-or decision, voice is essentially an *art* constantly evolving in new directions' (Hirschman, 1970: 43).

The articulation of voice is more complex than exit because active participation and influence is a skill and an art that typically requires some form of institutional support. It is also often overlaid by questions of loyalty, and consideration of the relationship between loyalty and voice introduces new complexities to the relationship of people to organizations. Loyalty can also be a means by which managers, and others whose own short-term interests may diverge from those of society more generally, can manipulate the exercise of exit and voice:

> While feedback through exit or voice is in the long-run interest of organization managers, their short-run interest is to entrench themselves and to enhance their freedom to act as they wish, unmolested as far as possible by either desertions or complaints of members. Hence management can be relied on to think of a variety of institutional devices aiming at anything but

> the combination of exit and voice which may be ideal from the point of view of society. (Hirschman, 1970: 92–3)

Hirschman's account of exit and voice is important in the creative industries context, as it alerts us to the limits of reliance upon markets (exit) as a primary driver of cultural development, without presenting the alternative (voice) as a universal alternative or panacea. In some contexts, consumer power as expressed through purchasing decisions can be a powerful and a positive force for innovation and change, whereas in others it may be associated with the disempowerment of citizens and the atrophying of voice. The qualities of 'voice' as an alternative to 'exit' are also contingent upon the quality of political institutions and the willingness of states to enable their citizens to freely express their views and to be heard by key decision makers. The relationship between forms of the modern nation-state and the capacity to develop the creative industries will be discussed in more detail in chapter 6.

International Trade in Cultural Products

For as long as there has been trade among nations, there has been trade in culture. The global expansion of the creative industries is an important contemporary manifestation of such trends. In its *Creative Economy Report 2010*, UNCTAD has observed that creative industries exports grew by 14 per cent per annum between 2002 and 2008, with an 11.7 per cent average annual increase in exports of cultural goods, and 17 per cent annual growth in exports of cultural services (UNCTAD, 2010: 128).

While such trends may have new ways of being measured in terms of the creative economy, they are contemporary manifestations of longstanding debates. The dominance of the United States over audiovisual trade in particular, which has been a feature of the global economy and global culture since the 1920s, has triggered sharp debates about whether international cultural trade can threaten national sovereignty and a sense of national cultural identity, particularly if the 'rules of the game' in world trade do not operate equally in their impact on all players. The issues at stake have been played out in various international forums (Flew, 2007: 191–7; 2012a: 125–32):

- The campaign through UNESCO for a 'New World Information and Communication Order' (NWICO), and a more equitable global distribution of communication resources, in the 1970s and early 1980s.

- Disagreements between the United States and the European Union over whether a 'cultural exemption' should apply in the General Agreement on Trade in Services (GATS) and in the rules and guidelines of the World Trade Organization (WTO).
- The UNESCO Convention on Cultural Diversity, passed in 2005, which states that 'market forces alone cannot guarantee the preservation and promotion of cultural diversity' (UNESCO, 2005).

Growing trade in creative goods and services is indicative of trends towards globalization. The economic geographer John Dunning (2001) has argued that the current stage of capitalism is properly seen as a global one since:

1. cross-border transactions are deeper, more extensive and more interconnected than ever before;
2. resources, capabilities (both knowledge and skilled workers), goods and services are more spatially mobile, with advances in transport and communication;
3. multinational corporations have become more central to wealth creation and distribution, and they both originate from and produce in a wider range of countries;
4. there is a much greater volume of transactions, and resulting volatility, in global capital and financial markets;
5. ICTs and electronic commerce have transformed the nature of cross-border transactions, particularly in services and intangible products.

One indicator of the growth of trade over the last three decades is the faster growth in exports as compared to global gross domestic products over the period 1982–2005, as shown in table 4.3.

A stronger indicator of the significance of globalization can be seen in the rapid growth of global foreign direct investment (FDI) in the period from the 1990s onwards. The UNCTAD data in figure 4.1 shows two surges in FDI, from the early 1990s to 2000, and from 2002 to 2007. Importantly, the share of FDI going to developing economies (including the former

Table 4.3. Global GDP and exports 1986–2005

	Annual growth rate (per cent)			
	1986–90	1991–5	1996–2000	2001–5
Global gross domestic product	10.8	5.6	1.3	9.3
Exports of goods and non-factor services	15.6	5.4	3.4	13.8

Source: Flew, 2007: 69.

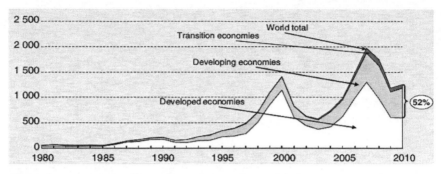

Figure 4.1. Foreign direct investment (FDI) inflows, global and by group of economies, 1980–2010 (US$bn)

Source: UNCTAD, 2012: 3.

Communist countries, or transitional economies) increased from 25 per cent in 2000 to 52 per cent in 2010 (UNCTAD, 2012). The total assets of foreign affiliates grew by 4,176 per cent in real terms between 1982 and 2005, from US$1,092 billion in 1982 to US$45,564 billion in 2005 (Flew, 2007: 69).

The conceptual underpinnings of the main theories of international trade in cultural products are to be found in media and cultural economics on the one hand, and critical political economy on the other. In media economics, the *theory of comparative advantage* is drawn upon, which proposes that nations benefit from trade if they specialize in producing one good or service rather than another, based on the relative efficiency of production of two goods or services. This is not the same as being the lowest cost or most efficient producer; in two-nation trade, one nation may have an absolute advantage in the production of both goods/services, but if it produced both goods/services, its trading partner would have no revenues with which to buy its products. Instead, the theory proposes that nations should specialize in producing goods and services where the opportunity cost of producing it is less. If nations specialize on the basis of where their comparative advantage lies, and rely on trade to access other goods and services from other nations, it is proposed that all can benefit from such *free trade*, and it will raise overall global wealth.

Hoskins et al. (2004) apply the theory of comparative advantage to global film and television production and trade. They note that in some industries, comparative advantages arise out of natural resource endowments; e.g., Australia is rich in agricultural and energy resources, which it can trade with Japan, which in turn is a leading producer of motor vehicles and consumer electronic goods. In other instances, it may be the relative weighting of labour- and capital-intensive production; e.g., China has an abundant supply of rural labourers prepared to work in relatively low-wage manufacturing jobs in its cities, producing goods at a low cost, and China trades profitably with Germany, which specializes in producing complex capital goods that require highly skilled labour and engineering expertise.

Some of these examples indicate that comparative advantages are by no means 'natural' or fixed in time. Drawing on the work of business economist Michael Porter (1990), we can note the importance of *competitive advantage*, where nations develop leadership in particular industries by means of effective public policy, concentration of resources, or acquisition of knowledge and expertise. Hoskins et al. (2004: 317) observe that 'new industries . . . are thought to depend more on human knowledge and the competitive environment than on physical factor endowments . . . characteristics of a country's demand and operating environment can be a source of competitive advantage'. As we will see in chapter 5, it has been argued that sources of competitive advantage can be geographically specific, located in particular cities or regions on the basis of successful industry clustering; it has been argued that clustering dynamics may be particularly strong in the creative industries.

Hoskins et al. (1997, 2004) observe the dominance of the United States in global film and television production, and attribute this to:

- benefits the US derived from its large domestic market size, which is a combination of a relatively large population and high per capita incomes;
- the size of the English language market, which is the largest global linguistic market, and which the US dominates;
- first mover advantages from being the world's first major exporter of film and television product;
- the geographical concentration of production in Los Angeles (Hollywood), where a highly competitive environment enables sophisticated supply chain relationships to develop between producers, providers of ancillary services and distributors, making it a centre for knowledge sharing and innovation;
- the Hollywood system itself, which is a highly effective media industry cluster of skilled technicians, actors, the 'star system' and relevant infrastructure, which generates synergistic gains resulting from a concentration of creative talents (cf. Scott, 2005).

The United States also accrues advantages in global audiovisual trade by nature of the types of cultural product it develops, as part of what Hoskins et al. refer to as 'cultural discount'. They note that, whereas cultural hardware products (TVs, cameras, sound recording equipment, etc.) bear few direct cultural traces, and can be produced anywhere through global production networks, cultural 'software' products are typically 'rooted in one culture, and thus attractive in the home market where viewers share a common knowledge and way of life'. They argue that such cultural products from other societies 'will have diminished appeal elsewhere, as viewers find it difficult to identify with the style, values, beliefs, history, myth, institutions, physical environment, and behavioural patterns' (Hoskins et al., 1997: 32). The question this raises is why would US audiovisual products experience less cultural discount than those from other countries? Among the reasons that have been proposed are:

- The *multicultural nature of US society*. As US society is itself very culturally diverse – if not linguistically diverse – success in the US domestic market often correlates with the ability to reach other international markets.
- *Narrative transparency*. Olson (2004) has argued that Hollywood producers have developed over time the capacity to produce media cultural products which can 'seem a part of one's culture, even though they have been crafted elsewhere' (Olson, 2004: 120).
- *Blockbuster productions*: Not all US audiovisual product does well internationally – comedies, for instance, tend to do much better in the US domestic market than they do overseas. However, high-budget science fiction, historical epics or action-adventure films can do well internationally, as they require low awareness of US cultural context. A film such as *Avatar*, for example, is set in a space colony in the twenty-second century, even if those who rule it look suspiciously like the US military.
- *Dominance over international distribution*: Political economists have drawn attention to the role played by US media majors in controlling international distribution, and how this has intersected with aspects of US foreign policy, such as demands for free trade in audiovisual services, to secure structural dominance in international markets (O'Regan, 1992; Miller et al., 2005).

The important point to be made about comparative and competitive advantages is that they are neither absolute nor permanent, even when they are reinforced by international market power. In the English language market alone, Hollywood may specialize in the action blockbuster and long-form television, but Britain has a notable global ascendancy in historical dramas, Australia has been a leader in serial dramas ('soaps'), and

Canada has become a centre for telemovie production. Moreover, when we consider the global context, we need to note the centrality of production centres such as Brazil, Mexico, India, China, Hong Kong and South Korea (Curtin, 2007; McMillin, 2007; Fung, 2009; Sinclair, 2009).

Indeed, there is now a considerable literature suggesting we are at the twilight of Hollywood dominance, as a result of the rising prominence in the global economy of the BRICS nations[3] and endemic cost inflation in Hollywood production. Jeremy Tunstall (2008) has argued that the peak of US media dominance was the mid twentieth century, and that the rise of economies other than those of Europe and the US has stimulated the rise of national and regional media production in Asia, Africa, Latin America and the Middle East. Tyler Cowen has observed that 'Hollywood holds a potentially vulnerable market position, given how much it spends on celebrity salaries and marketing. While these expenses give Hollywood movies a huge global boost, they also mean that American moviemakers have lost their ability to control their costs' (Cowen, 2002: 99). In tracking the rise of greater China as the world's largest film and television market, Michael Curtin has wondered whether 'Hollywood has dominated for so long that . . . the global future is commonly imagined as a world brought together by homogeneous cultural products produced and circulated by American media' (Curtin, 2007: 4). The significance of alternative centres of media and cultural production, and how they are changing the global creative industries landscape, will be considered in the next chapter.

Conclusion

This chapter has worked from a general understanding of the role played by markets to develop an understanding of the particularities of markets in the media and creative industries. In doing so, it has observed a range of competing perspectives on markets, from the dominant neoclassical approaches to those associated with political economy and the new institutionalist economics. It has also observed debates around markets for cultural goods and services, with the emergent concept of social network markets challenging some of the traditional 'market failure' approaches that have come from media and cultural economics. Extending market theories to the international level, it has also considered debates around international trade in cultural products, with the rise of creative industries being connected to economic globalization and the intensified circulation of cultural goods and services around the world. Again, there are notable differences of approach between theories of comparative advantage, those of competitive advantage, and those which see the play of power as being critical in shaping global geo-cultural flows.

In presenting this material, the chapter has been somewhat agnostic in determining the relative value of mainstream economic approaches as compared to those from critical political economy. One reason for outlining theories of how markets are meant to operate in principle is that, even if one is critical of the impact of market forces on the production and circulation of culture, and sees the need for a continuing strong role for governments in managing cultural flows, there remains merit in developing a detailed understanding of how markets work in relation to the creative industries. Operating primarily though what Albert Hirschman identified as the exercise of consumer power through 'exit', markets can constitute a powerful force for innovation, dynamism and change. At the same time, market society can generate its own 'negative externalities' – to use a favoured phrase among economists – and the capacity of social, political and cultural institutions to enable citizens to exercise 'voice' marks a source of countervailing power that is of continuing significance in both domestic and international economic relations.

5   Places

Introduction: The Century of Cities

The twenty-first century has been described as a century of cities; a 'new metropolitan age' (Isar et al., 2012: 1), where global, national, regional and local forces coalesce in densely populated metropolitan centres. The 2000s saw, for the first time in human history, the number of people living in cities exceed the number living outside of them, and the number of people living in cities is expected to increase from 3 billion in the early 2000s to 5 billion people, or 70 per cent of the world's population, by 2030, with the urban populations of the developing world being four times as large as those in the more economically developed countries (Worldwatch Institute, 2007; Donald, 2011). It has been argued that cities, and associated city-regions, have become the 'motors of the global economy' (Scott et al., 2001), and that the shift from manufacturing industries to knowledge, service and creative industries is integrally linked to such trends. This chapter will consider the relevance of cities as places of creative activity, and the extent to which urban form itself can act as a catalyst to the development of the creative industries. Noting worldwide trends, and in particular the rise of cities in the developing world, it will consider the role played by particular cities at certain historical junctures, as well as recent work on cities and globalization, and implications for urban cultural policy.

In addition to the economic and demographic trends concerning cities, the 2000s saw a resurgence of academic interest in the relationship between creativity and cities. Whereas the 1990s saw speculation that an Internet-driven economy that was 'post-industrial' or 'weightless' (Coyle, 1998) would see the significance of location decline, as technologically networked citizens could seemingly locate themselves anywhere to pursue their interests, the 2000s were marked by an energetic search by academics, artists, journalists, policy makers, entrepreneurs, investors, property developers, and many others to uncover the wellsprings of creativity and their relationship to place. Some of the most relevant concepts coming out of these debates, such as those of creative cities, media capitals and creative clusters, will be considered in this chapter.

At the same time, there will be discussion of whether some concepts were overcooked, particularly the claim that densely populated urban agglomerations are the natural home of the creative industries. As we will note, much of the world's urban growth is in fact suburban growth, or the outward expansion of city populations, and the Internet enables new manifestations of suburban creativity to emerge that do not fit with the 'imagined geography' of inner cities as the natural incubators of creative practice. Moreover, there is the need to consider potential downsides of the creative city, particularly the question of whether large inequalities within cities, as well as between cities, are consequences of such developments. The following chapter will consider whether public policy can act to ameliorate or reverse such trends towards uneven development (Sassen, 2001; Harvey, 2008) in an increasingly urbanized global economy.

Creative Cities in History

Cities have been at the core of globalization processes for much of human history, from the peak of the Roman Empire in the third century AD to the present day. Timberlake and Ma (2007) identify three reasons why cities are central to globalization. First, large cities are typically cosmopolitan places, with diverse populations from many other places in the world, and visited and experienced by people from all over the world. Second, cities typically exert considerable influence over the regions surrounding them, whether through the pull they exert over populations from rural areas and smaller towns as centres of economic opportunity, or through their role as administrative centres for corporations, governments and other institutions, which makes them concentrated sites of economic, political and cultural power. Finally, cities exist within a 'global system of cities', where there are hierarchies between the most influential, intermediate and smaller cities, which are connected into 'networks which span regions of various sizes . . . these networks are defined by the flows of people, information and things, such as commodities, among cities' (Timberlake and Ma, 2007: 255).

All of these forces that promote cities, and urban development, can be identified in the current global environment. People are moving on an unprecedented scale, from the countryside to the city and from one country to another: migrants to a new country more often than not settle in its major cities, and cities are also the primary destinations for tourists, students, business people and others who travel for work, leisure or education. The globalization of industry, finance and services makes the location of corporate headquarters an increasingly important decision, and much of global capital continues to cluster in what Sassen (1994), Castells (1996), Taylor (2004) and Friedmann (2006) have identified as *world cities*. World cities are structured as 'networks of urban places that are arranged hierarchically in terms of their relative importance as sites of corporate control' (Timberlake and Ma, 2007: 265): proxy measures for network density include the amount of traffic over communications networks, or the number of flights per day from international airports.

Historically, the growth of nation-states has been associated with the concentration of political and administrative authority in capital cities, and centres of economic and political power have also come to be centres for the arts, culture and entertainment industries. Moreover, with efficient transport and communication networks being a condition for urban development since the time of the Roman Empire, the revolution in networked ICTs has strengthened the role of cities as nodes in global networks enabling production, distribution, decision making and communication. Manuel Castells (1996) refers to these global networks as constituting a global *space of flows*, whose central nodes are what he terms *informational cities*.

There is much, then, to support Ash Amin's observation that globalization, the rise of information-based industries and networked ICTs promote the further development and expansion of cities:

> There appears little evidence to support the claim that cities are becoming less important in an economy marked by increasing geographical dispersal . . . [they] assert, one way or another, the powers of agglomeration, proximity, and density, now perhaps less significant for the production of mass manufactures than for the production of knowledge, information and innovation, as well as specialized inputs . . . in terms of the territorial base of the economy, there can be no question that the city remains the economic motor of postindustrial society. (Amin, 2000: 120)

Yet this was not inevitable. For much of the 1970s and 1980s, cities were seen as the sources of distinct 'urban problems'. If one looked at major cities such as New York and London in the 1970s, they appeared to be in decline, experiencing urban decay, rising crime, budgetary crises and the movement of people away from the urban centre (Fainstein and Harloe, 2000). Technological and economic developments such as electrification and rising motor vehicle use promoted the separation of home and work through suburbanization (Kotkin, 2006: 117–26), while the shift of traditional manufacturing industries to East Asia pointed towards deindustrialization in the West and, with it, the decline of once powerful industrial cities. By contrast, the 'new conventional wisdom' surrounding cities – to use Gordon and Buck's (2005) term – involves a shift from seeing them as 'essentially problematic residues of nineteenth- and early twentieth-century ways of organizing industrial economies' towards 'the idea that they could again be

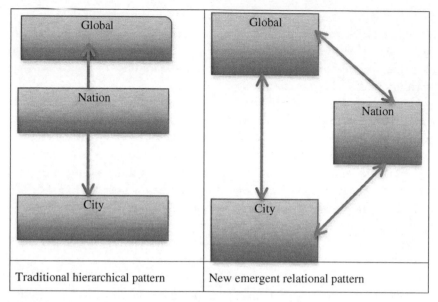

Figure 5.1. Dynamics of local and global relational patterns

Source: Isar et al., 2012: 2.

exciting and creative places in which to live and work' (Gordon and Buck, 2005: 6).

Scott (2008) describes the 1970s and 1980s as a period of crisis for the 'Fordist' city, built upon mass production of industrial goods. Scott sees the 'resurgent city' of the early twenty-first century as being connected to the rise of what he terms 'the cognitive-cultural economy', or the particular combinations of information-based industries, advanced services and creative industries that have been on the rise in the global economy. Isar et al. connect this to a shifting set of spatialized power relations, where it is cities, rather than nations, that are becoming the 'leading *loci* of cultural policy and governance' (2012: 2). In line with authors such as Sassen (1994), Castells (1996), Held et al. (1999) and Taylor (2004), Isar et al. identify cities as increasingly central global political-economic forces in their own right. As figure 5.1 indicates, this challenges the state-centric logic of twentieth-century political economy, where it was the nation-state, the national economy and national culture that were central, and which exerted leadership both over sub-national levels such as those of cities and regions, and within a global system that was understood as a system of states. In the twenty-first century, this traditional hierarchical pattern has been challenged by a networked relational model where power is increasingly 'shared and brokered' (Held et al., 1999) between the global, national and city-regional levels.

Cities can become world cities for a variety of reasons. In his review of world city literature, Taylor (2004: 40–1) observed that 85 cities had been cited as world cities in 16 different reference sources, with only four cities appearing in all registers: New York, London, Paris and Tokyo. There is also typically a correlation between world cities and creative cities, both historically and in the current context, but not all world cities are creative cities. For example, Paris, Frankfurt and Zurich appear in most registers of world cities, but of these three, only Paris would be seen as being a major centre for the arts, culture and creativity. A creative city has been defined by Throsby in the following way:

> The concept of a 'creative city' describes an urban complex where cultural activities of various sorts are an integral component of the city's economic and social functioning. Such cities tend to be built upon a strong social and cultural infrastructure; to have relatively high concentrations of creative employment; and to be attractive to inward investment because of their well-established arts and cultural facilities. (Throsby, 2010: 139)

Creative cities are not simply the by-product of historical legacies, such as a rich heritage of architectural monuments, nor are they simply places with a large amount of creative industries employment. Peter Hall (2000: 642) has made the observation that 'having creative industries is not at all the same thing as being creative', and the critical question for researchers to address is 'whether a city can have creative industries for very long without being creative'. Throsby proposes that:

> At its best . . . a creative city strategy will pay attention to cultural infrastructure, local cultural participation and involvement, the development of a flourishing and dynamic creative arts sector, community-oriented heritage conservation, and support for wider creative industries that are fully integrated into the local economy. (Throsby, 2010: 140)

From a historical perspective, Hall identified six cities that were centres of artistic and cultural creativity: Athens in the fifth century BC; Florence in the fourteenth century; London in the late sixteenth to early seventeenth century; Vienna in the late eighteenth to early nineteenth century; Paris between 1870 and 1910; and Berlin in the 1920s. In seeking to identify some common features of these cities, Hall observed the following features:

- a context of rapid economic and social transformation, in cities that were major centres of production, commerce and trade;
- a significant number of wealthy individuals who could financially support new ventures;

- a strong presence for high culture, in which 'culture was fostered by a minority and catered for the tastes of that minority' (Hall, 2000: 645);
- high levels of migration from many places, making these cities highly cosmopolitan and culturally diverse;
- a context of reaction to prevailing conservative forces and values, that is widespread and in which creative people are playing a central role.

In the cities considered above, there is a paradox: they are 'bourgeois cities', characterized by high disparities of wealth and life opportunities, but they are also 'places of great social and intellectual turbulence'. Hall observed that:

> What is critical is that this disjuncture is experienced and expressed by a group of creative people who feel themselves outsiders, because they are young or provincial or either foreign, or because they do not belong to the established order of power and prestige . . . A creative city will therefore be a place where outsiders can enter and feel a certain state of ambiguity: they must be neither excluded from opportunity, nor must they be so warmly embraced that the creative drive is lost. (Hall, 2000: 646)

Hall's account deals primarily with the classical European centres of the arts and culture, but it is acknowledged that the twentieth century saw a different kind of creative city emerge, born out of the capacity to combine art and technology, and whose epicentre was the United States. He notes that the United States had developed a distinct ability to convert its inventions into commercially useful innovations, and this was nowhere more apparent than in the cultural sphere where 'the American system of manufacturing' was combined with 'a populist concept of culture and entertainment, far removed from the European patrician attitude that public corporations should give the masses what was good for them' (Hall, 2000: 647). Such combinations, when combined with massive demographic flux, saw the rise of New York as a centre for music, the arts, advertising and fashion, the emergence of Los Angeles as the global centre for film and television, and music centres such as Memphis and Nashville.

Hartley et al. (2012) observe the central role played by *entrepreneurs* in these processes, be they the business entrepreneurs discussed by Joseph Schumpeter, who identified the commercial opportunities from mass entertainment that would lead to the Hollywood studios, Elvis Presley, etc., and artist-entrepreneurs such as Alfred Hitchcock, Andy Warhol and The Rolling Stones, who 'created not just new art, but a new art market and business model'. Swedberg (2006) has also observed that there are parallels in this regard between the artist and the entrepreneur in their willingness to challenge the *status quo* in pursuit of new opportunities:

the economic entrepreneur who works in the creative industries can . . . be conceptualized as someone who makes combinations, where art is one of the elements in the entrepreneurial combination. Or the artist who is interested in economic success may be conceptualized as someone who tries to link up his or her work with other elements in some combination that works. (Swedberg, 2006: 250)

Swedberg follows Schumpeter in identifying parallels between Schumpeter's figure of the entrepreneur and that of the artist, as those who:

- break out of equilibrium situations;
- seek to lead rather than follow;
- put together new combinations;
- feel no inner resistance to change;
- make intuitive choices among a multitude of new alternatives; and
- command no resources but borrow what they need (Swedberg, 2006: 250).

Creative Clusters

When we refer to creative cities, one issue of contention is whether we are referring to the whole city, or to particular parts of it. A classic instance of this is Los Angeles. When it is said that Los Angeles is the global centre of film and television, this is usually shortened to refer to Hollywood. Hollywood was where most of the major film production studios were located in the 1930s and 1940s, and has since been synonymous with movie stars and the film business. Today, most large film production studios are located outside of Hollywood, although they remain strongly concentrated in Greater Los Angeles: Hollywood today largely functions as a tourist destination, although the adult film industry retains a strong presence in the suburb. When we speak of Hollywood, then, we are talking about something more than a geographical location where films are made – far more films are now made in Burbank, Studio City and Culver City, or even Vancouver in Canada – than in Hollywood as such. Instead, we refer to 'Hollywood' as a cultural production system that has come to be spatially agglomerated in a particular place. As Scott (2005) observes, Hollywood – or to be more precise, Greater Los Angeles – functions as such a place. In the economic geography literature, such agglomeration dynamics are known as clustering, and it has been argued that the creative industries are particularly likely to be shaped by the dynamics of locational clustering.

The concept of *clusters* has its origins in the work of the British economist Alfred Marshall (1920 [1890]), who identified the positive externalities arising from the co-location of firms and workers in related industries; examples from his time include the Sheffield textiles industry and the wool textiles industry of South Yorkshire. There was renewed interest in the concept in the 1990s, particularly through the work of business management theorist Michael Porter. Porter defined a cluster as 'a geographically proximate group of interconnected companies and associated institutions in a particular field, linked by commonalities and complementarities' (Porter, 2000: 254). Porter argued that sustainable competitive advantage lay less in cutting costs and production efficiencies, than in promoting productivity growth and innovation over time. Following Marshall's original insight, Porter (1998, 2000) proposed that the location of firms in related and supporting industries in a particular cluster generated spillover benefits, including:

1. *productivity gains* arising from access to specialist inputs and skilled labour, specialized information and industry knowledge within particular locations, as well as the development of complementary relationships among firms and industries, and the role played by universities and training institutions in enabling knowledge transfer;
2. *innovation opportunities* stemming from proximity to buyers and suppliers, sustained interaction with others in the industry, and pressures to innovate in circumstances where cost factors facing competitors are broadly similar;
3. *opportunities for new business formation*, arising from access to information about opportunities, better access to resources required by business start-ups (e.g., venture capitalists, skilled workforce), and reduced barriers to exit from existing businesses, as they can be bought out by others within the cluster.

Many examples of successful clusters are cited, including the fashion industry in Milan, jewellery makers in Paris, financial services in London, wine making in northern California, and country music in Nashville. Other terms used in the extensive literature on clusters are 'industrial districts' (Amin, 2000) and learning regions (Cooke, 2002). Such places have been described as being 'sticky' (Markusen, 2008), in that their competitiveness in a global economy derives from what Michael Storper (1997) has termed 'untraded interdependencies', or 'the conventions, informal rules, and habits that coordinate economic actors under conditions of uncertainty . . . [and] constitute region-specific assets' (Storper, 1997: 4–5). Features of such successful clusters typically include:

- dense networks of small, locally owned firms;
- low barriers to entry and exit for new firms;
- established relations of trust and reciprocity among buyers and suppliers across the value chain;
- an institutional infrastructure that promotes knowledge sharing among participants (e.g., a local university may play a key brokering role, or a regional business association);
- strong movements of skilled people into the region, with low levels of out-migration;
- specialist sources of finance, technical expertise and business services in the city or region;
- strong local government that is supportive of the industry cluster while maintaining good governance practices.

Such factors are seen as particularly conducive to innovation, both in the sense of developing new ideas of value to the industry, and disseminating these new ideas among relevant knowledge communities. One feature of successful clusters is their combination of 'hard' and 'soft' infrastructure. Landry (2000: 133) observes that while the 'hard infrastructure' includes buildings, institutions, transport facilities, communications infrastructure, etc., the less tangible and more place-specific 'soft infrastructure' includes 'the system of associative structures and social networks, connections and human interactions, that underpins and encourages the flow of ideas between individuals and institutions'.

The most widely discussed clusters in terms of possible emulation globally are the Silicon Valley ICT cluster in Palo Alto–San Jose, where Apple, Hewlett-Packard and many other global ICT firms are located, and Hollywood. In his historical geography of Hollywood, Allen Scott (2005) identifies five critical elements in the rise of Hollywood as the world's pre-eminent audiovisual media cluster:

1. The rise of Hollywood was by no means inevitable – New York was the major US film production centre in the 1910s – but those who did establish their production bases in Hollywood developed superior business strategies, based around feature films and the star system. This ensured that, by the 1920s, Hollywood had developed a superior community of producers that in turn formed the basis for the further concentration of resources in the region.
2. While Hollywood's growth from the 1920s to the 1940s was based around the vertically integrated studio system, the break-up of the studio system after the Paramount anti-trust decision of 1948 paradoxically strengthened Hollywood as a production centre. It promoted new

competition between the big studios and smaller independent producers, the turn away from 'all under one roof' production houses towards
vertically disintegrated production networks, the rise of complex inter-
firm networks[4] and new competition for talent and resources arising
from the expansion of the television industry (cf. Christopherson and
Storper, 1989; Christopherson, 2011b).

3. Hollywood as an industrial district specializing in audiovisual media
   production is a cluster not only of producers and creative talent. It is
   also a cluster of specialist service and supply firms, engaged in activities
   as diverse as supplying soundstages, set design and construction, digital
   visual effects, agents and specialist business services (legal, financial,
   etc.), as well as government agencies and institutional actors who support the industry's development in various ways.

4. Hollywood has developed dynamic and distinct local labour markets,
   with a large number of potential employees and a diverse array of skills
   being clustered in the Greater Los Angeles area. The clustering of a
   large number of creative workers in a concentrated geographical locale
   means that Hollywood is also an intensive learning region, with massive
   amounts of tacit knowledge, the fast diffusion of new ideas and information (Cooke, 2002), and the serendipitous meetings and exchanges that
   Storper and Venables (2004) identify as 'buzz'.

5. The efficient production base of Hollywood is matched by effective
   marketing and distribution strategies that generate tendencies towards
   industry concentration and oligopoly within the domestic industry,
   while making it a formidable force in international markets.

In a global media industry 'characterized from a geographical point of
view by a heavy concentration in a limited number of cities, where large
media clusters have emerged' (Karlsson and Picard, 2011: 3), Hollywood
represents the archetypal creative media cluster. Drawing upon Lorenzen
and Frederiksen (2008), we can identify it as possessing three types of innovation economies:

1. *Localization economies*, where externalities derive from the co-location
   of firms in related industries, meaning that they develop associated spe-
   cializations of labour markets and associated institutions (e.g., government support agencies, universities and educational institutions) – these
   are industry clusters of the classic sort first identified by Alfred Marshall.

2. *Urbanization economies*, arising from a diverse spread of firms and industries in a particular location, which generate a diverse range of labour,
   skills, knowledge and ideas, as well as concentrated investment in large-
   scale infrastructure (particularly related to transport, communication

and education), the incentives for professional services to cluster in large cities, and the attractiveness of cities as sites for migration.

3. *Global city economies*, whereby radical product innovation can acquire support due to the depth of institutional and investor support, the search for novelty and new experiences, and links to sources of both political and economic power. In the creative industries, global cities such as New York, London, Los Angeles, Paris and Tokyo are both the headquarters for major corporate conglomerates and major sites for the arts and entertainment, including the critical *avant garde* (Landry, 2005; Currid, 2006, 2007).

The rise of creative clusters is indicative of the 'tight interweaving of place and production system' (Scott, 2008: 94), that is characteristic of the cultural economy of the creative industries. But it varies from place to place, and there is evidence that it tends to scale up, i.e. the larger a city, the more innovations per resident it tends to develop (Florida, 2007: xvii–xxvi). Lorenzen and Frederiksen (2008) identify different capacities for innovation in these clusters, from the incremental innovations that characterize industrial districts which draw upon localization economies, to the radical product innovations that typically arise out of global cities.

Drawing upon Hartley (2009) we can suggest that this is, at least in part, due to the locus of innovation in such urban centres. In a traditional industrial district, it is the direct producers themselves who drive innovation, meaning that it typically involves innovations within an established field. In large cities, there is a strong supportive infrastructure of providers of inputs and services to the creative industries, so that innovation is distributed more widely across the value chain. Global cities are, however, centres of greater consumer productivity, or more densely developed social network markets (Potts et al., 2008), and places where the flows of knowledge, new information, and original products and ideas are most rapid. In this respect, global cities also benefit from populations that are typically both highly diverse – in terms of nationality, ethnicity, lifestyle, preferences, etc. – and highly educated, so these local flows of knowledge tap into both global knowledge networks and circuits of global trade.

There is not a predictable pattern to the emergence of creative clusters. In the case of cities such as Nashville and Memphis as centres of country and blues music, we can see in retrospect cultural influences that were driving such developments – particularly the migration of African-Americans from the American south in the mid twentieth century – but the cities themselves would not have been predicted to be major centres of the music business. Similarly, German migrant families had wineries in South Australia's

Barossa Valley for over a century before the region took off as an internationally significant wine producer. The key was a change in the drinking habits of Australians, where the traditional preference for beer began to be supplemented by a general interest in wine; the changing status of women in Australian society, and their increasing numbers in the paid workforce, was also relevant here.

Given that creative clusters can – at least in principle – be developed in many places, can public policy produce creative clusters? The ingredients are well known: as De Propris and Hypponen (2008: 268) observe, they consist of 'geographical proximity . . . face-to-face collaborations . . . the co-location of specialized activities . . . low transaction costs, thick networks of social business activities, high levels of competence and specialization, innovation, and a pool of skilled labour'. There was also considerable interest among policy makers in developing such formations. In Europe, the European Capitals of Culture movement acted as a catalyst for such developments (Campbell, 2011; Palmer and Richards, 2011), and it is also seen in the development of *cultural quarters* such as the Temple Bar in Dublin, the Museums Quarter in Vienna, and the Nottingham Lace Market (Roodhouse, 2006). China has undertaken a massive investment in creative clusters as a key element in developing urban economies that are based on the creative industries and not simply on low-cost manufacturing. In the city of Shanghai, 83 creative clusters, or 'creative industries parks', had been authorized by the city authorities by the late 2000s (Keane, 2011).

In observing some limitations to creative cluster strategies, it can be noted, as Frith et al. point out in their study of the Glasgow music scene, that 'cluster theory . . . is an entirely convincing *post facto* analysis . . . but rather more problematic as a prescriptive or diagnostic tool' (Frith et al., 2009: 79). Part of the problem arises in the propensity to conflate various elements of clustering, such as the co-location of industries in a particular place on the one hand, and the embedded social networks and knowledge transfer that epitomize dynamic industry clusters. As Gordon and McCann (2001) point out, agglomeration of similar firms in a particular place does not in itself demonstrate the positive effects of clustering; for example, warehousing facilities have long been clustered near ports and airports, but this does not give such places the attributes of a Silicon Valley or a Hollywood. Another risk of creative cluster strategies is that they become overly genericized, and driven by civic boosterism and property development opportunities, rather than tapping into genuine mainsprings of local culture and creativity (Oakley, 2004; Mommaas, 2009). Finally, there is the risk of clusters becoming victims of their own success, generating a 'groupthink' that is insufficiently responsive to new ideas generated from outside of that *milieu*. The point has been made that the fabled 'tacit knowledge' that exists within Hollywood about what audiences want from entertainment can be seen as resulting in 'recycled creativity' and formulaic, risk-averse cinema and TV product that can be at odds with the development of more creative products that appeal to more diverse audiences (De Propris and Hypponen, 2008: 275–81).

Case Study: Shanghai and Seoul as Creative Cities

In many respects, creative cities discourses precede those of the creative industries. In Britain, the identification of cultural industries as an alternative pathway for urban development with the decline of manufacturing was taken up by a number of left-wing city councils in the 1980s and 1990s, well before there was a national creative industries policy (Flew, 2012a: 15–17). Similarly, in Europe, the concept of culture-led urban regeneration had considerable currency. Perhaps the exemplar was the 'Barcelona model', where leading architects and urbanists worked with local authorities to position the city as a cosmopolitan centre in European and global cultural flows (Paz Balibrea, 2004; Isar, 2012).

Creative cities concepts were quickly taken up in East Asia. Yusuf and Nabeshima (2005) observed that urbanization, the rise of service industries, the development of high value-added business services and ICT-intensive industries, and a growing middle class all encouraged the promotion of East Asian cities as creative industries centres. Gibson and Kong (2005) noted that the take-up of creative economy strategies took root in urban centres such as Hong Kong, Seoul, Singapore and Taipei in the 1990s and 2000s as markers of place competitiveness as the competition for global capital and creative talent in the region intensified. They argued that the 'normative creative economy script' had considerable appeal to policy makers in these cities, which had 'already established national broadcasting, arts and cultural industries, but [had] aspirations for "world city" status' (Gibson and Kong, 2005: 550).

In the first instance, it was the city-state of Singapore and the city-region of Hong Kong SAR that were most receptive to creative industries policy discourses, choosing to replicate significant elements of the UK model (Kong et al., 2006). But creative industries policies gathered momentum throughout East Asia, particularly as the end of the ICT boom in 2001 indicated weaknesses in technology-driven strategies that lacked an associated investment in creative capacity and 'cultural software', and as China continued to rise as both the major economic competitor and the largest potential market in the region.

The city of Shanghai was the most globalized and cosmopolitan Chinese city in the 1920s and 1930s, and from the late 1980s onwards, the city has become a global financial and commercial as well as industrial centre, particularly with the rapid development of the Pudong New Area to the city's east (Yusuf and Wu, 2002). The Shanghai municipal government has been a leader in China in adopting a creative industries strategy, with the establishment of a Shanghai Creative Industry Centre (SCIC) in 2004, and over 80 creative clusters being developed by 2008 (Keane, 2011).[5] Promoting the creative industries in Shanghai was identified as a priority in the national government's 11th Five-Year Plan, and it is estimated that creative industries now account for 7–10 per cent of Shanghai GDP (UNCTAD, 2008: 181). The five main areas of creative industries development have been:

- *R&D*, including advertising, animation, software and industrial design;
- *architectural design*, including engineering and interior design;
- *culture and media*, including art, books, newspaper publishing, radio, television, film, music and performing arts;
- *business services*, including education, training and consulting services; and
- *lifestyle*, including fashion, leisure, tourism and sports.

In her assessment of Shanghai's creative industries clusters, Zheng (2011) finds that they are consistent with Shanghai's positioning as an entrepreneurial city with a global orientation, as befits its historical standing as a highly commercial city, less driven by political factors than the other great Chinese city, Beijing. Zheng found that creative clusters had transformed the urban landscape of Shanghai, acting as a major attractor to creative talent both in China and internationally, and they were a key part of the city's branding and a driver of cultural activities and tourism. They have, however, been less successful in promoting new creative businesses, and have arguably functioned more as enclaves for middle-class professionals and as profitable real estate ventures, rather than as innovation hubs and catalysts for small and medium-sized enterprise (SME) development, as envisaged in the creative clusters literature (cf. Keane, 2011: 135–6).

The city of Seoul in South Korea marks a contrasting approach to creative city development. As South Korea's capital and leading urban centre, it grew rapidly from the late 1950s onwards, with the success of export-led industrialization and large-scale rural–urban migration (Kim and Han, 2012). Its emergence as a significant cultural centre in Asia is, however, more recent, and two factors have been critical. First, there has been the 'Korean wave' (*hallyu*) and the growing popularity of Korean films, TV series, games, music and other forms of popular culture throughout Asia and internationally over the course of the 2000s (Choi, 2008). Second, there has been a strong and consistent commitment on the part of local and national governments to establishing South Korea generally, and Seoul in particular, as a global leader in high-speed wireless and broadband connectivity, making Seoul one of the most digitally networked places in the world. This has in turn promoted a 'Korean digital wave' (Goldsmith et al., 2011), with all forms of digital culture flourishing, from mobile games to online participatory culture (Hjorth, 2011).

The development of Seoul as a global creative city has been more driven by digital technology developments, and less focused upon state-led cluster development, than that of Shanghai. There have been initiatives to promote the creative industries in particular locations, as with the 'culturenomics' strategy enunciated in the Creative and Cultural City Seoul strategy, and the promotion of the Hong-Dae area as a cultural district (Cho, 2010). But perhaps more indicative is the Seoul Digital Media City development, which aims to 'utilize the advanced Korean IT sector and tries to integrate urban development with digital technologies' (Kim and Han, 2012: 152). Less overtly 'cultural' than Shanghai's creative clusters, the development of digital creative industries in this context is more likely to be an outgrowth of 'the technosocial environment of contemporary Seoul' (Choi, 2010: 82), with its ubiquitous digital technology interfaces and distributed community engagements and interactions.

Media Capitals

The concept of *media capitals* is a variant of creative cluster theories developed by media theorist Michel Curtin (2003, 2007, 2009). Observing that the global centres of media production are not so much nations as cities, and that there is no necessary correspondence between city and nation in terms of being a production centre,[6] Curtin argues that media capitals are:

> Cities . . . [that] function less as centres of national media than as central nodes in the transnational flow of culture, talent and resources. Rather than asking about relations among and between nations, we should explore the ways in which media industries based in particular cities are participating in the restructuring of spatial and cultural relations worldwide. (Curtin, 2009: 111)

In proposing media capitals as an alternative framework to that of media or cultural imperialism, Curtin posits its value as 'a concept that at once acknowledges the *spatial* logics of capital, creativity, culture, and policy without privileging one among them' (Curtin, 2009: 117).

Curtin's framework identifies four key variables that shape the spatial dimensions of media and the emergence of media capitals. First, there is *the logic of accumulation*. The classic capitalist logic of accumulation, identified by classical political economists such as Adam Smith and Karl Marx, as well as geographers such as David Harvey, is to seek concentration of production resources on the one hand and to maximize the extension of markets on the other, in order to realize the greatest possible returns on investment in the shortest period of time. There are thus centripetal (localizing) tendencies in the sphere of production and centrifugal (dispersing) tendencies in distribution, that promote the rise of production clusters on the one hand, and relentless pressures for geographical expansion by companies on the other. Such dynamics are central to the rise of Hollywood as the quintessential media and creative cluster whose cultural products have global reach, but can be identified with second-tier media capitals such as Mumbai, Cairo, Miami and Hong Kong, which have developed distributional reach through privileged access for their products through territorially and linguistically related regions.

Second, there are *trajectories of creative migration*. The clustering of media production into media capitals means that these urban locations act as 'talent magnets' for particular types of creative workers. While this has been well documented by those authors who deal with patterns of migration to 'creative cities' (e.g., Florida, 2008), Curtin identifies a weakness of this literature as being a lack of consideration of the significance of political stability or expressive freedom for creative workers as a driver of such migration. This may not be such an issue where the competition is for creative workforce within nation-states, but it was a significant historical factor in the rise of Hong Kong as a destination for Chinese-speaking creative workers. It is a pertinent consideration in the aspirations of other East Asian urban centres to become leading creative cities, such as Beijing, Shanghai, Taipei and Singapore.

The third set of factors Curtin identifies involve *forces of socio-cultural variation*. Both the film and television industries have been strongly shaped by legal, institutional and policy frameworks that have for the most part been nationally based, although strongly influenced by international developments. The rise of Hollywood from the 1920s onwards meant that governments in many parts of the world prioritized the development of a national film industry as a countervailing force to Hollywood, as well as an outlet for the creative expression of national culture. Governments were even further implicated in the development of television, as they were required to provide basic infrastructure for broadcasting and to adjudicate on who could hold a licence to broadcast. In many parts of the world, this involved the development of a public service monopoly, or a strong public service broadcaster that was to be a conduit for national culture, values and information. Straubhaar (2007) has observed how communications technologies, global media economics and popular audience preferences that promote access to imported television material – particularly from the United States – mean that many national television systems develop in a relationship of *asymmetrical interdependence* to the imported content. They are neither fully independent nor fully subject to cultural domination: rather, the relationship between local and imported media content shifts over time, with the imported content acting as a force that helps to shape local media production. Thus, national media capitals – which are often also government and political power bases – become linked to transnational media content networks, which can further facilitate the movement of capital and creative workers.

Finally, there is the role played by *national media policies*. From the 1980s in particular, with the development of cable and satellite television and the popularization of the Internet, media has been seen as being increasingly subject to dynamic forces associated with globalization. Contrary to perceptions that this equals the end of the nation-state and the slide of national cultures into cultural homogenization, it remains the case, as Nitin Govil argues, that 'the national remains a powerful mode for engaging the spatial and temporal practices that organize the contemporary media industries across varied economies of scale' (Govil, 2009: 140). The national space remains central to defining the legal and institutional conditions of production and reception (ownership laws, content regulations, intellectual property, communications infrastructures), it provides a repertoire of vernacular forms that mark out media content as belonging to particular places and cultures, and it anchors particular media industries to media capitals and to governments who can provide supporting 'hard' and 'soft' infrastructure for the further development of media production.

The relationship between national, regional and global levels of media capital formation can be a complex one. At one end, there is a city such as Miami, which has become a centre of the Latin American film and *telenovela* trade (Mato, 2002; Sinclair, 2003). Miami brings together a network of Latin American media producers and the Spanish-speaking population of North America, but is not particularly integrated into the US media sector, where its product is niche and not in direct competition with Hollywood, New York or other English-language media capitals in the United States.

A contrasting case is that of Beijing which, as Huang (2012) points out, is the pre-eminent national media capital in China, as it is the headquarters of China Central TV (CCTV), has high-quality production facilities and creative workforce, and is of course the centre of political power in the country. The paradox for Beijing, which speaks to the wider contradiction of Chinese media being both highly commercialized and a highly regulated instrument of state ideological control, is that one reason for locating in Beijing is close proximity to key decision-making state agencies, in order to manage the inherent degree of structured uncertainty in the relationship of media companies to state authorities. At the same time, the forms of media content most likely to gain the approval of state bureaucrats are not those with the strongest appeal to audiences; this is true even in the highly con-strained Chinese media markets, and has proven to be the case internation-ally. Thus, the institutional arrangements that still prevail in Chinese media act as fetters upon Beijing's capacity to achieve global media capital status, and to bolster its media exports and international standing as producer of innovative media content.

Creative Cities and their Discontents

The various insights surrounding cities, creativity and culture were brought together around the concept of *creative cities*. Creative cities have formed one of the most influential concepts in urban development in the 2000s, identifying as it does the opportunity to combine a rich and diverse urban culture with the successful branding of particular locations as leading global sites, in the context of heightened global place-based competition between cities. In his influential early formulation of the concept, Landry (2000: 7) observed that 'cultural resources are the new materials of the city and its value base . . . creativity is the method of exploiting these resources and helping them grow'. It was widely observed that culture-led urban develop-ment offered new opportunities for post-industrial cities, and that the crea-tive industries can make a contribution to cities that is over and above that which is measured by income, employment and other economic indicators: they contribute to the '"feel" of the city . . . [that] may be imagined as an intangible, non-discursive quality that acts as an impulse to creative action' (Bassett et al., 2005: 145).

In her account of the cultural economy of New York City, Currid iden-tified how this was different from the industrial economy, as this 'atmos-phere' was in fact the driver of economic interactions, rather than their by-product:

> Economists often talk of the agglomeration of labour pools, firms, suppliers, and resources as producing an ensuing social environment where those involved in these different sectors engage each other in informal ways . . . But this informal social life that economists often hail as a successful by-product (what they call a positive spillover or externality) of an economic cluster is actually the central force, the *raison d'être*, for art and culture. *The cultural economy is most efficient in the informal social realm and social dynamics underlie the economic system of cultural production. Creativity would not exist as successfully or efficiently without its social world – the social is not the by-product – it is the decisive mechanism by which cultural products and cultural producers are generated, evaluated and sent to the market.* (Currid, 2007: 4; emphasis added)

The most influential arguments relating to creative cities in the 2000s were developed by the US economic geographer Richard Florida, with his theory of the rise of the *creative class*. Defining creative work as that which 'produces new forms and designs that are readily transferable and widely useful' (Florida, 2002: 7), Florida argued that there exists what he terms a 'creative class', which has grown in size from 10 per cent of the US workforce in 1900 to 30 per cent by 1990, thereby making it a numerically larger group than the traditional working class (Florida, 2002: 73, 330). He argues that the creative sectors account for 47 per cent of wealth generated in the US economy, so this creative class makes a disproportionately large contribution to contemporary economic growth (Florida, 2007: 29). He argued that creativity had become '*the* decisive source of competitive advantage' in the global economy, but that it was a paradoxical source of human capital since 'it is not a "commodity". Creativity comes from people. And while people can be hired or fired, their creative capacity cannot be bought or sold, or turned on and off at will' (Florida, 2002: 5).

The rise of the creative class was associated with a new *power of place*, where creative people sought out amenities-rich urban environments that had a vibrant nightlife, an engaging cultural 'scene' and a diverse range of experiences and opportunities. In contrast to arguments that people moved to where jobs were, Florida argued that creative people can create their own economic opportunities, and 'prefer places that are diverse, tolerant and open to new ideas . . . diversity increases the odds that a place will attract different types of people with different skill sets and ideas' (Florida, 2002: 249). He developed what was termed the 'Three T's Index' – technology, talent and tolerance – to argue that places with the highest concentrations of creative class workforce were characterized by: (1) the presence of high-technology firms and industries; (2) a highly educated population and significant levels of migration; and (3) a high proportion of gays and lesbians among their population, as well as artists and 'bohemians' (Florida, 2002:

249–51). In Florida's creative class thesis, the most dynamic cities in the United States are those such as San Francisco, Boston, Seattle, Portland, Oregon and Austin, Texas.

Extending this framework internationally, Florida argues that large city-regions are becoming disconnected from the nations they are part of, and that internationally mobile creative class workers choose cities to live in rather than nations:

> While in the aggregate statistical sense, it often seems to be nations that compete for creative talent, when it comes down to it, creative people choose *regions*. They don't simply think of the United States versus England, Sweden versus Canada, or Australia versus Denmark. They think of Silicon Valley versus Cambridge, Stockholm versus Vancouver, or Sydney versus Copenhagen. (Florida, 2007: 10)

Florida's arguments about creative cities and the creative class have been very widely debated and critiqued. They had strong appeal in urban planning circles in the 2000s, not least because investment in the 'soft infrastructure' of the arts and culture was a considerably lower-cost urban redevelopment strategy than the large-scale 'entrepreneurial city' strategies of the 1980s and 1990s that involved constructing large convention centres, sports facilities and entertainment precincts in order to attract tourism (Grodach and Loukaitou-Sideris, 2007).

At the same time, critics argue that this is very much a *consumption-led* urban strategy that loses sight of the complex production ecologies that form the basis for city-based creative clusters (Pratt, 2008a). The argument also became highly genericized, and open to the criticism made by Oakley (2004) of promoting a 'cookie-cutter' approach to urban cultural development: the image of the bike-wielding urban hipster and/or gay artist seeking intense urban experiences quickly moved from archetype to cliché when it translated to urban cultural policy. Moreover, it is far from clear that artists and other creative workers, rather than urban professionals in a more general sense, are the beneficiaries of such strategies. In so far as they promote gentrification of inner cities, their effect may well be to drive out artists, musicians and others engaged in cultural activities who are unable to afford rising property prices, thereby threatening to kill off the creative *milieu* that gave rise to creative city strategies in the first place (Hamnett, 2003; Badcock, 2009).

Florida's theory of creative cities and the creative class can be seen as one of a number of theories that stress the role played by *amenities* in promoting urban growth. Storper and Scott (2009) identify other variants of amenity-based urban growth theories, including those emphasizing the natural attributes of cities (sunshine, warm winters), diverse entertainment opportunities and cultural facilities. They conclude that such consumption-based theories of cities fail to identify the 'important forces endogenous to urban growth' (Storper and Scott, 2009: 153), most particularly the relationship between inter-firm networks, local labour markets and the institutional frameworks supporting innovation and coordination that exist in such cities. Their argument is that more prosperous cities will be able to provide a higher level of cultural and other forms of amenity, and hence will be attractive places to migrate to, but that it is the relationship between production and consumption that prevails in the city itself that drives its future growth trajectory. It may be argued, then, that Florida's theory both overstates the mobility of 'creative class' workers – particularly by conflating well-paid managers and professionals with less well-paid artists and other creative workers – and understates the significance of production networks to the success of cities. It would follow that, however desirable cultural amenities are to those who live in cities, they will not in and of themselves drive the economic performance of those cities. As a result, investing in cultural amenities by urban policy makers in order to achieve a turnaround in a city's economic performance is likely to be money that is poorly spent.

Finally, we need to observe that many of the world's leading creative cities are also among the most socially divided and unequal. Kotkin has argued that:

> An economy oriented to entertainment, tourism, and creative functions is ill suited to provide upward mobility for more than a small slice of its population . . . they are likely to evolve ever more into 'dual cities', made up of a cosmopolitan elite and a large class of those, usually at low wages, who service their needs. (Kotkin, 2006: 154)

Storper and Scott make a similar observation about new economy-based cities:

> The emerging new economy in major cities has been associated with a deepening divide between a privileged upper stratum of professional, managerial, scientific, technical and other highly qualified workers on the one side, and a mass of low-wage workers – often immigrant and undocumented – on the other side. The latter workers are not simply a minor side effect of the new economy or an accidental adjunct to the creative class. Rather, high-wage and low-wage workers are strongly complementary to one another in this new economy. (Storper and Scott, 2009: 164)

Reasons for this are many and varied, and relate in part to both the attractiveness of global cities to rich and poor migrants alike, the often 'winner-take-all' nature of the creative industries themselves, and the functional requirements of such cities for 'janitors, security guards, transport workers, short-order cooks, child-minders and so on, who maintain the networks, infrastructures and services that help to keep the entire urban system in operation' (Storper and Scott, 2009: 164). Cities such as Los Angeles, Paris and London have all seen rioting in recent years that may be seen as a reaction on the part of those perceiving themselves to be socially excluded from the wealth of the urban metropolis of which they are a part. In this respect, policies that focus on the provision of services and amenities aimed primarily at highly educated, high-income and highly mobile individuals may exacerbate urban economic and social divides, particularly if funded as an alternative to investing in jobs, education and the provision of basic infrastructure. Cities that seek to project themselves as being global and creative run the risk of doing so at the expense of significant segments of their local population, in ways that may ultimately threaten their social cohesion.

Conclusion

The reasons why some cities emerge as key hubs of creative activity are in part a variety of intangible factors, that can include history, culture, physical geography, demography, density and the ethnic composition of the population. This emergence can also be driven in a variety of important ways by public policy. This is not to say that governments can 'make' cities creative, or be identified as core global nodes for cultural innovation and creative industries activity. But they can be facilitators of developments that promote creative activity in particular cities and regions. In the 1990s and 2000s, supply-side strategies to develop creative clusters were an important element of the urban cultural policy agenda, as were consumption-led measures to provide cultural amenities that were seen as being particularly sought after by the 'creative class'. As this chapter has indicated, the report card on such policies is decidedly mixed, and even where successful, it can be noted that so-called creative cities can have their own problems, such as rising urban inequality and declining levels of social cohesion and a sense of shared identity.

6   Policies

Rethinking Cultural Policy

It can be argued that, historically, the origins of modern cultural policy lie with the French Revolution of 1789, with the transfer of the Royal art collections from the Palace of Versailles to the Louvre, and the more general movement of historically significant art works from the palaces of the nobility to the newly created public museums and galleries. What such actions established was the idea that artistic and creative works should be the property of the nation-state, and the cultural patrimony and common cultural heritage of its citizens. Thus a relationship between culture and the state was established, whereby it would be the role of the state to stimulate the development of new works, to ensure that access to culture is opened up to the whole population, and cultural institutions such as art galleries, libraries and museums have a central role in the cultural education of citizens and the formation of a common national cultural heritage (Gellner, 1983; Hobsbawm, 1990; Bennett, 1995).

Cultural policy in its more contemporary form took shape in the second half of the twentieth century. In Britain, the first chair of the Arts Council of Great Britain – established in 1946 – was the famous economist John Maynard Keynes, who was also an enthusiast of, and champion of, the arts. Keynes believed that the purpose of arts policy was to promote creative excellence, and that government had a key ongoing role in ensuring that this occurred (Skidelsky, 2000: 286–99). Keynes believed that, while public patronage was essential to enable artistic activity to take place without being dependent solely upon the market, and government initiatives were vital to ensuring the widest public access to and appreciation of the arts and culture, it was also essential that governments maintained an 'arm's length' relationship from the creative process itself. Keynes was a champion of what has come to be termed the *patron model* of arts and cultural policy, where government funds are distributed through a specialist arts council that relies on peer evaluations of cultural practitioners' excellence or worthiness (Craik, 2007). This model has been most influential in countries of the British Commonwealth, such as Canada, Australia and New Zealand, as well as in the Scandinavian nations.

In France, the formation of the Fifth Republic in 1958 acted as a catalyst to the development of a more activist cultural policy. President Charles de Gaulle appointed the famous novelist and art theorist André Malroux as France's first Minister of Cultural Affairs, and his vision for cultural policy saw a key role for the state in:

- making the nation's cultural heritage available to the whole population through a national network of theatres, museums, galleries, libraries and public exhibition spaces;
- using public funding to promote the creation of new artistic and cultural works, and providing financial support to artists and cultural workers;
- addressing inequalities of access to the arts and culture through active measures to democratize access to cultural works, as well as promoting community-based arts and culture (Looseley, 1995).

The French model of cultural policy is more characteristic of continental European nations, and has differed from the British one in three key respects. First, it promoted a more inclusive definition of culture, closer to the anthropological understanding of culture as 'a marker of how we live our lives, the senses of place and person that make us human . . . grounded by language, religion, custom, time and space' (Miller and Yúdice, 2002: 3), whereas the British approach has tended to focus more specifically upon the arts. Second, it is closer to what Craik (2007: 19) termed the *architect model* of cultural policy, where 'culture becomes the responsibility of a dedicated ministry . . . [with an] interventionist approach in which the rhetoric and aims of arts and cultural policy might be broadly aligned with social welfare and national culture objectives'. Finally, the French and European approaches have always seen film and media policy as an integral part of cultural policy, whereas the British approach, as well as that of the United States, has tended to bracket off media and communications policy from arts and cultural policy.

National cultural policies were developed by a number of newly independent nations in the 1960s and 1970s, and UNESCO played an active role in assisting developing countries in creating such policies. While much of this work was initially focused upon development of the arts and maintenance of cultural heritage, by the 1970s there was more attention being given to media and communications policies, and particularly to inequalities in the global distribution of information and communication resources. With the call for a New World Information and Communication Order (NWICO) in the 1970s and 1980s, UNESCO was highly critical of perceived Western 'cultural imperialism', seeing this as a barrier to the development of national cultural sovereignty commensurate with the political sovereignty arising from independence from colonial rule (Mattelart, 1994; Flew, 2007: 201–4). Throsby (2010: 2) has observed that UNESCO's cultural policy statements of the 1970s 'contained few if any references to the *economics* of culture, beyond an occasional reference to the administrative means for obtaining and deploying cultural funds for cultural purposes'. At the same time, developing countries have long been alert to the global dimensions of culture, and the interconnectedness of arts and media in questions of cultural development.

A growing interest in the economics of cultural policy has been accompanied by a shift in perspective over time from 'a concern solely with the arts and heritage to a broader interpretation of culture as a way of life . . . [and] an anthropological or sociological definition of culture as the expression of shared values and experiences' (Throsby, 2012: 2). In observing the policy implications of such a broadening in the scope of cultural policy, Craik et al. (2000) identified four key domains of cultural policy:

1. *arts and culture*, including direct funding to cultural producers, support for cultural institutions and the funding of cultural agencies;
2. *communications and media*, including support for film and broadcast media (both publicly funded and commercial), as well as policies related to new media technologies, publishing and intellectual property;
3. *citizenship and identity*, including language policy, cultural development policy, multiculturalism and questions of national symbolic identity;
4. *spatial culture*, including urban and regional culture and planning, cultural heritage management, and cultural tourism, leisure and recreation.

This series of domains could be extended even further: culture and the arts have in recent years been seen as important in addressing issues of social cohesion, social exclusion, physical and mental health and well-being, and making people more employable (Flew, 2012a: 168–9). The dilemma for cultural policy theorists and decision makers has long been one of how to conceive of the relationship between these levels of cultural policy. It was observed in chapter 1 that one approach is what is known as the *concentric circles* model, which places the creative and performing arts at the core of the system, with its influences (e.g. on creativity) radiating outwards to the wider creative industries, such as media, design, advertising, fashion, games, etc. The policy implication of the concentric circles approach is typically that the bulk of direct public subsidy would go to the 'core arts', as they are primarily associated with aesthetic excellence and cultural identity, whereas the latter sectors tend to receive more indirect support through content quotas for distributors, competitive production funds, business skills development, enabling better access to digital technologies, and so on.

Critics of traditional cultural policy, such as Garnham (1990), Lewis (2000) and Hesmondhalgh (2013) have argued that prioritizing the 'core arts' in cultural policy tends to be exclusive rather than inclusive, and generates inequitable funding outcomes whereby 'the majority subsidises the leisure activities of the privileged few' (Lewis, 2000: 86–7). Lewis has argued that 'a realistic cultural policy . . . should engage with the things that our society does, not with what we feel our society ought to be doing' (Lewis, 2000: 88). It is argued that the main justifications for cultural policies which privilege the core arts are significantly flawed:

1. Claims that the core arts are of superior artistic quality or aesthetic value are seen as circular and self-fulfilling, with such judgements frequently being made by those who are already invested in maintaining the cultural *status quo*.
2. Arguments that the core arts would not survive without public subsidy, whereas more commercial forms can exist in the marketplace, may or may not be true – there is a large amount of commercially oriented live theatre and classical music, for instance – but whether this necessitates a concentration of public funding around these activities may neglect the extent to which cultural innovation is occurring in all forms of cultural production, both commercial and non-commercial, elite and popular, analogue and digital.
3. The equity argument that public support for the core arts makes them more affordable to ordinary people again becomes circular, since it has been observed that cost is not the primary factor behind class-based patterns of cultural consumption (Lewis, 2000).

Development of the creative industries is both connected to and disruptive of traditional forms of cultural policy. It has its origins in the reorientation of the British government's relationship to culture in the late 1990s and 2000s, moving away from an 'arts and heritage' model towards one that more actively engaged with the economic possibilities of creativity across a wider range of industry domains. Internationally, creative industries were often associated with a turn towards 'joined-up government' (Pollitt, 2003), where cultural policy was expected to be better coordinated with other policy fields, including economic policy, education policy, trade policy, innovation policy and urban and regional policy (Pratt, 2004; Throsby, 2010).

As was discussed in chapter 1, the creative industries approach saw both commercial and state-supported forms of cultural activity as wellsprings of creativity, and hence warranting attention from a policy viewpoint. It rejects a binary opposition between the arts and media industries, incorporates new perspectives such as those from design, and is linked to the growing fuzziness of boundaries between tangible and digital culture. The creative industries approach also opens up – without necessarily resolving – debates about the cultural value of one activity as compared to another, which have a long history in a field such as cultural studies (Frow, 1995; Holden, 2009).

From Government to Governance

One factor that sets limits to traditional forms of cultural policy, and which is particularly apparent in the context of creative industries developments, is the problematic nature of binary oppositions between the state and the market. As Pratt (2005) has observed, the traditional framing of cultural policy around the state-subsidized arts on the one hand, and commercially driven culture and entertainment on the other, has led to policy discourses that have at different times prioritized aesthetic judgements, political judgements and economic judgements: the challenge now is 'one of creating a frame of reference within which all of these elements can be considered' (Pratt, 2005: 39). Pratt recommends the term 'governance' over that of 'policy', as it can better capture both 'the institutions and agencies charged with governing (government), and the modes and manner of governing (governance)' (Pratt, 2005: 39).

In relation to media policy, Freedman (2008: 13–14) has proposed the following tripartite distinction between policy, regulation and governance:

- *Policy*: the goals and norms that inform and underpin relevant legislation, and the intentions and instruments associated with shaping the structure and behaviour of actors within a bounded policy system (e.g., media policy, cultural policy).
- *Regulation*: the operations and activities of specific agencies that have responsibility for oversight of the policy instruments that have been developed to manage a policy system.
- *Governance*: the totality of institutions and instruments that shape and organize a policy system – formal and informal, national and supranational, public and private, large-scale and smaller-scale.

The concept of governance has a long history in corporate law, as well as in international relations. In relation to business, the complex nature of corporations – in terms of both their multidivisional structures and the separation of ownership and control – has meant that legal regulation itself can provide only a limited guide to corporate conduct. Moreover, it has an 'after the fact' quality, in that it can only be applied in cases of legal breaches and cannot provide a basis for ongoing monitoring of performance; it also only recognizes those with a legal stake in the corporation – primarily its shareholders – whereas modern large corporations engage with a diverse range of stakeholders, including employees, consumers, governments, suppliers and financiers. In that sense, corporate governance is recognized as a multi-layered structure, with legal regulation at its core, but also entailing stock exchange listing requirements, accounting practices, the role and responsibilities of Boards of Directors, codes of conduct, statements of accountability and commitments to ethical business practice. As a result, there is a continuum of layers of governance, from the 'hard law' associated with legislation that governs corporate behaviour, to the 'soft law' associated with self-regulation and quasi-regulation, that seeks to guide and influence corporate behaviour towards preferred goals (Freiberg, 2010: 186–7).

The concept of *soft law*, and its relationship to governance, has a particularly important history in international relations. As it is not possible for a supranational entity to exercise rule over sovereign nation-states, a network of treaties, charters, agreements, conventions, deliberative forums, and forms of cosmopolitan law have emerged as alternative forms of governance. Collectively, these constitute forms of 'soft law' that aim to align the conduct of individual nation-states to shared international rules and norms, with the scope to apply legal sanctions as a last resort. As Held et al. observed in the context of globalization theories, the impact of these regional and global forms of governance is that 'the locus of effective political power can no longer be assumed to be national governments – effective power is shared and bartered by diverse forces and agencies at national, regional and international levels' (Held et al., 1999: 80).

The concept of governance has become increasingly influential in economics and public policy. As discussed in chapter 4, the New Institutional Economics gives an important role to governance arrangements as the link between institutions and markets, as well as the embedded nature of such arrangements within and between national economies, and how the resulting forms of path dependence and institutional 'lock-in' generate differences in the economic performance of nations. Williamson (2000: 599) argued that governance arrangements as they pertained to contracts in particular were central to managing transaction costs between economic agents, in order to shape incentives and thus to 'craft order . . . mitigate conflict and realize mutual gains'. In the related field of public policy studies, authors such as Stewart-Weeks (2006) and Eggers (2008) have also argued that networked governance approaches are increasingly displacing traditional hierarchical models of government and command-and-control policy approaches. Summarizing the importance of the New Institutional

Economics to contemporary economic development theories, Oman and Arndt have concluded that it demonstrates the

> importance of a country's system of governance – its formal and informal institutions (the latter including its culture and unwritten values) and their interaction with the behaviour of economic and political entrepreneurs and organizations – for the country's success in terms of its long-term economic growth, enhancement of human welfare and societal development. (Oman and Arndt, 2010: 7)

The relevance of the concept of governance can be seen in relation to both creative industries development and media regulation. In relation to the creative industries, it points to the need to think more innovatively about how to provide support for both emergent sectors and those traditionally outside of the cultural policy mix. For example, a subsidy-based approach to support would not be appropriate for popular music sectors, where there are typically a large number of creative producers and a dynamic and highly competitive production, distribution and performance environment, whereas it may continue to be appropriate for the public support of orchestras and other major performing arts companies. Engaging with creative industries sectors such as popular music would be an example of what Pratt describes as the need for cultural policy to 'be drawn into a new conception of governance that acknowledges the existence of the market, but is actively involved in the shaping of that market' (Pratt, 2005: 41). A related question is that of how to open up cultural policy, so that it is not simply driven by patron–client relationships between the funding bodies and those who represent the long-established art forms, in order to broaden the scope of policy support and enable the development of 'a whole new infrastructure of public participation' (Pratt, 2005: 42).

In considering the range of creative industries policies developed worldwide, we can see the extent to which they have drawn upon innovative forms of governance. Table 6.1 indicates the diverse array of strategies we have considered, that include not only creative industries strategies as they were originally conceived in Britain, but also creative cluster, creative economy and creative cities strategies (cf. Hartley, 2009). Much of the academic debate surrounding creative industries has dealt with questions of definition – is 'creativity' an appropriate alternative term to 'culture' – and which industries themselves should be included? Is there a priority to be given to the 'core arts', or should commercial creative industries in the media and design sectors be given equal weighting in terms of importance? There has been less discussion of the policy innovations associated with such initiatives, even though table 6.1 shows evidence of a diverse array of

Table 6.1. Creative industries strategies as forms of policy

	Major policy goals	Policy instruments	Success indicators	Level of government	Engagement with creative producers	Examples
Cultural policy	Artistic excellence; Cultural heritage; Access and participation	Public subsidy (grants, fellowships, etc.); Art-form based advisory boards	Audiences for arts and culture; Public participation in the arts; International recognition of national cultural forms	National	Direct – support for particular individuals and institutions	National cultural policies; EU Culture Programmes; *Creative Australia*
Creative industries	Economic, employment and export growth in cultural sectors; Innovative new forms of intellectual property	Mapping of creative industries' size and significance; Industry/sectoral development policies	Economic, employment and export growth; New forms of copyrighted creative product; Linkages of CIs to other sectors (e.g., manufacturing, services)	National/regional	Indirect – engages with industry representatives to promote policy communities/networks	UK DCMS Mapping documents; Singapore Creative Industries Development Strategy; New Zealand Growth and Innovation Framework; Jamaica Creative Industries Strategy
Creative clusters	Innovative city-regions; Social cohesion and local jobs growth	Local infrastructure investment (e.g., communications, education);	Movement of new producers into city-region; Employment growth;	Local	Direct – government acts as a broker of inter-industry co-operation	Hollywood/Los Angeles film & TV industry; Milan fashion industry; Beijing central business district media cluster; Shanghai creative clusters

		Ability to 'fast-track' projects (e.g., locational film shoots); Facilitating local networks of industry, government and other local stakeholders	Enhanced role for culture in identity of the city-region; New forms of creative intellectual property		(NB: clusters can form independently of government, but supportive government is generally a condition for sustainability)	
Creative economy	Economy-wide applications of creativity; New skills and human capital development	Promotion of creativity across all activities (e.g., through education reform); Encouraging entrepreneurship and innovation in cultural sectors	Linkages of CIs to other sectors (e.g., manufacturing, services); Collaboration between arts and sciences; Advances in educational outcomes	National	Indirect – impact is on creative industries inputs (e.g., creative talent) and outputs (changing consumer demand in social network markets)	UK Creative Economy strategy; UNCTAD Creative Economy reports; Taiwan 'Twin Star' programme
Creative cities	Global city-brands; Tourism and overseas investment; Attracting talented professionals	Investment in cultural infrastructure; Promotion of cultural amenities, particularly in inner city areas; Changing local regulations to promote 'night-time economy'	Hosting of major international festivals and events; Growth of tourism and migration of skilled professionals; Participation in cultural activities	Local	Indirect – aim is to facilitate a 'creative environment' by reducing barriers to engagement and an open, tolerant local culture	Various US city strategies (e.g., 'Creative 100'); Creative City Berlin; Brisbane Creative City strategy; European Capitals of Culture

policy approaches existing under the broad banner of creative industries policies.

Two factors are particularly worth noting: (1) the extent to which the rise of new forms of creative industries policies marks a shift in the locus of policy from the national to the sub-national level, with the rise of cities and city-regions as cultural policy actors (Scott, 2008; Isar et al., 2012); and (2) the extent to which creative industries policy initiatives rely upon indirect measures to promote behavioural change as much, and in some instances more, than their reliance upon direct government financial support to creative producers or 'command-and-control' regulations of institutional conduct. In this latter respect, creative industries policies can be seen as exemplifying new ways of thinking about regulation and policy design, where 'it is the objective or the effectiveness of the intervention, not its form, that is important', and where regulations are defined as 'intentional measures or interventions that seek to change the behaviour of individuals or groups' (Freiberg, 2010: 4).

The work of Freiberg (2010), Braithwaite (2008) and others on *regulatory capitalism* is useful in drawing attention to the extent to which creative industries policies, as with other policy fields, are no longer constituted around simple state/market, public/private binaries that constrain behaviour (for an overview, see Flew 2012b). It is instead the case that:

- application of a diverse range of policy instruments in order to achieve policy goals is the norm, as is experimentation with institutional forms;
- government regulation is only one element of regulation: just as power is dispersed among social institutions, the capacity to regulate exists among non-government as well as government institutions;
- regulation is not limited to laws and rules, but also includes market-based instruments, regulation through contracts, licensing and accreditation requirements, regulation through design rules, and informational regulation including ratings and performance indicators;
- regulation is not just restrictive or coercive, but can also be facilitating or enabling, and can act to constitute a field – it can make things happen, as well as stopping things from happening;
- regulation can shape markets and create new markets, as well as being a controlling factor on the behaviour of participants within already existing markets.

Case Study: Popular Music and Urban Cultural Policy

There has been a growing interest in recent years in developing government policies that support popular music (Frith et al., 2009; Homan,

2012). At the same time, it has proved difficult to bring popular music into national cultural policies. Most funding for music by national governments is already committed to flagship institutions such as orchestras, with a smaller amount available for artistic experimentation: there are simply too many musicians around to be supported by government. Moreover, many musicians are themselves suspicious of government and its ability to 'pick winners': popular music is an archetypal creative industries 'micro business' where audience appeal and chance will always remain critical variables to determining who succeeds.

There has been a surge of interest worldwide in developing strategies for popular music as a core element of urban cultural policies. There has been a realization that approaches to live music that identified its presence primarily in terms of generating urban problems (noise, public nuisance, etc.) failed to recognize its significance to a wider 'night-time economy' of cities, where work and leisure practices are blurring, and where significant numbers of people are seeking to live in inner-city areas on the basis of their cultural activities and 'buzz' (Storper and Venables, 2004; Rowe and Bavinton, 2011). This is associated with a growing awareness on the part of urban authorities of the importance of music to the creative economy of cities, and to their international profile and 'branding' (Kornberger, 2010). Music scenes were seen as forming a vital part of what Charles Landry (2000) and others have termed the 'soft infrastructure' of cities, and were very much at the forefront of the 'creative cities' movement described in the previous chapter. This renewed interest among city policy makers in popular music has also been associated with a gradual abandonment of *ad hoc* governance, and the development of cultural plans and whole-of-government approaches to music, covering aspects as diverse as planning and zoning, support for festivals and live music events, and marketing and business development support for those in the local music industry (Frith et al., 2009; Homan, 2012).

In the early 2000s, I was involved in advising the Brisbane City Council on development of a music industry policy for the city of Brisbane, Australia (Flew, 2008). A fast-growing city of about 2.5 million, Brisbane had historically been a leading source of musicians, but a city where few remained, due to a combination of its second-tier status in circuits of cultural production and distribution, its perceived social conservatism, and government indifference or active hostility to cultural development. Coinciding with new opportunities for Brisbane-based musicians to get national exposure through the music festivals circuit and the national networking of youth radio station Triple J, and the election of more progressive labour governments at state and local level, Brisbane embarked upon a creative city urban development strategy that saw a key role for the live music scene as a vital part of the city's cultural infrastructure, making it a more attractive location for both professional workers and business investors (Gregg, 2011: 23–30).

The policy challenge was how to promote sustainability in the city's music culture that could build upon a range of short-term advantages to promote the development of producer and distribution services that are associated with major music cities worldwide. It coexisted with a problem for the local government authorities, as the redevelopment of inner-city warehouses and lofts as apartment blocks in close proximity to major live music venues had triggered noise complaints which in turn threatened the existence of these venues. This problem of gentrification of previously run-down inner-city areas that had become havens for artists and musicians – a common issue worldwide (Hamnett, 2003) – was particularly concentrated in the Fortitude Valley nightclub precinct.

The report, titled *Music Industry Development and Brisbane's Future as a Creative City* (Flew et al., 2003) made recommendations to the Brisbane City Council relating to:

- music and entertainment industry stakeholder engagement in city planning, zoning, licensing and noise regulations;
- development of the Fortitude Valley areas as a designated entertainment precinct with different noise regulations from other parts of the city;
- ongoing support for music industry events, such as the annual 'Big Sound' conference, that encourage national industry networking in Brisbane;
- collaboration between local and state government agencies in enhancing music industry business skills development.

While most proposals from the report were taken up, it has proven difficult over time to maintain a focus on music industry development in Brisbane, and some of the reasons can be extrapolated to other instances where urban cultural policy has identified a key role for popular music (Frith et al., 2009). Music faces a paradoxical issue in terms of visibility to policy makers and other key decision makers, in that since it appears to be everywhere and to be happening regardless of government decisions, there is little impetus to develop ongoing policy support for it. This is in contrast to a sector such as the film industry, which typically has a few high-profile projects, and where it is very clear what the current health of the production sector is. Moreover, the historical lack of engagement with government, combined with suspicions born out of past dealings with enforcement agencies, means that the contemporary music industry has often not built the sorts of government lobbying infrastructures associated with the film and television industries, or other areas of the creative and performing arts.

There is also the 'chicken-and-egg' question related to thriving local music scenes and a supportive industry infrastructure: which generates the other? In their survey of popular music policies as they developed in the city of Glasgow, Frith et al. (2009: 80–1) argued that 'it is a healthy musical culture that leads to a flourishing music industry and not an investment in music industry infrastructure that creates a flourishing musical culture'. Echoing the critiques of creative cluster theories discussed in chapter 5, they observe that music policies for cities often have a *post hoc* quality to them – policy makers retrospectively claim credit for the emergence of successful music scenes that in reality emerged for the most part independently of their interventions.

Creative Industries and Development

Many of the most significant discussions about creative industries are taking place in the developing world. The United Nations Conference on Trade and Development (UNCTAD) has led a global conversation about the possibilities for development strategies based around the creative economy (UNCTAD, 2008, 2010). It has proposed that 'adequately nurtured, creativity fuels culture, infuses a human-centred development and constitutes the key ingredient for job creation, innovation and trade while contributing to social inclusion, cultural diversity and environmental sustainability' (UNCTAD, 2010: xix). One of the factors which makes creative economy strategies potentially appealing is that they can draw upon human capacities and small-scale initiatives, rather than being dependent upon large-scale capital investment, thus drawing upon the manner in which 'every society has its stock of intangible cultural capital articulated by people's identity and values' (UNCTAD, 2008: 3). By drawing upon local cultural practices rather than needing to bring in expertise from the outside, creative industries strategies can maintain cultural diversity and promote cultural sustainability. Moreover, the rapidly falling costs of production and distribution associated with the global dissemination of networked digital media technologies further enhances such possibilities by opening up new markets for such cultural products and practices.

At the same time, as UNCTAD notes, 'despite the richness of their cultural diversity and the abundance of creative talent, the great majority of developing countries are not yet fully benefiting from the enormous potential of their creative economies to improve development gains' (UNCTAD, 2008: 6). In this respect, digital technologies and globalization present both opportunities and significant threats to developing nations. The enhanced speed of flows of, and greater global access to, global cultural products present the significant risk that cultural production in smaller developing nations will be overwhelmed by the products of the global media and entertainment industries, who can take advantage of scale economies in production and global reach in distribution.

This dystopian scenario, where the incorporation of developing countries into the global creative economy is nothing more than one of providing low-cost labour and secondary markets to 'Global Hollywood' (Miller et al., 2005) and other metropolitan creative industries centres, has been a catalyst to international measures that aim to maintain global cultural diversity, in the face of potential pressures towards cultural homogenization and the diminution of local and national cultures. Most notable among these has been the UNESCO Convention on the Protection and Promotion of Diversity of Cultural Expressions, which proposes among its guiding principles that:

- cultural activities, goods and services have both an economic and a cultural nature, because they convey identities, values and meanings, and must therefore not be treated as solely having commercial value; and
- while the processes of globalization, which have been facilitated by the rapid development of information and communication technologies, afford unprecedented conditions for enhanced interaction between cultures, they also represent a challenge for cultural diversity, namely in view of risks of imbalances between rich and poor countries (UNESCO, 2005).

One of the features of creative economy strategies is that they stress a multifaceted and incremental approach to cultural policy. UNCTAD has associated creative economy strategies with a broad conception of cultural policy, while noting that cultural policy is seen in some countries as being primarily about the creative arts, and in others as being largely to do with preserving and protecting cultural heritage – both tangible, such as culturally significant sites, and intangible, such as languages. It is argued that 'in line with the cross-cutting and multidimensional nature of the creative economy, cultural policy in its broader interpretation embraces aspects of a number of other areas of economic and social policy' (UNCTAD, 2008: 173). In particular, industry policy towards the creative industries is now seen as a core element of cultural policy in developing nations:

> Consideration of the creative economy becomes a key element of industrial policy, whereby industrial development strategies can exploit the potential

dynamism of the creative industries in generating growth in output, exports and employment. A positive outlook for industrial policy in which creativity and innovation are important drivers of growth is well suited to the contemporary economic conditions of globalization and structural change. (UNCTAD, 2008; 173–4)

This view of creative industries policies as a form of industry policy is consistent with other analyses of the creative economy. Jaguaribe (2008) has argued that the global dissemination of ICT innovations has made it more possible for developing countries to pursue 'niche' strategies for their creative industries with products able to reach global markets, and that they have allowed for 'leapfrogging' technological innovations, such as the massive adoption of mobile media in countries where access to fixed-line telephony remains restricted. She argues that 'while it is not possible to have a knowledge economy without scientific and technological accumulation, it is possible to have a creative economy and creative industries which benefit from technological innovations but do not depend on the formal accumulation of scientific and technical knowledge' (Jaguaribe, 2008: 310). Venturelli (2005) has argued that the shift from an industrial economy to an information-based one moves our understanding of culture from a 'legacy' one associated with the preservation of cultural heritage to a more dynamic one, associated with the capacity to generate and lever off new ideas and forms of creative practice that can then be distributed at near-zero cost through digital information networks. In such an information-driven or creative economy, she observes, 'the environmental conditions most conducive to originality and synthesis, as well as the breadth of social participation in forming new ideas, comprise the true test of cultural vigour and the only valid basis of public policy' (Venturelli, 2005: 395).

Policies that are identified as promoting the creative economy in developing countries (UNCTAD, 2008. 176–85; Barrowclough and Kozul-Wright, 2008: 26–9) include:

1. Investment in education and human capital, with particular reference to the intersection between creative capacities and relevant technical skills, in order to better facilitate the transition to digital production and distribution models.
2. Provision of improved infrastructure at all levels, but particularly digital infrastructure and access to high-speed broadband networks and ICTs.
3. Strategies for cultural asset management and community cultural development, including cultural heritage management as well as promoting new opportunities for artists and creative workers.
4. Innovations in financing small to medium-sized enterprises in the

creative industries, and enabling better access to micro-finance, as well as tailored programmes for business skills development (Cunningham et al., 2008b).

5. Establishment of creative clusters that can constitute gathering points that bring together those engaged in both the formal and non-formal sectors of the creative industries, and where public resources can be concentrated to maximize potential impact.

6. A whole-of-government approach to cultural policy, that recognizes points of intersection with education, trade and industry policies, and the role played by local, regional and national governments in developing the creative industries.

7. Advances in data gathering in order to better understand the size, significance and linkages arising in national creative industries, along the lines recommended by UNESCO in its revised *Framework for Cultural Statistics* (UNESCO, 2009). In particular, there is a need to better capture the role played by the non-formal sector in order to promote better understanding on the part of policy makers.

Creative industries policies are seen as being better pursued by an *enabling state* (Mulgan and Wilkinson, 1994), rather than one that seeks to grow the creative industries by means of planning targets or command-and-control regulations. Along such lines, UNCTAD referred to what it termed the *creative nexus*: an intersecting set of interactions between policies that nurture and develop creative capacities, and strategies to promote private investment, technology adoption, entrepreneurship and trade (UNCTAD, 2008: 49–50). Such an approach resembles the highly successful creative economy strategies adopted in the Scandinavian countries (Denmark, Norway, Sweden and Finland), where the focus has been less upon development of the creative industries as a discrete industry sub-sector than on the intersections between creative entrepreneurship, growing creative businesses, creative cluster development and creative place making (Power, 2009; Flew, 2012a: 37–9).

The Developmental State and the Creative Industries

In surveying global economic development theory from the 1950s onwards, one of the striking features of early development theory was the absence of explicit thinking about the institutions of the state. Early development theories were characterized by a pragmatic and a-historical approach to such questions as the apparent urgency of developmental tasks such as poverty alleviation, the reluctance in a 'Cold War' context to question the politics of development, and the assumption that economic management techniques could simply be adopted from advanced industrial societies and applied in the Third World (Leys, 1996). The result was 'a very practical, short-term, state-oriented conception of development', where 'the goal of development was growth [and] the agent of development was the state' (Leys, 1996: 110). Assumptions about 'the neutrality and effectiveness of the state as an agent of social change' (Radice, 2008: 1164) applied not only to economic policy, where the goal was industrialization, but also in relation to media and culture. *Modernization* theories of communication proposed that the mass media, urbanization and the entrepreneurial initiatives of Western-educated 'change agents' would enable values and orientations among the population to shift away from those associated with traditional society towards those closer to an idealized version of Western modernity (Sparks, 2007; Melkote, 2010).

By the late 1960s, however, considerable discontent had set in with the limited gains arising from development models, amid concerns that political colonialism had simply been replaced by an economically driven neo-colonialism, that was failing to meet the needs of the majority of the population. One marker of the change was found in the work of economist Albert Hirschman; in the 1950s and 1960s he was an enthusiastic champion of industrial development models in Latin America, but by the 1970s he was critically reflecting on how such development strategies could promote 'antagonistic growth', whereby elites used development models to capture state resources for their own ends, hence increasing economic inequalities and promoting the rise to power of political dictatorships (Hirschman, 1995). Similarly, Everett Rogers, who was a pioneer of development communications, had by the 1970s accepted critiques of the ethnocentric nature of its underlying assumptions, and was drawing out the need for alternative development paradigms that stressed social equality and popular participation, promoted self-reliance, and drew upon indigenous knowledge frameworks (Rogers, 1974).

Dependency theories emerged in the 1960s and 1970s as the basis for a critique of mainstream development theories, out of a synthesis of Latin American structuralism, Marxist theories of imperialism, and world systems theories developed by Immanuel Wallerstein and others (Palma, 1973; Brewer, 1980). Dependency theorists argued that the absence of industrial development in the Third World was not the consequence of a lack of resources or entrepreneurial attitudes. Rather, it was the systemic consequence of an unequally structured capitalist world economy, whereby the Western metropolitan powers appropriated economic surplus from the

nations of the periphery, through enforcement of unequal trade and investment relations. In doing so, they were aided and abetted by what Andre
Gunder Frank (1973) termed a 'comprador bourgeoisie' – economic, political, military and intellectual elites who identified more with the metropolitan powers than with their own people. The result was the proliferation of
'client states', kept in power through US military hegemony and beholden
to Western corporate and political interests. As was discussed in chapter 4,
the corollary in the media and cultural sphere was the dominance of global
media conglomerates in the fields of information and entertainment, whose
programming promoted Western views and capitalist values, maintaining
the structure of cultural dependency and cultural imperialism critiqued by
Herbert Schiller (1976) and others.

The dependency paradigm provided in many ways the polar opposite of
the modernization paradigm. Where modernization theories saw the lack of
development as the result of negative internal factors (prevalence of traditional values, overpopulation, etc.), dependency theories saw underdevelopment as the direct consequence of the unequal structuring of the capitalist
world economy. While traditional development theories saw the role that
could be played by Western capital, technology and expertise as a positive
one, filling gaps in the local economy, dependency theories saw such an
opening up to Western imports as further entrenching unequal power relations and economic inequalities. And while development theories promoted
greater integration into the world economy, dependency theorists spoke of
delinking from the capitalist world system, promoting of self-reliant development, and strengthening political-economic links among the nations of
the 'Global South', on the basis of a common colonialist legacy. But for all
of these differences, there were important shared principles: both theories
defined development in primarily economic terms, giving a particularly
important role to developing manufacturing industries; both saw such economic development as being critical to strengthening national sovereignty
and the nation-state; and both continued to look to the state to be the pilot
of economic development, whether of a capitalist or a state-socialist kind,
focused on directing capital to large-scale nation-building development
projects (Brewer, 1980: 274–94; Leys, 1996; Radice, 2008).

The influence of the dependency paradigm was seriously weakened in the
1980s, with the demise of campaigns for a New International Economic
Order (NIEO) and a New World Information and Communication
Order (NWICO) that had been pursued through agencies of the United
Nations. At the same time, developments in East Asia in particular – and to
a lesser degree in some parts of Latin America – were making it questionable whether it was still possible to speak of a homogeneous 'Third World',

of developing nations who continued to be disadvantaged in the world economy through the legacies of colonialism and unequal global power relations. The rise of the so-called 'Tiger' economies of East Asia – South Korea, Taiwan, Singapore and Hong Kong – generated considerable interest in the manner in which they had achieved industrial development. Following from Chalmers Johnson's (1982) pioneering analysis of Japanese industrialization, authors such as Amsden (1989), Wade (1990) and Evans (1995) identified the key role played by the 'developmental state' in these countries in organizing resources and managing relations between business, finance and labour to achieve national development goals. Associated with this was a rethinking of the role of the state in relation to globalization, rejecting the proposition that economic globalization invariably rendered the nation-state powerless, and pointing to the role played by developmental states in positioning their local industries in the global economy (Weiss, 1998, 2003).

Peter Evans (1995) identified three archetypal state forms in developing nations: (1) non-cohesive or predatory states; (2) fragmented intermediate states; and (3) developmental states. The *predatory state* tends to be formed around an absolutist ruler and a small clique of supporters, where the bureaucracy is weak and corrupt, state power is used to appropriate resources from the rest of society, civil society is deliberately disorganized (frequently by force), and where personal ties are the primary source of social and economic advancement. An example of such a state would be the Democratic Republic of Congo, which has one of the lowest *per capita* incomes in the world, despite being rich in natural resources.

The *fragmented intermediate state* frequently has pockets of bureaucratic professionalism coexisting with other state agencies where personal ties and/ or corruption predominate, and where state authority is fragmented and both intra-elite and elite–mass conflicts are common – the latter sometimes leading to populist movements. India is often cited as an example of such a state, where the gap between developmental aspirations and the on-the-ground experience speaks to weaknesses in state capacity to deliver on ambitious policy goals.

The *developmental state* is characterized by four features:

1. governments having sufficient power in the society to direct and prioritize development projects;
2. government leaderships with a coherent development vision, such as the export-led industrialization policies pursued in Taiwan and South Korea, or the strategies of Hong Kong and Singapore to be leaders in commercial services;

3. a competent and coherent bureaucracy, where merit-based appointments prevail, where agencies work together around shared goals, and rule-based conduct is the norm; and

4. a state that is *embedded* in civil society, with strong links to the wider community, but where it possesses sufficient *autonomy* to be able to pursue collective interests above short-term sectional interests, particularly those of individual businesses and business sectors.

For Evans, this last point about what he termed *embedded autonomy* was critical, and is difficult to achieve without fortuitous historical and social circumstances. At the same time, there are lessons to be learned from the successful developmental states, and it is interesting to consider the extent to which countries as diverse as China, Brazil, South Africa and Indonesia have been taking on at least some of these lessons in recent years. In doing so, they can draw upon what is known as the 'Gerschenkron thesis' – after the economic historian Alexander Gerschenkron (1962) – who observed that late developers can benefit from adopting the lessons of early developers: Germany learnt from Britain, Japan learnt from Germany and Britain, South Korea learnt from Japan, etc. In the East Asian context, this has been referred to as the *'flying geese' hypothesis*, where late developers can engage in partial institutional emulation, effectively 'free-riding' from the successes and failures of others (Ozawa et al., 2001).

The relevance of the developmental state debates to creative industries policy strategies lies in a paradox of creative industries. The bulk of creative industries initiatives emerge in the private sector rather than the public sector, and this is particularly the case in developing countries, where the elaborate cultural policy infrastructures that characterize regions such as Europe have not been developed. Indeed, in many developing countries, the key drivers of creative industries development can be found in the informal economy, through 'economic production and exchange occurring within capitalist economies but outside the purview of the state' (Lobato, 2012: 39–40). The African music industry is an often-cited example, where transforming the potential that exists from vibrant and creative local communities to a successful local music industry requires better linkages between the formal and informal economies (Loew, 2006–7; Pratt, 2008b; Schultz and van Gelder, 2008–9; UNCTAD, 2008: 78–80). As Andy Pratt observed from his study of the music industry in Senegal:

> While there is general cultural policy in Senegal . . . there is no explicit coordinated policy for music . . . In part, this is because, unlike most art forms, contemporary music exists almost exclusively in the private sector. The tradition of public policy-making in Senegal, as in most other nations, has been a

grant-giving culture; a music policy, if it existed, would have to have more of an industrial character. (Pratt, 2008b: 133)

At the same time, a key historical lesson from the developmental state literature is that governments need to play an active role in fostering the conditions for developing new industries that gain a foothold in a highly competitive global economy. The gaps in size between creative industries as a share of national income in developed and developing countries are not the result of less creative activity taking place in the developing world – there may very well be more – but rather the failure to effectively harness this creativity to developmental goals. As Kohli (2004) has observed:

> Private investors in late-late-developing countries need organized help, help that effective states are most able to provide to overcome such obstacles as capital scarcity, technological backwardness, rigidities in labour markets, and to confront the overwhelming power of foreign corporations and of competitive producers elsewhere . . . state intervention . . . varies, not so much by quantity as by type and quality. It is therefore patterns of state intervention in the economy that are key to explaining successful late-late development. (Kohli, 2004: 377)

In the language of the New Institutional Economics, institutions matter, and the governance framework that develops in particular countries will be of vital importance in shaping the performance of their creative industries, as it will for the economy overall (North, 1990). But whereas this has in some instances been associated with neoliberal development prescriptions about the need to 'get relative prices right', and reduce the role of government bureaucracies in setting priorities and harnessing resources for national development goals, the developmental state literature notes the continuing importance of government in promoting such priorities in the developing world. At the same time, what neoliberals term rent-seeking behaviour, and what the developmental state theorists refer to as the fragmented or predatory state, can see such public resources misallocated to serve particular interests against the general interest. The wisdom and integrity of policy makers, and indeed the governments for which they work, remain variables for which there is no 'off-the-shelf' measure or prescription that can be offered from outside of societies themselves.[7]

Case Study: Nollywood

After the United States (Hollywood) and India (Bollywood), the third largest film-producing nation in the world is the African state of Nigeria.

The Nigerian film industry, which has been termed 'Nollywood' (Nigeria + Hollywood), produces over 1,000 films annually, and is estimated to be worth about US$2.5 billion, and to employ over 350,000 people (UNCTAD, 2010: 250; Miller, 2012). Given the gulf that exists between creative activity in Africa and the economic performance of its creative industries, the rise of Nollywood has attracted considerable interest throughout Africa as well as international attention.

The rise of Nollywood was integrally connected to the accessibility of video technology. Nigeria had a strong history of government support for television, but its film industry was in dire straits by the early 1990s because of film production that made use of celluloid becoming unaffordable with the economic crisis; rising crime in the major cities such as Lagos also made going to the cinema more hazardous (Onuzulike, 2007). In 1992, the low-budget production *Living in Bondage* was shot on videotape, and proved to be extremely popular when distributed directly to consumers for home viewing on VHS machines. The direct-to-video production model proved to be the key to local success, as it allowed for production of an enormous number of films – over a film a day was being made in Lagos by the late 1990s – which attracted a strong local audience, drawn to stories that were based upon recognizable local themes and popular genres such as supernatural horror (Haynes, 2007).

The Nollywood production model has been rooted in the informal economy, with locally made films sold in street markets, first as VHS, but more recently as DVDs. Films are viewed at home, but also in shops, bars, hairdressers, at market stalls and through informal 'video clubs'. As Lobato (2012) has observed, it is a mistake to see Nollywood as a single national market: there are Hausa, Yoruba, Igbo and English-language productions speaking to Nigeria's different language communities, with the major cities such as Lagos, Abuja and Kano having their own local industries; there is also a degree of integration with the neighbouring Ghanaian film industry, and with other West African states. The films have attracted a large international following, not only in Africa, but also among a wide range of immigrant communities in the United States, Europe and elsewhere. At the same time, the audiences for these movies outside Nigeria are not primarily diasporic; rather, 'Nollywood' cinema has come to be part of alternative global networks and a part of what Miller (2012: 131) terms 'informal globalization'.

Lobato has referred to a *formalizing imperative* in the Nigerian film industry since the late 2000s. This is partly a matter of being able to make better-quality movies as commercial success allows for higher production budgets; it also reflects some tiredness among local audiences with formulaic genres and low production values. It also reflects the wishes of some of the more successful producers to 'see Nollywood shed its informal skin and become a mature business with global reach . . . the aim is to create bigger budget, conventionally funded movies, and to integrate the rough-and-ready video industry into the world of formal finance and banking' (Lobato, 2012: 60). Formalization presents a series of major challenges for the Nigerian film industry, ranging from film-makers dealing with government censors, market sellers dealing with tax collectors, and distributors developing more transparent international networks. It would also require a clear commitment on the part of the Nigerian state to view the local industry as a central part of its economy, rather than as a problem from the point of view of morality, a potential cash cow for corrupt officials, or as something that the nation's rulers need to worry about as an outlet for popular discontent. It requires thinking along the lines of a developmental state, in ways that have thus far eluded the otherwise resource-rich nation of Nigeria.

UNCTAD has observed that 'the film and video industry, if properly developed, could be a very significant source of wealth for any country, particularly its contribution to GDP [but] it is also a very powerful tool for communication, education, cultural integration and image projection' (UNCTAD, 2010: 250). At the same time, the resulting tensions between a 'privatized' media sector and the desire of the state for a greater contribution to nation-building should not be underestimated, nor should the issues of corruption and cronyism within the Nigerian government agencies. Formalization will certainly involve more robust action being taken against film piracy, which has long been a core feature of Nollywood's development, which is at odds with the 'weak copyright economy' (Lobato, 2010) around which the Nigerian film industry has grown. The relationship between copyright and creative industries in developing nations will be considered below.

Intellectual Property and Development

One area where the question of the institutional arrangements that best promote creative industries development arises sharply is that of copyright and intellectual property laws. It was observed in chapter 1 that the creative industries are sometimes also termed the *copyright industries*, and the rights of creators to derive income from their original creative works has long been enshrined in the concept of authorship, with copyright providing the basis for ongoing income streams in the form of royalties long after the original work was created. Copyright law has involved balancing a complex series of rights between creators, distributors and users of copyrighted works, since the passing of the Statute of Anne in Britain in 1709 and the US Copyright Act of 1790. Copyright laws derive from the principle that neither the creators of a new work nor the general public should be able to appropriate all of the benefits that flow from the creation of a new, original work of authorship. Creators have both a moral right over the work, and a legitimate economic right to derive material benefit from its use by others, thus providing them with an economic incentive to create new works. At the same time, by recognizing that original ideas and works derive from an existing pool of knowledge and creativity, and that access to the widest possible pool of information, knowledge and forms of creative expression is a public good and a right of a democratic citizenry, there is a need to ensure that such works are accessible in the public domain and that there are guaranteed rights to fair use by others.

The challenge of how to balance private ownership and public use is even more intense in the contemporary global economy for several reasons. First, copyrighted works are not necessarily owned by their creators; ownership has typically been assigned contractually to the giant media, information and entertainment corporations who derive the primary benefits from copyright laws in their current form (Vaidhyanathan, 2001; Drahos and Braithwaite, 2002). Second, the passing of the TRIPS (Trade-Related Aspects of Intellectual Property Rights) Agreement as part of the World Trade Organization (WTO) negotiations in 1995 expedited the development of a common global intellectual property framework that has been described as 'a stunning triumph for commercial interests and industry lobbyists who had worked so tirelessly to achieve the global agreement' (Sell, 2002: 172).

Almost all developing nations are net importers of intellectual property, while the US has a dominant position as a net intellectual property exporter, through creative industries such as software and entertainment as well as many of the world's most important trademarks. Observing this asymmetry, Drahos and Braithwaite (2002) wondered why over 100 developing nations would sign the TRIPS Agreement as they 'had nothing really to gain by agreeing to terms of trade for intellectual property that would offer so much protection to the comparative advantage the US enjoyed in intellectual property-related goods' (Drahos and Braithwaite, 2002: 11). Sell (2002: 185) argued that the TRIPS Agreement was reflective of 'unchecked industry dominance over the intellectual property agenda' in the 1990s, which only subsequently came to be more effectively challenged by 'an increasingly vociferous and mobilized civil society campaign' to challenge such dominance.

The third major issue is the digitization of media content, which has dramatically reduced the cost of reproducing digital works, while enabling their rapid dissemination through the Internet as well as in tangible forms such as CDs and DVDs. One consequence of this is that media piracy is rampant: up to 80 per cent of the DVDs in global circulation may be pirated copies, with piracy defined as 'the unauthorized copying, distribution, performance or other use of copyrighted material' (Lobato, 2012: 69). Piracy is most prominent in the developing world where, as Lobato has observed, piracy can be seen not simply as theft, but as free enterprise in action in the informal economy, or possibly even as resistance to the attempts by transnational media and entertainment conglomerates to appropriate wealth from the developing world, by setting prices at such a premium relative to the falling costs of production and distribution (Lobato, 2012: 74–6, 80–2). In this sense, digital technologies may be a 'power of the weak', providing street-level entrepreneurs with a chance to apply counter-power in the face of international agreements such as TRIPS severely constraining the scope for national discretion in the application of copyright and intellectual property laws.

The case for strengthening intellectual property rights (IPR) in developing countries, as part of enhancing the quality of the overall institutional and governance framework, is two-fold. First, it is argued that laws governing intellectual property in developing countries that are similar to those of developed economies will encourage businesses to invest in the developing world, and particularly to develop production facilities and promote the transfer of technology to these countries (Loew, 2006–7: 180–1). The second concerns growing the creative economy in developing countries themselves. It has often been noted that widespread piracy in developing countries has its major impacts, not upon global media conglomerates whose blockbuster films are being pirated, but upon local creative producers, as a culture develops that does not consider paying for creative works to be necessary.

The latter has been a consistent finding in work on the music industry in Africa (Pratt, 2008b; Schultz and van Gelden, 2008–9) and the Caribbean (James, 2008). Here it is argued that, because pirate distribution chains are well resourced, and local enforcement regimes are weak, piracy subverts development of a sustainable local music industry, making it difficult to invest in music production and distribution facilities and support local artists. Moreover, it denies local creators access to a revenue stream outside of the live performance circuit, in an environment that differs from the situation in developed nations, where live performance typically complements sales and royalties, and where it may make more sense to offer 'free' product as a 'hook' to consumers. It discourages local creators from staying in their own country, leading to an exodus of creative talent and the loss of local capacity to further develop the sector, as well as the lack of development of intra-regional and South–South trade.

As the case of Nigerian film production above indicates, there comes a point where the ongoing development of local creative industries requires a shift from low-cost, fly-by-night arrangements in the informal economy, which typically coexist with widespread piracy, towards formalization of a successful local industry with a sustainable value chain. That said, the extent to which committing considerable resources to enforcement of IPRs that pertain primarily to stamping out cheap copies of Hollywood blockbusters is money well spent, where there are so many demands on the public purse, is debatable. Enhancing public education about the value of supporting local creative artists, combined with reliable collection agencies that can ensure money gets back to the producers themselves, is key to using IPRs to develop sustainable local creative industries in developing nations. This would help to enable their creative economies to achieve the scale of operations, with resulting employment benefits and other spillover effects, commensurate with the abundant evidence of flourishing local creativity in many parts of the developing world.

Conclusion

This book has noted many challenges, tensions and ambivalences that surround the development of global creative industries. It was observed that the origins of the field in policy discourse have tended to give creative industries debates something of a national orientation – can one country advance its economy and culture through a national creative industries policy? – at a time when economic and cultural globalization are associated with the development of global production networks and more complex and intensified global circuits of culture. Strategies to promote new opportunities through the creative industries for employment, innovation, urban development and foreign trade also need to keep a wary eye on the sorts of jobs that are created in the creative industries and on whether, as critics have argued, they are characterized by precarity and 'flexploitation' rather than being sites for new forms of creative expression.

There is also the issue, which has most recently been raised by Maxwell and Miller (2012), about the ecological sustainability of the global creative industries, particularly those engaged with digital culture. While we focus upon the new forms of globally networked interconnectivity and creative engagement enabled by smart phones, mobile computing and tablet devices, there is much less discussion of 'the myriad ways that media technology consumes, despoils, and wastes natural resources' (Maxwell and Miller, 2012: 1). Similarly, in our discussions of 'smart cities' and 'creative clusters', there are fewer questions being asked about the long-term sustainability of such urban forms. The ecological risks associated with large car-dependent mega-cities are readily apparent. Perhaps more surprising are findings that it is not necessarily the suburbanite in the gas-guzzling SUV who may be engaging in the most environmentally damaging activities. Evidence suggests that it may in fact be the more affluent, ecologically aware inner-city 'creative class' types whose activities emit the most carbon and consume the most resources, as a commitment to recycling, bike riding, and green politics is being overwhelmed by their no less strong commitment to owning the latest electronic gadgets, frequent air travel, and living in smaller households (ACF, 2012).

From the late 1990s to the mid 2000s, creative industries debates were primarily associated with the advanced industrial economies. Advocates of creative industries policy strategies pointed to the long-term decline of manufacturing in higher-wage nations, and argued that culture-led regeneration of cities and regions, combined with strategies to promote innovation and entrepreneurship in the arts, media and design-based industries, could provide new opportunities for the post-industrial nations of Europe, North America, Asia and Australasia (Flew, 2012a). Their critics wondered about the quality of creative industries jobs, the sustainability of such industries in the face of boom-and-bust capitalist economic cycles, patterns of social exclusion both in these industries and in the cities that sought to promote them, and whether a degree of definitional confusion may have been associated with overstating the size and significance of creative industry sectors, e.g. by including quite different industries such as computer software (Garnham, 2005).

These debates are continuing, particularly in those countries where governments are seeking to reinvigorate national cultural policies to account for media convergence, and develop alternatives to arts subsidy-based models. For example, the economic crisis in the European Union has seen the member states strengthen commitments to a 'Creative Europe' strategy that can harness new opportunities for the creative industries (European Union, 2012). This is a response to the growing need to diversify the economic base of the region in the face of digital technologies and global competition, as well as better matching policy priorities to where there is increasing activity taking place, particularly among younger people in the European Union.

From the mid 2000s, however, the geographical locus of creative industries debates has been shifting from the advanced industrial nations to the developing world. In this respect, the growing interest in creative industries in China can be seen as pivotal. While some aspects of Chinese creative industries strategies were about branding cities such as Shanghai and Beijing as creative cities and media capitals, there was also considerable attention being given to how to transition the Chinese economy from one based upon low-wage, high-polluting manufacturing industries towards more value-added sectors that incorporated creativity and design, in order to develop leading global brands and achieve a more sustainable growth trajectory (Keane, 2011). Since that time, there has been considerable international attention given – particularly by UNCTAD – to creative economy strategies as alternative development pathways. Countries as diverse as Brazil, South Africa, Jamaica, Thailand and Senegal have been developing strategies to capitalize upon the high levels of creative activities among their populations, to promote more culturally and socially inclusive development models.

It has been a contention of this book that, while the unequal structures of the global economy can act as barriers to creative industries development, a consideration that is no less important is the institutional arrangements within the countries in question. The wider development literature, as well as the experience of nations such as the 'Tiger' economies of East Asia, points to the importance of a developmental state capable of setting rules of the game that are equitable and transparent, as well as being able to mobilize social and economic resources towards preferred national goals. While culture is sometimes positioned as being in opposition to economic development, the lessons of the developing world are increasingly that effective governance and institutional rules that are both accepted and observed within a society will be the keys to promoting the creative industries in a global context, converting the significant amount of creative activity taking place throughout these countries into realized development outcomes.

Some findings from this book may challenge some accepted wisdom in the creative industries field. An interesting case in point is that of intellectual property. While early Western theories of the creative industries championed copyright and intellectual property laws as being at the core of developing the creative industries (e.g., Howkins, 2001), others saw these intellectual property regimes as little more than an iniquitous tool for transferring wealth and resources from the developing world to the rich nations, and from Internet-savvy consumers to global media conglomerates. In those countries where content piracy is widespread, however, it may be necessary to use these laws to enable creative producers to secure income from their work, and achieve the basic conditions of sustainability for local creative industries.

For example, the impact of free music downloads on artists in the major culture-producing nations is mitigated to some extent by their ability to derive a growing proportion of their income from concerts, festivals, etc. By contrast, in much of the developing world, live performance has long been the only option available for musicians due to rampant piracy of their recorded creative works. Providing these artists with greater security of access to income from sales is a necessary condition for developing a local music industry, and hence being able to keep them in the music business and, in many cases, to remain in the country. Similar issues can be identified in the fast-booming Nigerian film industry ('Nollywood') where a degree of formalization of industry structures, including distribution networks, is now the key to being able to enhance the quality of local film productions, and the ability to enforce copyright arrangements may well be a part of this.

As Lobato (2012) has observed, we need to be careful not to idealize the informal economy; it frequently involves exploitation of the vulnerable and the undermining of more collective solutions that engage the local creative producers themselves. But we need to recognize that any form of cultural policy now involves a complex articulation between state actors and the informal economy; it is not simply a question of how government funds are distributed to established artists and creative producers, media organizations or formal cultural institutions. Crackdowns on copyright infringement are also not the only means of engaging the informal sectors with the formal cultural economy, and it remains the case that popular sympathy for cracking down on sales of pirated copies of *Avatar* so that James Cameron can build new extensions to his Hollywood mansion remains low, and with good reason.

The challenge in developing nations is how to harness the undoubted energies that arise out of informal arrangements in the creative industries, but enable them to become 'formalized' to the degree necessary to build local sectors that can be viable and can provide equitably distributed opportunities for more of a nation's citizens over the medium term. In addressing the institutional conditions necessary for meeting such a challenge, there will be no simple 'off-the-shelf' model applicable under all circumstances. To speak of global creative industries, then, is to acknowledge the complexities of local, national and regional circumstances. Creative industries strategies need to be considered in the wider context of debates about public policy, development, and the institutional capacities of nation-states in the context of globalization.

Notes

1 Bilton also notes the influence of popular management books, business magazines and feature films in promoting an image of the 'celebrity CEO' who
'represents management as it likes to see itself – as entrepreneurial free spirits
who don't play by the rules' (Bilton, 2007: 81). Much is made of figures such as
Richard Branson, the late Anita Roddick and the late Steve Jobs as mavericks,
who reject the formalities of organizational culture and 'resolve to empower the
workforce by purging bureaucrats, encouraging risk-taking and seeking inspiration from the lowliest employee' (Bilton, 2007: 81). Very often, the business
side of a creative activity is treated almost as an afterthought. A classic case
study of the latter is the 2010 film *The Social Network*, which presents Facebook
founder and CEO Mark Zuckerberg as someone who is self-absorbed, impa-
tient with others and indifferent to business practicalities, and presents these
not as attributes to be overcome, but as being at the core of Facebook's commercial success. The death of Steve Jobs in 2011 also saw an extensive debate
about whether his style of management at Apple was an example of visionary
leadership or an autocratic style that was personally damaging to those around
him.

2 A notable critic of the application of HHI to media law was C. Edwin Baker,
who argued in *Media Concentration and Democracy* that the index itself had an
inherent problem in determining what was the relevant industry variable to
evaluate (e.g., newspapers nationally, newspapers in a particular location, the
media as a whole), but that the focus on price and product variables lost sight
of what was the key issue for a democratic society, which was access to a diverse
range of voices and opinions (Baker, 2007: 58–71).

3 BRICS is a term used to describe the emergent economies of Brazil, Russia,
India, China and South Africa. Another formulation is the BRIICS, including
Indonesia, and BRICKS, including (South) Korea. The growth rates of these
economies have accelerated since the 1990s, and were three times those of the
United States and the major European economies in the 2000s. With such
growth comes, of course, a rising middle class of prospective media consumers.

4 De Propris and Hypponen (2008: 281) observe that while Hollywood is typically associated with the large film studios, 80 per cent of firms in the Hollywood
film cluster employ fewer than four people.

5 The hybrid term 'cultural creative industries' (*wenhua chuangyi chanye*) is sometimes used in China. The term 'cultural industries' has typically been associated
with the arts and cultural heritage as aspects of Chinese civilization, as well
as sectors such as publishing, film and TV where state control over content

remains significant. By contrast, 'creative industries' is often associated with less culturally valued and/or politically sensitive entertainment-related fields such as games, advertising and cultural tourism. Significantly, the hybrid 'cultural creative industries' has been more commonly used in the political capital of Beijing, whereas 'creative industries' has more currency in the more commercially oriented Shanghai (Keane, 2007).

6 The example of Miami is instructive in this regard. Miami has come to be a central point in the distribution, and more recently the production, of *telenovelas* throughout Latin America. Within the United States, its influence is confined to the Spanish-speaking population, which is nonetheless sizable. Miami is a common nodal point for distribution of *telenovelas* from countries such as Mexico, Argentina, Colombia and Venezuela, in the absence of a shared centre outside of the United States for such distribution (Mato, 2002; Sinclair, 2003).

7 A more institutionally oriented use of the term neoliberalism may rescue the concept from its current parlous intellectual state, where it has become a generic term of denunciation for anything and everything that a particular author may find morally objectionable, from reality TV shows to university restructurings, or where it simply becomes a synonym for economic discourse or talk about markets (Flew, 2012a: 176–82). From a developmental perspective, a neoliberal approach may be said to be one that associates the development of a successful market economy with particular institutional arrangements and state forms, and promotes the view that the required institutional infrastructure of capitalism does not vary on the basis of history, social structure or context. Heller (2009) provides an example of such an approach, and it was key to the so-called 'Washington Consensus' held among key international institutions in the 1980s and 1990s. By contrast, the 'developmentalist state' approach tends to accept that there will be a diverse array of institutional forms associated with capitalist development, that there is no single 'best model', and that any national strategy needs to be context-sensitive. The rise of China since the late 1970s has provided a fascinating case study through which to consider these approaches, as its institutional forms are highly divergent from the neoliberal ideal: see Hutton and Desai (2007) for a debate about the institutional sustainability of Chinese capitalism.

References

ACF (Australian Conservation Foundation) (2012) *Consumption Atlas.* http://www.acfonline.org.au/sites/default/files/resource/index67.swf

Adorno, T. and Horkheimer, M. (1979) The Culture Industry: Enlightenment as Mass Deception. In J. Curran, M. Gurevitch and J. Woollacott (eds.), *Mass Communication and Society.* London: Verso, pp. 349–83.

Albarran, A. (2010) *The Media Economy* (2nd edn). New York: Routledge.

Albarran, A. and Dimmick, J. (1996) Concentration and Economies of Multiformity in the Communication Industries. *Journal of Media Economics* 9(4): 41–50.

Aldridge, A. (2003) *Consumption.* Cambridge: Polity Press.

Amin, A. (2000) The Economic Base of Contemporary Cities. In G. Bridge and S. Watson (eds.), *A Companion to the City.* Oxford: Blackwell, pp. 115–29.

Amin, A. (2003) Industrial Districts. In E. Sheppard and T. Barnes (eds.), *A Companion to Economic Geography.* Oxford: Blackwell, pp. 149–68.

Amsden, A.H. (1989) *Asia's Next Giant: South Korea and Late Industrialization.* New York: Oxford University Press.

Andrews, G., Yeabsley, J. and Higgs, P. (2009) *The Creative Sector in New Zealand: Mapping and Economic Role: Report to New Zealand Trade and Enterprise.* Auckland: New Zealand Institute of Economic Research.

Ang, I. (1996) Global Media/Local Meaning. In *Living Room Wars: Rethinking Media Audiences for a Postmodern World.* New York: Routledge, pp. 50–61.

Appadurai, A. (1990) Disjuncture and Difference in the Global Cultural Economy. In M. Featherstone (ed.), *Global Culture: Nationalism, Globalization and Modernity.* London: Sage, pp. 295–310.

Appleby, J. (2003) Consumption in Early Modern Social Thought. In D.B. Clarke, M.A. Doel and K.M.L. Housiaux (eds.), *The Consumption Reader.* London: Routledge, pp. 31–9.

Arvidsson, A., Malossi, G. and Naro, S. (2010) Passionate Work? Labour Conditions in the Milan Fashion Industry. *Journal for Cultural Research* 14(3): 295–309.

Badcock, B. (2009) Gentrification. In R. Hutchison (ed.), *Encyclopedia of Urban Studies.* Thousand Oaks, CA: Sage, pp. 306–10.

Baker, C.E. (2007) *Media Concentration and Democracy: Why Ownership Matters.* Cambridge: Cambridge University Press.

Banks, M. and Hesmondhalgh, D. (2009) Looking for Work in Creative Industries Policy. *International Journal of Cultural Policy* 15(4): 415–30.

Baran, P. and Sweezy, P. (1968) *Monopoly Capital.* Harmondsworth: Penguin.

Barber, B. (2000) Jihad versus McWorld. In F.J. Lechner and J. Boli (eds.), *The Globalization Reader*. Malden, MA: Blackwell, pp. 21–6.

Barnet, R. and Müller, R. (1974) *Global Reach: The Power of the Multinational Corporations*. New York: Simon & Schuster.

Barney, D. (2004) *The Network Society*. Cambridge: Polity.

Barrowclough, D. and Kozul-Wright, Z. (2008) Voice, Choice and Diversity through Creative Industries. In D. Barrowclough and Z. Kozul-Wright (eds.), *Creative Industries and Developing Countries: Voice, Choice and Economic Growth*. London: Routledge, pp. 1–36.

Barthes, R. (1973) *Mythologies*. London: Methuen.

Bassett, K., Smith, I., Banks, M. and O'Connor, J. (2005) Urban Dilemmas of Competition and Cohesion in Cultural Policy. In N. Buck, I. Gordon, A. Harding and I. Turok (eds.), *Changing Cities: Rethinking Urban Competitiveness, Cohesion and Governance*. Basingstoke: Palgrave, pp. 132–53.

Baudrillard, J. (1988) For a Critique of the Political Economy of the Sign. In M. Poster (ed.), *Jean Baudrillard: Selected Writings*. Cambridge: Polity Press, pp. 57–97.

Beck, U. and Lau, C. (2005) Second Modernity as a Research Agenda: Theoretical and Empirical Explorations in the 'Meta-Change' of Modern Society. *British Journal of Sociology* 56(4): 525–57.

Beinhocker, E. (2006) *The Origin of Wealth: Evolution, Complexity, and the Radical Remaking of Economics*. Boston, MA: Harvard University Press.

Benkler, Y. (2006) *The Wealth of Networks*. New Haven, CT: Yale University Press.

Bennett, T. (1995) *The Birth of the Museum*. London: Routledge.

Bennett, T., Emmison, M. and Frow, J. (1999) *Accounting for Tastes: Australian Everyday Cultures*. Cambridge: Cambridge University Press.

Berger, W. (2009) *Glimmer: How Design Can Transform Your Business, Your Life, and Maybe Even the World*. London: Random House.

Berger, W. (2010) The Four Phases of Design Thinking. *HBR Blog Network*, 29 July. http://blogs.hbr.org/cs/2010/07/the_four_phases_of_design_thin.html.

Best, M. (1990) *The New Competition: Institutions of Industrial Restructuring*. Cambridge: Polity Press.

Bielby, W. and Bielby, D. (1994) 'All Hits are Flukes': Institutionalized Decision Making and the Rhetoric of Network Prime-Time Program Development. *American Journal of Sociology* 99(5): 1287–1313.

Bilton, C. (2007) *Management and Creativity; From Creative Industries to Creative Management*. Oxford: Wiley-Blackwell.

Bilton, C. and Leary, R. (2002) What Can Managers Do for Creativity? Brokering Creativity in the Creative Industries. *International Journal of Cultural Policy* 8(1): 49–64.

Blackshaw, T. (2010) Bauman's Challenge to Sociology. In M. Davis and K. Tester (eds.), *Bauman's Challenge: Sociological Issues for the 21st Century*. Basingstoke: Palgrave Macmillan, pp. 70–91.

Bocock, R. (1993) *Consumption*. London: Routledge.

Boggs, J. (2009) Cultural Industries and the Creative Economy – Vague but Useful Concepts. *Geography Compass* 3(4): 1483–98.

Boltanski, L. and Chiapello, E. (2005) *The New Spirit of Capitalism* (trans. G. Elliott). London: Verso.

Bourdieu, P. (1984) *Distinction: A Social Critique of the Judgement of Taste* (trans. R. Nice). London: Routledge.

Braithwaite, J. (2008) *Regulatory Capitalism*. Cheltenham: Edward Elgar.

Brewer, A. (1980) *Marxist Theories of Imperialism: A Critical Survey*. London: Routledge & Kegan Paul.

Brown, T. (2008) Design Thinking. *Harvard Business Review* 86(6): 84–92.

Bruns, A. (2008) *Blogs, Wikipedia, Second Life, and Beyond: From Production to Produsage*. New York: Peter Lang.

Bulow, J. and Summers, L. (1986) A Theory of Dual Labour Markets with Application to Industrial Policy, Discrimination, and Keynesian Unemployment. *Journal of Labor Economics* 4(3): 376–414.

Callus, R. and Cole, M. (2002) Live for Art – Just Don't Expect to Make a Living from It: The Worklife of Australian Visual Artists. *Media International Australia* 102: 77–92.

Campbell, P. (2011) Creative Industries in a European Capital of Culture. *International Journal of Cultural Policy* 17(5): 510–22.

Canclini, N.G. (2001) *Consumers and Citizens* (trans. G. Yúdice). Minneapolis, MN: University of Minnesota Press.

Carter, M. (2003) *Fashion Classics: From Carlyle to Barthes*. Oxford: Berg.

Castells, M. (1996) *The Rise of the Network Society*. Vol. I of *The Information Age: Economy, Society and Culture*. Oxford: Blackwell.

Castells, M. (2001) *The Internet Galaxy: Reflections on the Internet, Business, and Society*. Oxford: Oxford University Press.

Castells, M. (2009) *Communication Power*. Oxford: Oxford University Press.

Castells, M. and Aoyama, Y. (1994) Paths towards the Informational Society: Employment Structure in G-7 Countries, 1920–90. *International Labour Review* 133(1): 5–33.

Caust, J. (2003) Putting the 'Art' Back into Arts Policy Making: How Arts Policy has been 'Captured' by the Economists and the Marketers. *International Journal of Cultural Policy* 9(1): 51–63.

Caves, R. (2000) *Creative Industries: Contracts between Art and Commerce*. Cambridge, MA: Harvard University Press.

Centre for International Economics (CIE) (2009) *Creative Industries Economic Analysis: Final Report*. Canberra: Centre for International Economics.

Chavance, B. (2009) *Institutional Economics*. New York: Routledge.

Cho, M. (2010) Envisioning Seoul as a World City: The Cultural Politics of the Hong-dae Cultural District. *Asian Studies Review* 34(3): 329–47.

Choi, J. (2008) The New Korean Wave of U. In H. Anheier and Y.R. Isar (eds.), *The Cultural Economy*. Cultures and Globalization Series, Vol. 2. London: Sage, pp. 148–54.

Choi, J. (2010) The City in Connections: Seoul as an Urban Network. *Multimedia Systems* 16: 75–84.

Christensen, C. (2003) *The Innovator's Dilemma.* New York: HarperCollins.

Christopherson, S. (2011a) Hard Jobs in Hollywood: How Concentration in Distribution Affects the Production Side of the Media Entertainment Industry. In D. Winseck and D.Y. Jin (eds.), *The Political Economies of Media: The Transformation of the Global Media Industries.* London: Bloomsbury, pp. 123–41.

Christopherson, S. (2011b) Connecting the Dots: Structure, Strategy, and Subjectivity in Entertainment Media. In M. Deuze (ed.), *Managing Media Work.* Thousand Oaks, CA: Sage, pp. 179–90.

Christopherson, S. and Storper, M. (1989) The Effects of Flexible Specialization on Industrial Politics and the Labour Market. *Industrial and Labour Relations Review* 42(3): 331–47.

Clegg, S., Kornberger, M. and Pitsis, T. (2005) *Managing and Organizations.* London: Sage.

Coe, N., Kelly, P. and Yeung, H.W.C. (2007) *Economic Geography: A Contemporary Introduction.* Malden, MA: Blackwell.

Collins, J. (1993) Postmodernism and Television. In R.C. Allen (ed.), *Channels of Discourse, Reassembled.* London: Routledge, pp. 327–53.

Collins, R., Garnham, N. and Locksley, G. (1988) *The Economics of Television: The UK Case.* London: Sage.

Compaine, B. (2001) The Myths of Encroaching Global Media Ownership. *Open Democracy,* 8 November. Available at http://www.opendemocracy.net/media-globalmediaownership/article_87.jsp.

Compaine, B. and Gomery, D. (2000) *Who Owns the Media? Competition and Concentration in the Media Industry.* Mahwah, NJ: Lawrence Erlbaum Associates.

Cooke, P. (2002) *Knowledge Economies: Clusters, Learning and Cooperative Advantage.* London: Routledge.

Couldry, N. (2010) *Why Voice Matters: Culture and Politics after Neoliberalism.* London: Sage.

Cowen, T. (2002) *Creative Destruction: How Globalization is Changing the World's Cultures.* Princeton, NJ: Princeton University Press.

Coyle, D. (1998) *The Weightless World.* London: Capstone.

Craik, J. (2007) *Re-visioning Arts and Cultural Policy: Current Impasses and Future Directions.* Canberra: ANU e-Press.

Craik, J. (2009) *Fashion: The Key Concepts.* Oxford: Berg.

Craik, J., Davis, G. and Sunderland, N. (2000) Cultural Policy and National Identity. In G. Davis and M. Keating (eds.), *The Future of Governance.* Sydney: Allen & Unwin, pp. 177–202.

Csikszentmihalyi, M. (1996) *Creativity: Flow and the Psychology of Discovery and Invention.* New York: Harper Perennial.

Cunningham, S. (2011) Developments in Measuring the 'Creative' Workforce. *Cultural Trends* 20(1): 25–40.

Cunningham, S. (2013) *Hidden Innovation: Policy, Industry and the Creative Sector*. Brisbane: University of Queensland Press.

Cunningham, S., Banks, J. and Potts, J. (2008a) Cultural Economy: The Shape of the Field. In H. Anheier and Y.R. Isar (eds.), *The Cultural Economy*. Cultures and Globalization Series, Vol. 2. London: Sage, pp. 15–26.

Cunningham, S., Ryan, M.D., Keane, M. and Ordonez, D. (2008b) Financing Creative Industries in Developing Countries. In D. Barrowclough and Z. Kozul-Wright (eds.), *Creative Industries and Developing Countries: Voice, Choice and Economic Growth*. London: Routledge, pp. 65–110.

Currid, E. (2006) New York as a Global Creative Hub: A Competitive Analysis of Four Theories on World Cities. *Economic Development Quarterly* 20(4): 330–50.

Currid, E. (2007) *The Warhol Economy: How Fashion, Art and Music Drive New York City*. Princeton, NJ: Princeton University Press.

Curtin, M. (2003) Media Capital: Towards the Study of Spatial Flows. *International Journal of Cultural Studies* 6(2): 202–28.

Curtin, M. (2007) *Playing to the World's Biggest Audience: The Globalization of Chinese Film and TV*. London: University of California Press.

Curtin, M. (2009) Thinking Globally: From Media Imperialism to Media Capital. In J. Holt and A. Perren (eds.), *Media Industries: History, Theory, Method*. Malden, MA: Wiley-Blackwell, pp. 108–19.

Curtin, M. (2010) Comparing Media Capitals: Hong Kong and Mumbai. *Global Media and Communication* 6(3): 263–70.

Cutler & Co. (2008) *Venturous Australia: Building Strength in Innovation*, Report prepared for the Department of Innovation, Industry, Science and Research. Available at http://www.innovation.gov.au/Innovation/Policy/Documents/NISReport.pdf.

Dale, G. (2010) *Karl Polanyi: The Limits of the Market*. Cambridge: Polity.

David, P. and Foray, D. (2002) An Introduction to the Economy of the Knowledge Society. *International Social Science Journal* 171: 9–23.

Davis, H. and Scase, R. (2000) *Managing Creativity: The Dynamics of Work and Organization*. Buckingham: Open University Press.

De Mooij, M. (2010) *Global Marketing and Advertising: Understanding Cultural Paradoxes*. Los Angeles, CA: Sage.

Department for Culture, Media and Sport (1998) *Mapping the Creative Industries*. http://www.culture.gov.uk/reference_library/publications/4740.aspx (accessed 2 April 2009).

Department of Prime Minister and Cabinet (2011) *National Cultural Policy Discussion Paper*. Canberra: Australian Government Office of the Arts.

De Propris, L. and Hypponen, L. (2008) Creative Clusters and Governance: The Dominance of the Hollywood Film Cluster. In P. Cooke and L. Lazzeretti (eds.), *Creative Cities, Cultural Clusters and Local Economic Development*. Cheltenham: Edward Elgar, pp. 258–86.

Design Singapore Council (DSC) (2010) *Design for Enterprises*. Available at http://designforenterprises.sg/aboutus.aspx.

Deuze, M. and Fortunati, L. (2011) Atypical Newswork, Atypical Media Management. In M. Deuze (ed.), *Managing Media Work*. Thousand Oaks, CA: Sage, pp. 111–20.

Dicken, P. (2007) Economic Globalization: Corporations. In G. Ritzer (ed.), *The Blackwell Companion to Globalization*. Malden, MA: Blackwell, pp. 291–306.

Doeringer, P. and Crean, S. (2006) Can Fast Fashion Save the US Apparel Industry? *Socio-Economic Review* 4: 353–77.

Donald, A. (2011) The Paradoxical City. In A. Williams and A. Donald (eds.), *The Lure of the City: From Slums to Suburbs*. London: Pluto, pp. 1–12.

Drahos, P. and Braithwaite, J. (2002) *Information Feudalism*. London: Earthscan.

du Gay, P. and Pryke, M. (2002) *Cultural Economy: Cultural Analysis and Commercial Life*. London: Sage.

du Gay, P., Hall, S., Janes, L., Mackay, H. and Negus, K. (1997) *Doing Cultural Studies: The Story of the Sony Walkman*. London: Sage.

Dugger, W. and Sherman, H.J. (1994) Comparison of Marxism and Institutionalism. *Journal of Economic Issues* 28(1): 101–27.

Dunlop, P. (2012) Fashion, Ethics, Ethos. In E. Felton, O. Zelenko and S. Vaughan (eds.), *Design and Ethics: Reflections on Practice*. London: Routledge, pp. 193–203.

Dunning, J. (2000) Regions, Globalization and the Knowledge-Based Economy: The Issues Stated. In J. Dunning (ed.), *Regions, Globalization and the Knowledge-Based Economy*. Oxford: Oxford University Press, pp. 8–41.

Dunning, J. (2001) *Global Capitalism at Bay?* London: Routledge.

Eco, U. (1976) *A Theory of Semiotics*. Bloomington, IN: Indiana University Press.

Eggers, W. (2008) The Changing Nature of Government: Network Governance. In J. O'Flynn and J. Wanna (eds.), *Collaborative Governance: A New Era of Public Policy in Australia?* Canberra; ANU ePress, pp. 23–8.

El-Nawawy, M. and Iskandar, A. (2002) *Al-Jazeera: How the Free Arab News Network Scooped the World and Changed the Middle East*. Cambridge, MA: Westview.

Ernst, D. and Kim, L. (2002) Global Production Networks, Knowledge Diffusion, and Local Capacity Formation. *Research Policy* 31: 1417–29.

European Union (2012) *Creative Europe: Support Programme for Europe's Cultural and Creative Sectors from 2014*. http://ec.europa.eu/culture/creative-europe/index_en.htm.

Evans, P. (1995) *Embedded Autonomy: States and Industrial Transformation*. Princeton, NJ: Princeton University Press.

Fainstein, S. and Harloe, M. (2000) Ups and Downs in the Global City: London and New York at the Millennium. In G. Bridge and S. Watson (eds.), *A Companion to the City*. Oxford: Blackwell, pp. 155–67.

Featherstone, M. (1991) *Consumer Culture and Postmodernism*. London: Sage.

Featherstone, M. (2007) *Consumer Culture and Postmodernism* (2nd edn). London: Sage.

Ferguson, A. (1988) *Industrial Economics: Issues and Perspectives*. Basingstoke: Macmillan.

Flew, T. (2002) Beyond *ad hocery*: Defining Creative Industries. In M. Volkering (ed.), *Cultural Sites, Cultural Theory, Cultural Policy: Proceedings of the Second International Conference on Cultural Policy Research*. Wellington: Te Papa, 23–26 January, pp. 181–91.

Flew, T. (2003) Creative Industries and the New Economy. In G. Argyrous and F.J.B. Stilwell (eds.), *Economics as a Social Science*. Sydney: Pluto Press, pp. 309–14.

Flew, T. (2004) Creativity, the 'New Humanism' and Cultural Studies. *Continuum: Journal of Media and Cultural Studies* 18(2): 161–78.

Flew, T. (2006) The Social Contract and Beyond in Broadcast Media Policy. *Television and New Media* 7(3): 282–305.

Flew, T. (2007) *Understanding Global Media*. Basingstoke: Palgrave Macmillan.

Flew, T. (2008) Music, Cities and Cultural and Creative Industries Policy. In G. Bloustien, S. Luckman and M. Peters (eds.), *Sonic Synergies: The Place of Music in the Creative Knowledge Economy*. Aldershot: Ashgate, pp. 7–16.

Flew, T. (2009) The Cultural Economy Moment? *Cultural Science* 2(1): 2–11.

Flew, T. (2011a) Rethinking Public Service Media and Citizenship: Digital Strategies for News and Current Affairs at Australia's Special Broadcasting Service (SBS). *International Journal of Communication* 5: 215–32.

Flew, T. (2011b) Media as Creative Industries: Conglomeration and Globalization as Accumulation Strategies in an Age of Digital Media. In D. Winseck and D.Y. Jin (eds.), *The Political Economies of Media: The Transformation of the Global Media Industries*. London: Bloomsbury, pp. 84–100.

Flew, T. (2012a) *The Creative Industries, Culture and Policy*. London: Sage.

Flew, T. (2012b) *The Convergent Media Policy Moment*, Institute for Culture and Society Occasional Paper, Vol. 3 No. 3, University of Western Sydney.

Flew, T., Ching, G., Stafford, A. and Tacchi, J. (2003) *Music Industry Development and Brisbane's Future as a Creative City*. Brisbane: Creative Industries Research and Applications Centre.

Florida, R. (2002) *The Rise of the Creative Class*. New York: Basic Books.

Florida, R. (2007) *The Flight of the Creative Class*. New York: HarperCollins.

Florida, R. (2008) *Who's Your City? How the Creative Economy is Making Where to Live the Most Important Decision of your Life*. New York: Basic Books.

Foster, J.B. (2000) Monopoly Capital at the Turn of the Millennium. *Monthly Review* 51(11): 1–17.

Foucault, M. (2008) *The Birth of Biopolitics* (ed. M. Sennelart; trans. G. Burchell). Basingstoke: Palgrave Macmillan.

Frank, A.G. (1973) *Capitalism and Underdevelopment in Latin America*. New York: Monthly Review Press.

Freedman, D. (2008) *The Politics of Media Policy*. Cambridge: Polity.

Freiberg, A. (2010) *The Tools of Regulation*. Sydney: Federation Press.

Friedman, M. and Friedman, R. (1980) *Free to Choose*. Harmondsworth: Penguin.

Friedmann, J. (2006) The World City Hypothesis. In N. Brenner and R. Keil (eds.), *The Global Cities Reader*. London: Routledge, pp. 67–71.

Frith, S., Cloonan, M. and Williamson, J. (2009) On Music as a Creative Industry. In A. Pratt and P. Jeffcutt (eds.), *Creativity, Innovation and the Cultural Economy*. London: Routledge, pp. 74–89.

Fröbel, F., Heinrichs, J. and Kreye, O. (1980) *The New International Division of Labour*. Cambridge: Cambridge University Press.

Frow, J. (1995) *Cultural Studies and Cultural Value*. Oxford: Oxford University Press.

Fung, A. (2009) Globalized Televised Culture: The Case of China. In G. Turner and J. Tay (eds.), *Television Studies After TV*. London: Routledge, pp. 178–88.

Galbraith, J.K. (1973) Power and the Useful Economist. *American Economic Review* 63(1): 1–11.

Galloway, S. and Dunlop, S. (2007) A Critique of Definitions of the Cultural and Creative Industries in Public Policy. *International Journal of Cultural Policy* 13(1): 17–31.

Garnham, N. (1990) *Capitalism and Communication*. London: Sage.

Garnham, N. (1995) Political Economy and Cultural Studies: Reconciliation or Divorce? *Critical Studies in Mass Communication* 12(1): 62–71.

Garnham, N. (2005) From Cultural to Creative Industries: An Analysis of the Implications of the 'Creative Industries' Approach to Arts and Media Policy Making in the United Kingdom. *International Journal of Cultural Policy* 11(1): 15–29.

Garnham, N. (2011) The Political Economy of Communication Revisited. In J. Wasko, G. Murdock and H. Sousa (eds.), *The Handbook of Political Economy of Communications*. Chichester: John Wiley & Sons, pp. 41–61.

Gauntlett, D. (2011) *Making is Connecting: The Social Meaning of Creativity from DIY and Knitting to YouTube and Web 2.0*. Cambridge: Polity Press.

Gellner, E. (1983) *Nations and Nationalism*. Oxford: Blackwell.

Gerschenkron, A. (1962) *Economic Backwardness in Historical Perspective*. Cambridge, MA: Harvard University Press.

Giarini, O. (2002) The Globalisation of Services in Economic Theory and Economic Practice: Some Conceptual Issues. In J.R. Cuadrado-Roura, L. Rubalcaba-Bermejo and J.R. Bryson (eds.), *Trading Services in the Global Economy*. Cheltenham: Edward Elgar, pp. 58–77.

Gibson, C. and Kong, L. (2005) Cultural Economy: A Critical Review. *Progress in Human Geography* 29(5): 541–61.

Gill, R. (2011) 'Life is a Pitch': Managing the Self in New Media Work. In M. Deuze (ed.), *Managing Media Work*. Thousand Oaks, CA: Sage, pp. 249–62.

Goldsmith, B., Lee, K.-L. and Yecies, B. (2011) In Search of the Korean Digital Wave. *Media International Australia* 141: 70–7.

Goodman, D. (2007) Globalization and Consumer Culture. In G. Ritzer (ed.), *The Blackwell Companion to Globalization*. Malden, MA: Blackwell, pp. 330–51.

Gordon, I. and Buck, N.H. (2005) Cities in the New Conventional Wisdom. In N.H. Buck, I. Gordon, A. Harding and I. Turok (eds.), *Changing Cities: Rethinking Urban Competitiveness, Cohesion, and Governance*. Basingstoke: Palgrave Macmillan, pp. 1–21.

Gordon, I. and McCann, P. (2001) Industrial Clusters: Complexes, Agglomerations, and/or Social Networks? *Urban Studies* 37(3): 513–32.

Govil, N. (2009) Thinking Nationally: Domicile, Distinction, and Dysfunction in Global Media Exchange. In J. Holt and A. Perren (eds.), *Media Industries: History, Theory, Method*. Malden, MA: Wiley-Blackwell, pp. 132–43.

Granovetter, M. (1985) Economic Action and Social Structure: The Problem of Embeddedness. *American Journal of Sociology* 91(3): 481–510.

Gregg, M. (2011) *Work's Intimacy*. Cambridge: Polity.

Grodach, C. and Loukaitou-Sideris, A. (2007) Cultural Development Strategies and Urban Revitalization. *International Journal of Cultural Policy* 13(4): 349–70.

Habermas, J. (1992) Citizenship and National Identity: Some Reflections on the Future of Europe. *Praxis International* 12(1): 1–14.

Hall, P. (2000) Creative Cities and Economic Development. *Urban Studies* 37(4): 639–49.

Hall, S. and Held, D. (1989) Citizens and Citizenship. In S. Hall and M. Jacques (eds.), *New Times: The Changing Face of Politics in the 1990s*. London: Lawrence & Wishart, pp. 173–88.

Hamnett, C. (2003) Gentrification, Postindustrialism, and Industrial and Occupational Restructuring in Global Cities. In G. Bridge and S. Watson (eds.), *A Companion to the City*. Malden, MA: Blackwell, pp. 331–41.

Harney, S. (2010) Creative Industries Debate – Unfinished Business: Labour, Management, and the Creative Industries. *Cultural Studies* 24(3): 431–44.

Hartley, J. (1996) *Popular Reality: Journalism, Modernity, Popular Culture*. London: Arnold.

Hartley, J. (2009) From the Consciousness Industry to the Creative Industries: Consumer-Created Content, Social Network Markets, and the Growth of Knowledge. In J. Holt and A. Perren (eds.), *Media Industries: History, Theory, Method*. Malden, MA: Wiley-Blackwell, pp. 231–44.

Hartley, J. (2012) *Digital Futures for Media and Cultural Studies*. Malden, MA: Wiley-Blackwell.

Hartley, J. and Montgomery, L. (2009) Fashion as Consumer Entrepreneurship: Emergent Risk Culture, Social Network Markets, and the Launch of *Vogue* China. *Chinese Journal of Communication* 2(1): 61–76.

Hartley, J., Potts, J., Cunningham, S., Keane, M., Flew, T. and Banks, J. (2012) *Key Concepts in the Creative Industries*. London: Sage.

Harvard Business Essentials (2003) *Managing Creativity and Innovation*. Boston, MA: Harvard Business School Press.

Harvey, D. (1982) *The Limits to Capital*. Oxford: Blackwell.

Harvey. D. (2008) The Right to the City. *New Left Review* 55: 23–40.

Haynes, J. (2007) Nollywood: What's in a Name? *Film International* 5(4): 106–8.

Held, D., McGrew, A., Goldblatt, D. and Perraton, J. (1999) *Global Transformations: Politics, Economics and Culture*. Stanford, CA: Stanford University Press.

Heller, M. (2009) *Capitalism, Institutions, and Economic Development*. London: Routledge.

Henderson, J., Dicken, P., Hess, M., Coe, N. and Yeung, H.W.C. (2002) Global Production Networks and the Analysis of Economic Development. *Review of International Political Economy* 9(3): 436–64.

Herman, E.S. and McChesney, R.W. (1997) *The Global Media: The New Missionaries of Global Capitalism*. London: Cassell.

Hesmondhalgh, D. (2007a) *The Cultural Industries* (2nd edn). London: Sage.

Hesmondhalgh, D. (2007b) Creative Labour as a Basis for Critique of Creative Industries Policy. In G. Lovink and N. Rossiter (eds.), *MyCreativity Reader*. Amsterdam: Institute of Network Cultures, pp. 59–68.

Hesmondhalgh, D. (2013) *The Cultural Industries* (3rd edn). London: Sage.

Hesmondhalgh, D. and Baker, S. (2011) *Creative Labour: Media Work in Three Cultural Industries*. London: Routledge.

Higgs, P., Cunningham, S. and Pagan, J. (2007) *Australia's Creative Economy: Basic Evidence on Size, Growth, Income and Employment*. Technical Report. http://eprints.qut.edu.au/8241/ (accessed 20 March 2009).

Higgs, P., Cunningham, S. and Bakhshi, H. (2008) *Beyond the Creative Industries: Mapping the Creative Economy in the United Kingdom*. Technical Report. National Endowment for Science, Technology and the Arts (NESTA), February.

Hirschman, A. (1970) *Exit, Voice and Loyalty: Responses to Decline in Firms, Organizations, and States*. Cambridge, MA: Harvard University Press.

Hirschman, A.O. (1995) *A Propensity to Self-Subversion*. Cambridge, MA: Harvard University Press.

Hjorth, L. (2011) Locating the Online: Creativity and User-Created Content in Seoul. *Media International Australia* 141: 118–27.

HM Treasury (2006) *Cox Review of Creativity in Business: Building on the UK's Strengths*. London: HM Treasury.

Hobsbawm, E.J. (1990) *Nations and Nationalism since 1780*. Cambridge: Cambridge University Press.

Hobsbawm, E.J. (1996) *The Age of Revolution 1789–1848*. New York: Vintage.

Hodgson, G. (2000) Socio-economic Consequences of the Advance of Complexity and Knowledge. In Organization for Economic Co-operation and Development, *The Creative Society of the 21st Century*. Paris: OECD, pp. 89–112.

Hodgson, G. and Knudsen, T. (2010) *Darwin's Conjecture: The Search for General Principles of Social and Economic Evolution*. Chicago, IL: University of Chicago Press.

Holden, J. (2009) How We Value Arts and Culture. *Asia Pacific Journal of Arts and Cultural Management* 6(2): 447–56.

Homan, S. (2012) 'I Tote and I Vote': Australian Live Music and Cultural Policy. *Arts Marketing: An International Journal* 1(2): 96–107.

Horwitz, R. (1989) *The Irony of Regulatory Reform: The Deregulation of American Telecommunications.* New York: Oxford University Press.

Hoskins, C., McFadyen, S. and Finn, A. (1997) *Global Television and Film: An Introduction to the Economics of the Business.* Oxford: Clarendon Press.

Hoskins, C., McFadyen, S. and Finn, A. (2004) *Media Economics: Applying Economics to New and Traditional Media.* Thousand Oaks, CA: Sage.

Howard, M. and King, J. (1985) *The Political Economy of Marx.* Harlow: Longman.

Howard, M. and King, J. (2004) The Economic Contributions of Paul Sweezy. *Review of Political Economy* 16(4): 411–56.

Howe, J. (2009) Is Crowdsourcing Evil? The Design Community Weighs In. *WIRED. com,* 10 March. http://www.wired.com/business/2009/03/is-crowdsourcin/.

Howkins, J. (2001) *The Creative Economy: How People Make Money from Ideas.* London: Allen Lane.

Huang, A. (2013) Can Beijing Become a Global Media Capital? In T. Flew (ed.), *Creative Industries and Urban Development: Creative Cities in the 21st Century.* London: Routledge.

Hutton, W. and Desai, M. (2007) Does the Future Really Belong to China? *Prospect Magazine,* 130, January.

Hymer, S. (1975) The Multinational Corporation and the Law of Uneven Development. In H. Radice (ed.), *International Firms and Modern Imperialism.* Harmondsworth: Penguin, pp. 37–64.

Ichikawa, S. (2008) Creative Industries: The Case of Fashion. In H. Anheier and Y.R. Isar (eds.), *The Cultural Economy.* Cultures and Globalization Series, Vol. 2. London: Sage, pp. 253–9.

Isar, Y.R. (2012) Cultures and Cities: Some Policy Implications. In H. Anheier and Y.R. Isar (eds.), *Cities, Cultural Policy and Governance.* Cultures and Globalization Series, Vol. 5. London: Sage, pp. 330–9.

Isar, Y.R., Hoelscher, M. and Anheier, H. (2012) Introduction. In H. Anheier and Y.R. Isar (eds.), *Cities, Cultural Policy and Governance.* Cultures and Globalization Series, Vol. 5. London: Sage, pp. 1–12.

Jaguaribe, A. (2008) The Policy Parameters. In D. Barrowclough and Z. Kozul-Wright (eds.), *Creative Industries and Developing Countries: Voice, Choice and Economic Growth.* London: Routledge, pp. 305–29.

James, V. (2008) The IPRs and the Music Industry in the Caribbean. In D. Barrowclough and Z. Kozul-Wright (eds.), *Creative Industries and Developing Countries: Voice, Choice and Economic Growth.* London: Routledge, pp. 213–47.

Jenkins, H. (2006) *Convergence Culture: When New and Old Media Collide.* New York: New York University Press.

Johnson, C. (1982) *MITI and the Japanese Miracle.* Stanford, CA: Stanford University Press.

Karlsson, C. and Picard, R. (2011) *Media Clusters and Media Cluster Policies.* CESIS Electronic Working Papers Series, Paper No. 246. Stockholm: Centre of Excellence for Science and Innovation Studies.

KEA European Affairs (2006) *The Economy of Culture in Europe.* Study prepared for the European Commission (Directorate-General for Education and Culture), October. http://ec.europa.eu/culture/key-documents/doc873_en.htm.

Keane, M. (2007) *Created in China: The Great New Leap Forward.* London: Routledge.

Keane, M. (2011) *China's New Creative Clusters: Governance, Human Capital and Investment.* London: Routledge.

Kellner, D. (1995) Cultural Studies, Multiculturalism and Media Culture. In G. Dines and J.M. Humez (eds.), *Gender, Race, and Class in Media.* Thousand Oaks, CA: Sage, pp. 5–17.

Kellner, D. and Pierce, C. (2007) Media and Globalization. In G. Ritzer (ed.), *The Blackwell Companion to Globalization.* Malden, MA: Blackwell, pp. 383–95.

Kim, H.M. and Han, S.S. (2012) City Profiles: Seoul. *Cities* 29: 142–54.

Klein, N. (2001) *No Logo.* London: Flamingo.

Kohli, A. (2004) *State-Directed Development.* Cambridge: Cambridge University Press.

Kong, L., Gibson, C., Khoo, L. and Semple, A. (2006) Knowledge of the Creative Economy: Towards a Relational Geography of Diffusion and Adaptation in Asia. *Asia Pacific Viewpoint* 47(1): 173–94.

Kornberger, M. (2010) *Brand Society.* Cambridge: Cambridge University Press.

Korzeniewicz, M. (2000) Commodity Chains and Marketing Strategies: Nike and the Global Athletic Footwear Industry. In F.J. Lechner and J. Boli (eds.), *The Globalization Reader.* Malden, MA: Blackwell, pp. 155–66.

Kotkin, J. (2006) *The City: A World History.* New York: Random House.

Landry, C. (2000) *The Creative City.* London: Earthscan.

Landry, C. (2005) London as a Creative City. In J. Hartley (ed.), *Creative Industries.* Malden, MA: Blackwell, pp. 233–45.

Lash, S. and Urry, J. (1994) *Economies of Signs and Space.* London: Sage.

Leadbeater, C. (1999) *Living on Thin Air: The New Economy.* London: Penguin.

Lee, F. (2009) *A History of Heterodox Economics: Challenging the Mainstream in the Twentieth Century.* New York: Routledge.

Lee, M. (1993) *Consumer Culture Reborn: The New Cultural Politics of Consumption.* London: Routledge.

Lessig, L. (2004) *Free Culture: How Big Media Uses Technology and the Law to Lock Down Culture and Control Creativity.* New York: Penguin.

Levitt, T. (1983) The Globalization of Markets. *Harvard Business Review* 61(3): 92–102.

Lewis, J. (2000) Designing a Cultural Policy. In G. Bradford, M. Gary and G. Wallach (eds.), *The Politics of Culture.* New York: New Press, pp. 79–93.

Leys, C. (1996) *The Rise and Fall of Development Theory.* Bloomington, IN: Indiana University Press.

Lobato, R. (2010) Creative Industries and Informal Economies: Lessons from Nollywood. *International Journal of Cultural Studies* 13(4): 337–54.

Lobato, R. (2012) *Shadow Economies of Cinema: Mapping Informal Film Distribution.* London: BFI/Palgrave Macmillan.

Loew, L. (2006–7) Creative Industries in Developing Countries and Intellectual Property Protection. *Vanderbilt Journal of Entertainment and Technology Law* 9: 171–200.

Looseley, D. (2005) *The Politics of Fun: Cultural Policy and Debate in Contemporary France*. Oxford: Berg.

Lorenzen, M. and Frederiksen, L. (2008) Why do Cultural Industries Cluster? Localization, Urbanization, Products and Projects. In P. Cooke and L. Lazzeretti (eds.), *Creative Cities, Cultural Clusters and Local Economic Development*. Cheltenham: Edward Elgar, pp. 155–79.

Lury, C. (2011) *Consumer Cultures*. Cambridge: Polity.

Machin, S. and McNally, S. (2007) *Tertiary Education Systems and Labour Markets*. Paris: OECD.

Mandel, E. (1983) Consumption. In T. Bottomore, L. Harris, V.G. Kiernan and R. Miliband (eds.), *A Dictionary of Marxist Thought*. Oxford: Blackwell, pp. 92–3.

Marcuse, H. (1964) *One-Dimensional Man*. Boston, MA: Beacon Press.

Markusen, A. (2008) Sticky Places in Slippery Space: A Typology of Industrial Districts. In R. Martin and P. Sunley (eds.), *Economic Geography*, Vol. 2. London: Routledge, pp. 366–92.

Marshall, A. (1920 [1890]) *Principles of Economics* (8th edn). London: Macmillan.

Marx, K. (1973 [1857]) *Grundrisse* (trans. M. Nicolaus). Harmondsworth: Penguin.

Marx, K. (1976 [1867]) *Capital*, Volume One. Harmondsworth: Penguin.

Maslow, A. (1943) A Theory of Human Motivation. *Psychological Review* 50(4): 370–96.

Mato, D. (2002) Miami in the Transnationalization of the *Telenovela* Industry: On Territoriality and Globalization. *Journal of Latin American Cultural Studies* 11(2): 195–212.

Mattelart, A. (1994) *Mapping World Communication: War, Progress, Culture* (trans. S. Emanuel and J.A. Cohen). Minneapolis, MN: University of Minnesota Press.

Maxwell, R. and Miller, T. (2012) *Greening the Media*. New York: Oxford University Press.

McChesney, R.W. (2008) *The Political Economy of Media*. New York: Monthly Review Press.

McChesney, R.W. and Schiller, D. (2003) *The Political Economy of International Communication: Foundations for the Emerging Global Debate about Media Ownership and Regulation*. United Nations Institute for Social Development, Program Paper No. 11.

McIntyre, R. (1992) Consumption in Contemporary Capitalism: Beyond Marx and Veblen. *Review of Social Economy* 50(1): 40–60.

McKendrick, N. (2003) The Consumer Revolution of Eighteenth-Century Europe. In D. Clarke, M. Doel and K. Housiaux (eds.), *The Consumption Reader*. London: Routledge, pp. 40–2.

McLuhan, M. (1964) *Understanding Media*. New York: Mentor Books.

McLuhan, M. and Fiore, Q. (1967) *The Medium is the Message*. New York: Bantam.

McMillan, J. (2002) *Reinventing the Bazaar: A Natural History of Markets*. New York: Norton.

McMillin, D. (2007) *International Media Studies*. Oxford: Blackwell.

McNamara, A. (2002) How 'Creative Industries' Evokes the Legacy of Modernist Visual Art. *Media International Australia* 102: 66–76.

McRobbie, A. (2005) Clubs to Companies. In J. Hartley (ed.), *Creative Industries*. Oxford: Blackwell, pp. 375–90.

McWilliam, E. and Hatcher, C. (2004) Emotional Literacy as a Pedagogical Product. *Continuum: Journal of Media and Cultural Studies* 18(2): 179–89.

Meikle, G. and Young, S. (2012) *Media Convergence: Networked Digital Media in Everyday Life*. Basingstoke: Palgrave.

Melkote, S.R. (2010) Theories of Development Communication. In D.K. Thussu (ed.), *International Communication: A Reader*. London: Routledge, pp. 105–21.

Menger, P. (1999) Artistic Labour Markets and Careers. *Annual Review of Sociology* 25: 541–74.

Miller, D. (2010) The Poverty of Morality. In A. Warde (ed.), *Consumption*, Vol. 2. London: Sage, pp. 243–58.

Miller, J. (2012) Global Nollywood: The Nigerian Movie Industry and Alternative Global Networks in Production and Distribution. *Global Media and Communication* 8(2): 117–33.

Miller, T. and Yúdice, G. (2002) *Cultural Policy*. London: Sage.

Miller, T., Govil, N., McMurria, J., Maxwell, R. and Wang, T. (2005) *Global Hollywood 2*. London: BFI Publishing.

Mitchell, W., Inouye, A. and Blumenthal, M. (2003) *Beyond Productivity: Information Technology, Innovation, and Creativity*. Washington, DC: National Academies Press.

Mohun, S. (2003) Consumer Sovereignty. In D.B. Clarke, M.A. Doel and K.M.L. Housiaux (eds.), *The Consumption Reader*. London: Routledge, pp. 139–43.

Mommaas, H. (2009) Spaces of Culture and Economy: Mapping the Cultural-Creative Cluster Landscape. In L. Kong and J. O'Connor (eds.), *Creative Economies, Creative Cities: Asian-European Perspectives*. Dordrecht: Springer, pp. 45–59.

Montgomery, L. (2010) *China's Creative Industries: Copyright, Social Network Markets and the Business of Culture in a Digital Age*. Cheltenham: Edward Elgar.

Mosco, V. (2009) *The Political Economy of Communications* (2nd edn). London: Sage.

Moulier Boutang, Y. (2011) *Cognitive Capitalism* (trans. E. Emery). Cambridge: Polity.

Mulgan, G. and Wilkinson, H. (1994) The Enabling (and Disabling) State. In P. Ekins and M. Max-Neef (eds.), *Real-Life Economics*. London: Routledge, pp. 340–57.

Murdock, G. and Golding, P. (2005) Culture, Communications and Political Economy. In J. Curran and M. Gurevitch (eds.), *Mass Media and Society* (4th edn). London: Hodder Education, pp. 60–83.

Neff, G., Wissinger, E. and Zukin, S. (2005) Entrepreneurial Labor among Cultural Producers: 'Cool' Jobs in 'Hot' Industries. *Social Semiotics* 15(3): 307–34.

Negus, K. and Pickering, M. (2004) *Creativity, Communication and Cultural Value*. London: Sage.

NESTA (National Endowment for Science, Technology and the Arts) (2006) *Creating Value: How the UK Can Invest in New Creative Businesses*. Accessed at: www.nesta.org.uk/creating-value-how-the-uk-can-invest-in-new-creative-businesses-2/ (accessed 1 May 2008).

Noam, E. (2009) *Media Ownership and Concentration in America*. Oxford: Oxford University Press.

North, D. (1990) *Institutions, Institutional Change and Economic Performance*. Cambridge: Cambridge University Press.

North, D. (1994) *Understanding the Process of Economic Change*. Princeton, NJ: Princeton University Press.

Norton, A. (2012) *Graduate Winners: Assessing the Public and Private Benefits of Higher Education*. Melbourne: Grattan Institute.

Oakley, K. (2004) Not So Cool Britannia: The Role of Creative Industries in Economic Development. *International Journal of Cultural Policy* 7(1): 67–77.

Olson, S.R. (2004) Hollywood Planet: Global Media and the Competitive Advantage of Narrative Transparency. In R.C. Allen and A. Hill (eds.), *The Television Studies Reader*. New York: Routledge, pp. 111–29.

Oman, C. and Arndt, C. (2010) *Measuring Governance*. OECD Policy Brief No. 39. Paris: OECD.

Onuzulike, U. (2007) The Birth of Nollywood: The Nigerian Movie Industry. *Black Camera* 22(1): 25–6.

O'Regan, T. (1992) Too Popular by Far: On Hollywood's International Popularity. *Continuum* 5(2): 302–51.

O'Regan, T. (1996) *Australian National Cinema*. London: Routledge.

Ozawa, T., Castello, S. and Phillips, R. (2001) The Internet Revolution, the 'McLuhan' Stage of Catch-up, and Institutional Reforms in Asia. *Journal of Economic Issues* 35(2): 289–98.

Palma, G. (1973) Dependency: A Formal Theory of Underdevelopment or a Methodology for the Analysis of Concrete Situations of Underdevelopment? *World Development* 6: 881–924.

Palmer, R. and Richards, G. (2011) *Third European Cultural Capital Report*. Amsterdam: Elsevier.

Payne, A. (2012) Nourishing or Polluting: Redefining the Role of Waste in the Fashion System. In E. Felton, O. Zelenko and S. Vaughan (eds.), *Design and Ethics: Reflections on Practice*. London: Routledge, pp. 204–14.

Paz Balibrea, M. (2004) Urbanism, Culture and the Post-Industrial City: Challenging the 'Barcelona Model'. In T. Marshall (ed.), *Transforming Barcelona*. London: Routledge, pp. 205–44.

Petrovic, G. (1983) Alienation. In T. Bottomore, L. Harris, V.G. Kiernan and R. Miliband (eds.), *A Dictionary of Marxist Thought*. Oxford: Blackwell, pp. 9–15.

Pink, D. (2006) *A Whole New Mind*. New York: Reed Elsevier.

Polanyi, K. (1945) *The Great Transformation*. London: Gollancz.

Pollitt, C. (2003) Joined-Up Government: A Survey. *Political Studies Review* 1: 34–49.

Porter, M. (1990) *The Competitive Advantage of Nations*. London: Macmillan.

Porter, M. (1998) Clusters and the New Economics of Competition. *Harvard Business Review* 76(6): 77–91.

Porter, M. (2000) Locations, Clusters, and Company Strategy. In G. Clark, M. Feldman and M. Gertler (eds.), *The Oxford Handbook of Economic Geography*. Oxford: Oxford University Press, pp. 253–74.

Potts, J. (2011) *Creative Industries and Economic Evolution*. Cheltenham: Edward Elgar.

Potts, J. and Cunningham, S. (2008) Four Models of the Creative Industries. *International Journal of Cultural Policy* 14(3): 233–47.

Potts, J., Cunningham, S., Hartley, J. and Ormerod, P. (2008) Social Network Markets: A New Definition of the Creative Industries. *Journal of Cultural Economics* 32(2): 167–85.

Power, D. (2009) Culture, Creativity and Experience in Nordic and Scandinavian Cultural Policy. *International Journal of Cultural Policy* 15(4): 445–60.

Pratt, A. (2004) Mapping the Cultural Industries: Regionalization – the Example of South East England. In D. Power and A.J. Scott (eds.), *Cultural Industries and the Production of Culture*. London: Routledge, pp. 19–36.

Pratt, A. (2005) Cultural Industries and Public Policy. *International Journal of Cultural Policy* 11(1): 31–44.

Pratt, A. (2008a) Creative Cities: The Cultural Industries and the Creative Class. *Geografiska Annaler: Series B – Human Geography* 90(2): 107–17.

Pratt, A. (2008b) The Music Industry and its Potential Role in Local Economic Development: The Case of Senegal. In D. Barrowclough and Z. Kozul-Wright (eds.), *Creative Industries and Developing Countries: Voice, Choice and Economic Growth*. London: Routledge, pp. 130–45.

Pratt, A. and Jeffcutt, P. (2009) Creativity, Innovation and the Cultural Economy: Snake-Oil for the 21st Century? In P. Jeffcutt and A. Pratt (eds.), *Creativity, Innovation and the Cultural Economy*. London: Routledge, pp. 3–19.

Quiggan, J. and Potts, J. (2008) Economics of Non-Market Innovation and Digital Literacy. *Media International Australia* 128: 144–50.

Radice, H. (2008) The Developmental State under Global Neoliberalism. *Third World Quarterly* 29(6): 1153–74.

Rifkin, J. (2000) *The Age of Access*. London: Penguin.

Ritzer, G. (1998) Introduction. In J. Baudrillard, *The Consumer Society: Myths and Structures*. London: Sage, pp. 1–22.

Robertson, R. and White, K. (2007) What is Globalization? In G. Ritzer (ed.), *The Blackwell Companion to Globalization*. Malden, MA: Blackwell, pp. 54–66.

Rogers, E.E. (1974) Communication in Development. *ANNALS of the American Academy of Political and Social Science* 412: 44–56.

Roodhouse, S. (2006) *Cultural Quarters: Principles and Practice*. Bristol: Intellect.

Ross, A. (2003) *No Collar: The Humane Workplace and its Hidden Costs*. New York: Basic Books.

Ross, A. (2006) *Fast Boat to China: Lessons from Shanghai*. Princeton, NJ: Princeton University Press.

Ross, A. (2007) Nice Work If You Can Get It: The Mercurial Career of Creative Industries Policy. In G. Lovink and N. Rossiter (eds.), *MyCreativity Reader: A Critique of Creative Industries*. Amsterdam: Institute of Network Cultures, pp. 17–39.

Ross, A. (2009) *Nice Work If You Can Get It: Life and Labor in Precarious Times*. New York: New York University Press.

Rowe, D. and Bavinton, N. (2011) Tender for the Night: After-Dark Cultural Complexities in the Night-Time Economy. *Continuum: Journal of Media and Cultural Studies* 25(6): 811–25.

Ryan, B. (1992) *Making Capital from Culture*. Thousand Oaks, CA: Sage.

Sackrey, C., Schneider, G. and Knoedler, J. (2005) *Introduction to Political Economy*. Cambridge, MA: Economic Affairs Bureau.

Santagata, W. (2004) Creativity, Fashion and Market Behaviour. In D. Power and A.J. Scott (eds.), *Cultural Industries and the Production of Culture*. New York: Routledge, pp. 75–90.

Santagata, W. (2010) *The Culture Factory: Creativity and the Production of Culture*. Heidelberg: Springer.

Sassen, S. (1994) *Cities in a World Economy*. Thousand Oaks, CA: Pine Forge Press.

Sassen, S. (2001) *The Global City*. Princeton, NJ: Princeton University Press.

Schiller, D. (1999) *Digital Capitalism: Networking the Global System*. Cambridge, MA: MIT Press.

Schiller, H.I. (1969) *Mass Communications and American Empire*. Boston, MA: Beacon Press.

Schiller, H.I. (1976) *Communication and Cultural Domination*. New York: International Arts and Sciences Press.

Schiller, H.I. (1991) Not Yet the Post-Imperialist Era. *Critical Studies in Mass Communication* 8(1): 13–28.

Schiller, H.I. (1996) *Information Inequality: The Deepening Social Crisis in America*. London: Routledge.

Schultz, M. and van Gelder, A. (2008–9) Creative Development: Helping Poor Countries by Building Creative Industries. *Kentucky Law Journal* 97: 79–148.

Schumpeter, J.A. (1950) *Capitalism, Socialism and Democracy*. New York: Harper & Row.

Scolari, C. (2009) Transmedia Storytelling: Implicit Consumers, Narrative Worlds, and Branding in Contemporary Media Production. *International Journal of Communication* 3: 586–606.

Scott, A.J. (2005) *On Hollywood: The Place, the Industry*. Oxford: Oxford University Press.

Scott, A.J. (2008) *Social Economy of the Metropolis: Cognitive-Cultural Capitalism and the Global Resurgence of Cities.* Oxford: Oxford University Press.

Scott, A.J., Agnew, J., Soja, E. and Storper, M. (2001) Global City-Regions. In A.J. Scott (ed.), *Global City-Regions: Trends, Theory, Policy.* Oxford: Oxford University Press, pp. 11–30.

Sell, S.K. (2002) Intellectual Property Rights. In D. Held and A. McGrew (eds.), *Governing Globalization.* Cambridge: Polity, pp. 171–88.

Simmel, G. (1950) The Metropolis and Mental Life. In K. Wolff (ed.), *The Sociology of Georg Simmel.* New York: Free Press, pp. 410–24.

Simmel, G. (2003) The Philosophy of Fashion. In D. Clarke, M. Doel and K. Housiaux (eds.), *The Consumption Reader.* London: Routledge, pp. 238–45.

Sinclair, J. (2003) 'The Hollywood of Latin America': Miami as Regional Center in Television Trade. *Television and New Media* 4(3): 211–29.

Sinclair, J. (2009) Latin America's Impact on World Television Markets. In G. Turner and J. Tay (eds.), *Television Studies After TV.* London: Routledge, pp. 141–8.

Sinclair, J. (2012) *Advertising, the Media and Globalisation: A World in Motion.* London: Routledge.

Sinclair, J., Jacka, E. and Cunningham, S. (1996) Peripheral Vision. In J. Sinclair, E. Jacka and S. Cunningham (eds.), *New Patterns in Global Television: Peripheral Vision.* Oxford: Oxford University Press, pp. 1–32.

Singer, J. (2011) Journalism in a Network. In M. Deuze (ed.), *Managing Media Work.* London: Sage, pp. 103–10.

Siwek, S. (2006) *Copyright Industries in the US Economy – The 2006 Report.* International Intellectual Property Alliance, November.

Skidelsky, R. (2000) *John Maynard Keynes. Vol. 3, Fighting for Britain 1937–1946.* London: Papermac.

Sklair, L. (2000) Sociology of the Global System. In F. Lechner and J. Boli (eds.), *The Globalization Reader.* Malden, MA: Blackwell, pp. 64–9.

Smith, A. (1991) [1776] *The Wealth of Nations.* New York: Prometheus Books.

Smith, A. (1990) Towards a Global Culture? In M. Featherstone (ed.), *Global Culture.* London: Sage, pp. 171–91.

Smith, C. and McKinlay, A. (2009) Creative Industries and Labour Process Analysis. In A. McKinlay and C. Smith (eds.), *Creative Labour: Working in the Creative Industries.* Basingstoke: Palgrave Macmillan, pp. 3–28.

Sparks, C. (2007) *Globalization, Development and the Mass Media.* London: Sage.

Steger, M. (2003) *Globalization: A Very Short Introduction.* Oxford: Oxford University Press.

Stewart-Weeks, M. (2006) From Control to Networks. In H.K. Colebatch (ed.), *Beyond the Policy Cycle: The Policy Process in Australia.* Sydney: Allen & Unwin, pp. 184–202.

Stilwell, F. (2002) *Political Economy: The Contest of Economic Ideas.* Oxford: Oxford University Press.

Stoneman, P. (2010) *Soft Innovation: Economics, Product Aesthetics, and the Creative Industries.* Oxford: Oxford University Press.

Storey, J. (1999) *Cultural Consumption and Everyday Life*. London: Arnold.

Storper, M. (1997) *The Regional World*. New York: Guilford.

Storper, M. and Scott, A.J. (2009) Rethinking Human Capital, Creativity and Urban Growth. *Journal of Economic Geography* 9(1): 147–67.

Storper, M. and Venables, A. (2004) Buzz: Face-to-Face Contact and the Urban Economy. *Journal of Economic Geography* 4(2): 351–70.

Straubhaar, J. (2007) *World Television: From Global to Local*. Los Angeles, CA: Sage.

Swedberg, R. (2006) The Cultural Entrepreneur and the Creative Industries. *Journal of Cultural Economics* 30(2): 243–61.

Sweezy, P.M. (1968) *The Theory of Capitalist Development*. New York: Monthly Review Press.

Taylor, P.J. (2004) *World City Networks: A Global Urban Analysis*. London: Routledge.

Thomas, A.O. (2006) *Transnational Media and Contoured Markets: Redefining Asian Television and Advertising*. New Delhi: Sage.

Thompson, G. (2003) *Between Hierarchies and Networks: The Logic and Limits of Network Forms of Organization*. Oxford: Oxford University Press.

Thompson, J. (1991) *Ideology and Modern Culture*. Cambridge: Polity Press.

Thompson, J. (1995) *The Media and Modernity: A Social Theory of the Media*. Cambridge: Polity Press.

Throsby, D. (2001) *Economics and Culture*. Cambridge: Cambridge University Press.

Throsby, D. (2008a) The Concentric Circles Model of the Cultural Industries. *Cultural Trends* 17(3): 147–64.

Throsby, D. (2008b) Modelling the Cultural Industries. *International Journal of Cultural Policy* 14(3): 217–32.

Throsby, D. (2010) *The Economics of Cultural Policy*. Cambridge: Cambridge University Press.

Timberlake, M. and Ma, X. (2007) Cities and Globalization. In G. Ritzer (ed.), *The Blackwell Companion to Globalization*. Malden, MA: Blackwell, pp. 254–71.

Tomlinson, J. (1991) *Cultural Imperialism*. London: Pinter.

Tomlinson, J. (1999) *Globalization and Culture*. Chicago, IL: University of Chicago Press.

Tomlinson, J. (2007) Cultural Globalization. In G. Ritzer (ed.), *The Blackwell Companion to Globalization*. Malden, MA: Blackwell, pp. 352–66.

Towse, R. (2003) *A Handbook of Cultural Economics*. Cheltenham: Edward Elgar.

Towse, R. (2010) *A Textbook of Cultural Economics*. Cambridge: Cambridge University Press.

Tunstall, J. (2008) *The Media Were American: US Mass Media in Decline*. Oxford: Oxford University Press.

Turner, G. (2012) *What's Become of Cultural Studies?* London: Sage.

UNCTAD (United Nations Conference on Trade and Development) (2008) *Creative Economy Report 2008*. United Nations: Geneva.

UNCTAD (United Nations Conference on Trade and Development) (2010) *Creative Economy Report 2010*. United Nations: Geneva.

UNCTAD (United Nations Conference on Trade and Development) (2012) *World Investment Report 2012*. United Nations: Geneva.

UNESCO (United Nations Educational, Scientific and Cultural Organization) (2005) *Convention on the Protection and Promotion of the Diversity of Cultural Expressions*. Paris: UNESCO.

UNESCO (United Nations Educational, Scientific and Cultural Organization) (2009) *The 2009 UNESCO Framework for Cultural Statistics (FCS)*. Montreal: UNESCO Institute for Statistics.

Vaidhyanathan, S. (2001) *Copyrights and Copywrongs*. New York: New York University Press.

Veblen, T. (1970 [1899]) *The Theory of the Leisure Class: An Economic Study of Institutions*. London: Unwin Books.

Veblen, T. (2000) Conspicuous Consumption. In M. Lee (ed.), *The Consumer Society Reader*. Malden, MA: Blackwell, pp. 31–47.

Venturelli, S. (2005) Culture and the Creative Economy in the Information Age. In J. Hartley (ed.), *Creative Industries*. Oxford: Blackwell, pp. 391–8.

Volkmer, I. (1999) *News in the Global Sphere: A Study of CNN and its Impact on Global Communications*. Luton: University of Luton Press.

Wade, R. (1990) *Governing the Market: Economic Theory and the Role of Government in East Asian Industrialization*. Princeton, NJ: Princeton University Press.

Wang, J. (2008) *Brand New China: Advertising, Media and Commercial Culture*. Cambridge, MA: Harvard University Press.

Wasko, J. (2004) The Political Economy of Communications. In J. Downing, D. McQuail, P. Schlesinger and E. Wartella (eds.), *The SAGE Handbook of Media Studies*. Thousand Oaks, CA: Sage, pp. 309–30.

Waters, M. (2001) *Globalization* (2nd edn). London: Routledge.

Webb, J., Schirato, T. and Danaher, G. (2002) *Understanding Bourdieu*. Sydney: Allen & Unwin.

Weiss, L. (1998) *The Myth of the Powerless State*. Ithaca, NY: Cornell University Press.

Weiss, L. (2003) Introduction: Bringing Domestic Institutions Back In. In L. Weiss (ed.), *States in the Global Economy: Bringing Domestic Institutions Back In*. Cambridge: Cambridge University Press, pp. 1–33.

Williams, R. (1965) *The Long Revolution*. Harmondsworth: Penguin.

Williams, R. (1976) *Keywords: A Vocabulary of Culture and Society*. London: Fontana.

Williamson, O.E. (1975) *Markets and Hierarchies*. New York: Free Press.

Williamson, O.E. (1985) *The Economic Institutions of Capitalism*. New York: Free Press.

Williamson, O.E. (2000) The New Institutional Economics: Taking Stock, Looking Ahead. *Journal of Economic Literature* 38(3): 595–613.

Winseck, D. 2011. The Political Economy of the Media and the Transformation of the Global Media Industries. In D. Winseck and D.Y. Jin (eds.), *Political Economies of the Media: The Transformation of the Global Media Industries.* London: Bloomsbury, pp. 3–44.

Work Foundation, The (2007) *Staying Ahead: The Economic Performance of the UK's Creative Industries.* Available at: www.theworkfoundation.com/assets/docs/publications/176_stayingahead.pdf (accessed 1 May 2008).

World Intellectual Property Organization. 2012. Creative Industries – Economic Contribution and Mapping. Available at: http://www.wipo.int/ip-development/en/creative_industry/economic_contribution.html (accessed 16 February 2012).

Worldwatch Institute (2007) *State of the World 2007: Our Urban Future.* Washington, DC: Worldwatch Institute.

Yusuf, S. and Nabeshima, K. (2005) Creative industries in East Asia. *Cities* 22: 109–22.

Yusuf, S. and Wu, W. (2002) Pathways to a World City: Shanghai Rising in an Era of Globalization. *Urban Studies* 39(7): 1213–40.

Zamagni, S. (1987) *Microeconomic Theory: An Introduction.* Oxford: Basil Blackwell.

Zheng, J. (2011) 'Creative Industries Clusters' and the 'Entrepreneurial City' of Shanghai. *Urban Studies* 48(16): 3561–82.

Zieleniac, A. (2010) Georg Simmel. In R. Hutchinson (ed.), *Encyclopedia of Urban Studies.* Thousand Oaks, CA: Sage, pp. 718–22.

Zukin, S. and Maguire, J. (2004) Consumers and Consumption. *Annual Review of Sociology* 30(2): 173–97.

Zweimuller, J. (2000) Schumpeterian Entrepreneurs meet Engel's Law: The Impact of Inequality on Innovation-Driven Growth. *Journal of Economic Growth* 5(2): 185–206.

Index